THE LIFE AND DEATH OF MAL CUTPURSE

THE CASE OF MARY CARLETON

COUNTERFEIT LADIES

The Life and Death of Mal Cutpurse

The Case of Mary Carleton

Edited with Introduction and Notes by

JANET TODD

and

ELIZABETH SPEARING

LONDON

WILLIAM PICKERING

1994

Published by Pickering & Chatto (Publishers) Limited
17 Pall Mall, London SW1Y 5NB

British Library Cataloguing in Publication Data
Counterfeit Ladies: Life and Death of Mal
Cutpurse and the Case of Mary Carleton. –
(Pickering Women's Classics Series)
    I. Todd, Janet   II. Spearing, Elizabeth
    III. Series
    823

    ISBN 1–85196–087–2

Typeset by Waveney Typesetters
Norwich

Printed and bound in Great Britain by
Redwood Books
Trowbridge

CONTENTS

INTRODUCTION

Mary Frith ('Moll/Mal Cutpurse') and Mary Carleton ('the German Princess') were the most famous female 'rogues' of seventeenth-century England. Despite this, 'rogue' is not a title Mary Carleton would have claimed in her vindication, and Mary Frith seems to have seen herself primarily as a practical business person. Both became historical and mythical figures who attracted to themselves several extra stories of 'pranks' and trickery. These stories sometimes linked the two together in the public mind, and both were thus connected with other dubious and counterfeiting females such as Pope Joan.

The Case of Mary Carleton and *The Life and Death of Mrs. Mary Frith* were published only a year apart in the early 1660s, soon after the restoration of Charles II. The new regime still had traces of its original fascination and the public was not yet disillusioned with its self-indulgence and inefficiency; part of the attraction of the female 'rogues', as of many well-known and well-documented criminals, was that they openly espoused the royalist cause and associated themselves not only with royalist politics, but also with Stuart glamour. The nonchalant power associated with the image of the cavalier could be shared by the charismatic transgressor and the self-publicist seeking to legitimise her nonconformism.

Mary Carleton and Mary Frith both lived before the time when a Romantic interest in the self turned autobiography into a familiar literary form; even subjective biography was not common, memoirs rather than self-analysis were the order of the day. Nor would those who were writing about themselves have read many other examples; much of the autobiographical writing of the time was not published until later. As women from the lower classes, Frith and Carleton were among those least likely to portray themselves for posterity; those few who did so were almost always deeply religious women describing their spiritual lives, often at the behest of a pastor. Their most important precursor was in fact Margery Kempe, who had probably dictated her autobiography in the 1420s, and was, like them, a subversive woman who rejected enclosure and was frequently in conflict with the law. A sense of the gap between the assigned self and the experienced self seems to be one of the motives for autobiography in the period before autobiography existed as a recognised genre.

Generic issues are a concern of both texts. The readers of *The Case of Mary Carleton* are asked to 'cast a favourable eye upon these Novels of my life, not much unlike those of Boccace, but that they are more serious and tragical'. The address to the reader at the beginning of *The Life and Death of Mrs. Mary Frith* also considers the question of genre, feeling that Mal Cutpurse deserves 'a place in the *Rationale* and Account of Time...farre beyond *Prince Crispine* and his *Lady*, and the rest of that Leud rout, and band of Knight Errantry'. Mary Frith herself (if the narrative voice is indeed her own) is conscious that she is writing in a tradition of picaresque literature, 'following the laudable example of others, who have in part preceded me as *Seignior Gusman*, and the Spanish Tribe of Cheaters'.

One of the most important forms of narrative in the six-teenth and seventeenth centuries was romance, available to a much wider public since printed books had become more widespread. Various types of story of love and adventure, of ladies of matchless beauty and the knights of unequalled strength and skill in arms who wandered the world earning their hearts and hands, had been internalised and had probably be-come part of the imaginative baggage of most reading people. Margaret Cavendish, Duchess of Newcastle, may have claimed that she 'never read a Romancy Book throughout in all my life', but she nevertheless knew exactly what such a book was like. Both of the counterfeit ladies whose own stories are told in this volume give evidence not just of having read romances, but of sometimes identifying with the fictional beings who were the subjects of other narratives, and of trying to see how they or some version of their own personae might fit into such a story. If Carleton sees herself as a Lady Errant, giving lustre to a romance, Frith pretends that she is a 'squiresse' as she gallops across London on horseback for a wager. They are both also aware of rogue literature as romance's opposite as in Mary Frith's allusion, quoted above, to Mateo Alemán's *Guzmán de Alfarache*. The picaresque genre is often seen as defined by a kind of unromantic 'realism', yet the picaro is as much a fictional entity as the knight errant. Social historians such as J. A. Sharpe[1] suggest that there is more evidence for vagabond organisation, hierarchy and canting in literature than in reality, and he sees a lack of correspondence between the impression given by the rogue literature and the reliability of vagrant or metropolitan crime as it appears in court records. Popular ideas about crime were partly formed from literature, but this literature was perhaps more an indication of anxiety about social disruption and an attempt to deal with this anxiety by giving it a manageable form, than a reflection of reality.

The literary form which one would expect to correspond most closely with social reality is the criminal biography, which became increasingly popular in the late seventeenth and eighteenth centuries. It culminated in the famous fictional rogue biographies of Daniel Defoe, especially *Moll Flanders*, with its frequent echoes of the tale of Mary Carleton. However, as Ernest Bernbaum has pointed out when writing about the Mary Carleton narratives, 'from every attempt to distinguish between fact and fiction we return, as in the case of the other criminal biographies of the time, thoroughly baffled'.[2] The more one reads of such works, the more one sees the same episodes, the same anecdotes, even expressed in much the same words, recurring again and again. There seem to have been a number of free-floating stories which were incorporated among more authentic details. It is thus very difficult to judge how far the stories of Carleton and Frith belong to fact or fiction; like their protean protagonists, the narratives assume a variety of shapes.

THE LIFE AND DEATH OF MRS. MARY FRITH COMMONLY
CALLED MAL CUTPURSE

The figure of 'Moll Cutpurse' occurs repeatedly in various forms over a long period, but the present text is certainly the only one that gives anything like an account of the actual woman rather than a mythical figure, or that could derive from information given by the original 'Moll', Mary Frith herself. It was published in 1662, within three years of her death. Not only is the content unique, but the volume in the British Library is apparently the sole copy to have survived.[3] The present edition is based on close examination of the British Library copy, and an attempt has been made to relate the text in some detail to its historical context.

The extent to which this is possible is demonstrated by Appendix I, p. 157. Many events which figure in the narration can be followed up and fit not only into the general chronology, but can also be linked to the text with surprising precision. The first episode in Mary Frith's 'Diary', for example, an event which seems to have been critical in the formation of her identity, can probably be precisely located. Those responsible for her try to have Frith 'spirited' (kidnapped and deported) to America, but she realises what is happening and succeeds in taking charge of her own destiny. After the failure of Raleigh's Roanoke Island colony, another attempt had been made to establish a settlement in the New World. A company was formed and a charter granted by the King in 1606, and in the following year the construction of Jamestown began. Captain Newport brought home glowing reports of Virginia, and had already taken some colonists back, including the first two women in 1608. Then, in 1609, the company was reconstituted, with more than six hundred London investors buying into it; in May, five hundred men, women and children assembled in nine ships, expected to sail for 'New England' (a term used for any North American English colony in the early days). However, the departure was delayed for several weeks by contrary winds. This would have provided an opportunity for the enterprise to become well-known, and during the enforced wait social drinking aboard among crew, passengers and visitors would have been highly probable. Frith's 'private Merchant, the first beginner of this inhumane way of Merchandize', would have been one of the six hundred investors, hoping to make money from the new business opportunity offered by dealing in indentured labourers. Even the word 'Cannibals' applied to the crew could be more than a vague pejorative term: a survivor of the 'starving time' which followed wrote that 'so great was our famine, that a saluage we slew and buried, the poorer sort tooke him vp againe and eat him; and so did diuers one another boyled and stewed with roots and herbs: And one amongst the rest did kill his wife...and had eaten part of her before it was known'.[4]

The account of Mary Frith in the *History* is not only presented anonymously, it is not even clear how many hands are involved or to what extent Frith may have been responsible for telling her own story. The work is in three sections: an address 'To the Reader', a longer introductory section, and the main body of narrative, written in the first person and purporting to be the 'Diary' of Frith herself. The address, printed in italic and written in a tone of somewhat ostentatiously learned and sprightly irony, as though marking the distance between the writer and what is being presented, offers us Frith as a remarkable phenomenon: she is not actually condemned; rather, a new generation of thieves and bawds is to modify its behaviour by her example. The writer asks for the 'Abruptness and Discontinuance of the Matter, and the severall Independencies thereof' to be excused, ascribing this to the character of Frith herself; no hint is given as to the origin of the material, and this writer signs off with 'Vale' ('Farewell'). The typeface then changes to roman and an apparently different presenter supplies more detailed introductory material. This introduction is clearer in placing Frith in, or at least very close to, the criminal classes, and the never-failing justification of giving an account of shady practice out of' 'pleasant officiousness to the publique good' is produced. The writer assumes the voice of one considering and retailing second-hand information ('for I suppose her [when young] of very competent discretion', 'for I am not informed that it was out of any settled serious perswasion'), and seems to be of a younger generation ('or what the fashion of those times were for Girls to be dressed in'). It does, however, sound as though this is a narrator with personal knowledge of the subject in later life ('a spice she had even then, of prophane dissolute language, which in her old dayes amounted to down-right Swearing, which was in her not so malicious as customary'). An account is given of Frith's family background and childhood up to the point when she embarked on her career, then the writer breaks off; Frith's 'own person' will be 're-assume[d]', so that the rest of her life can be presented 'according to that tract of her own Genius, with which she pleasured her self and her discourses in all company'. The rest of the volume then consists of 'this Diary of her own here following'. How far the main body of the narrative can be said to be 'her own' is difficult to determine. There does, however, appear to be a distinctive voice, a voice of which an echo can be heard in Frith's will (indexed under 'Mary Markham' in the records of the Prerogative Court of Canterbury and dated 6 June 1659), in which she bequeaths her soul to God, and her body to the cart, 'whenever it come'. This sounds very like a woman who would also say, 'but if Mr. H——— be Squemish and will not Preach, let the *Sexton* mumble Two or Three Dusty Claiy words and put me in'.

It has been suggested that there is distinctive verbal redundancy in the introduction which reappears in two possible interpolations in the 'Diary', a diatribe against adultery and the account of Frith's last illness. But both of these passages also include features which might suggest more imaginative identification of the writer with the subject than seems characteristic from the introduction, if it is otherwise only the introduction which is supposed to be written by that particular narrator. The detailed evocation of Frith's swollen belly as a beauteous globe rather than 'a withered, dryed and wrinckled piece of Skin', a feeling of pride in this and the fanciful enjoyment of pregnancy, seems to have the ring of personal truth, and is consistent with other passages where Frith suggests her imaginative life.

It is certainly possible, even likely, that what we have is by and large a 'told to' autobiography. The introduction claims that the young Mary learnt to read 'perfectly', and the 'Diary' implies that Frith was not only able to read but accustomed to do so. This does not necessarily mean that she could write, however. In the seventeenth century there were many more who could read than could write, especially among women, and Frith's will is only signed with a shaky cross, though, as this document states that she is 'sick and weak in body', lack of a written signature is not conclusive. As has been noted, the reader is told that the story of Frith's life will be presented 'according to that tract of her own Genius, with which she pleasured her self and her discourses in all company', and whether written down personally, or 'told to' a biographer or amanuensis, the narration is distinctively oral in style. The 'Diary' rambles from one topic and register to another, incorporates much direct speech, addresses the reader familiarly in the second person, and is marked by breaks in chronological order and syntactical formality. The tone is that of a sociable and talkative person reminiscing over beer and tobacco in a tavern.

Although it is not, of course, possible to draw any firm conclusion from the evidence, it seemed appropriate to attempt the more scientific approach of 'cumulative sum' analysis of samples of the text. A computer programme which is used not only for purposes of literary investigation, but also to test the authenticity of the supposed confessions of twentieth-century law-breakers, was thus applied to the supposed confessions of a seventeenth-century predecessor. The resulting 'cusum' charts do, in fact, lend some support to the view that there may be three distinct voices, one for each section of the text.

utpurse' is probably most familiar to modern readers from the representation of her in Middleton and Dekker's *The Roaring Girl*, printed in 1611. A 'roaring boy' was, in the cant of the day, a noisy and riotous young man who terrorised decent people in the streets of London. Such youths evidently constituted a well-known and all-too-familiar class. The term 'roaring girl', on the other hand, must have been applied only to a tiny minority of individuals, and seems to have been used with somewhat wider connotations, denoting a young female whose behaviour was transgressive or assertive in some way. The heroine of Middleton and Dekker's play has great energy and charm; she wears masculine attire, wields a sword, frequents taverns and does business with thieves; she also sympathises with true love and with the lot of other women. The play's epilogue promises that if the audience is disappointed:

> The Roaring Girl herself, some few days hence,
> Shall on this stage [of the Fortune Theatre] do ample recompense....

An entry in *The Consistory of London Correction Book* for 27 January 1612 suggests that this promise was kept. (A consistory or bishop's court dealt, among other matters, with the sexual and moral transgressions of those in a diocese.) It runs as follows:

> This day & place the sayd Mary appeared personally & then & there voluntarily confessed that she had long frequented all or most of the disorderly & licentious places in this Cittie as namely she hath vsually in the habite of a man resorted to alehowses Tavernes Tobacco shops & also to play howses there to see plaies and pryses & namely being at a playe about 3 quarters of a yeare since at the ffortune in mans apparell & in her bootes & with a sword by her syde, she told the company there present that she thought many of them were of opinion that she was a man, but if any of them would come to her lodging they should finde that she is a woman & some other immodest & lascivious speaches she also vsed at that time And also sat there vppon the stage in the

publique viewe of all the people there presente in mans apparrell & playd vppon her lute & sange a songe. And she further confessed that she hath for this longe time past vsually blasphemed & dishonored the name of God by swearing & cursing & tearing God out of his kingdome yf it were possible, & hath also vsually associated her selfe with Ruffinly swaggering & lewd company as namely with cut purses blasphemous drunkardes & others of bad note & most dissolute behaviour with whom she hathe to the great shame of her sexe often tymes (as she sayd) drunke hard & distempered her heade with drinke And further confesseth that since she was punished for the misdemeanors afore mentioned in Bridewell she was since vpon Christmas day at night taken in Powles Church with her peticoate tucked vp about her in the fashion of a man with a mans cloake on her to the great scandall of diuers persons who vnderstood the same & to the disgrace of all womanhood And she sayeth & protesteth that she is heartely sory for her foresayd licentious & dissolute lyfe & giveth her earnest promise to carry & behave her selfe ever from hence forwarde honestly soberly & woma‹n›ly & resteth ready to vndergo any censure or punishement for her misdemeanors afor‹e›sayd in suche manner & forme as shalbe assigned her by the Lo: Bishop of London her Ordinary. And then she being pressed to declare whether she had not byn dishonest of her body & hath not also drawne other women to lewdnes by her perswasions & by carrying her self lyke a bawde, she absolutly denied that she was chargeable with eyther of these imputacions And therevppon his Lordship. thought fit to remand her to Bridewell from whence she nowe came vntill he might further examine the truth of the misdemeanors inforced against her without laying as yet any further censure vppon her.[5]

Frith also figures, though more briefly, in a play by Nathan Field published in 1618 but probably written and acted several years earlier. The title of the first edition simply reads: *Amends for Ladies*; the Huntington Library copy alone appears to have the title: *Amends for Ladies. / With the Hvmovr of Roring.* For the second edition the title was expanded to: *Amends for Ladies. With the merry prankes of Moll Cut-Purse: Or, the humour of roaring....* In this play the character of Moll Cutpurse makes only one brief appearance; it must have seemed that her notoriety would be good box office or good for the publisher's receipts, and she is brought on to deliver a message and exchange some rather ambivalent backchat in a play which otherwise has nothing to do with her. The real Moll must at this point have been in her twenties and clearly already well-known to Londoners. Frith and Field were probably childhood neighbours, as Field was born in 1583, son of the minister of the parish in which Frith was supposedly born (no baptismal entry has so far been found).

The *Stationers' Register* has an entry for August 1610 of 'A Booke called the Madde Prancks of Merry Mall of the Bankside, with her Walks in Mans Apparel and to what Purpose. Written by John Day', which supports the impression that Frith, in her twenties, had emerged as a well-known figure at that point; no copy of any such work survives, however, and it may never have been printed. From these years on, though, Frith occurs again and again, not just in published works of all kinds, but also in private writing. John Chamberlain's letter of February 1612, for example, gives a rather different view of Frith's penance at Paul's Cross from that in the 'Diary':

> ...and this last Sonday Mall Cut-purse a notorious bagage (that used to go in mans apparell and challenged the feild of divers gallants) was brought to the same place, where she wept bitterly and seemed very penitent, but yt is since doubted she was maudelin druncke, beeing discovered to have tipled of three quarts of sacke before she came to her penaunce: she had the daintiest preacher or ghostly father that ever I saw in pulpit, one Ratcliffe of Brazen Nose in Oxford, a likelier man to have led the revells in some ynne of court then to be where he was, but the best is he did extreem badly, and so wearied the audience that the best part went away, and the rest taried rather to heare Mall Cutpurse then him.[6]

Mal Cutpurse's World

By 1610, then, Frith appears to be at the beginning of a promising career of social transgression. What sort of criminal world might she have entered? By 1630, the population of England had nearly doubled in little more than a hundred years, while opportunities for gainful employment had not increased at the same rate; for many people, begging or crime must have been the only way to stay alive. London was developing fast at the time, and there does seem to have been a more organised criminal world there than in other cities. There were certainly whole areas of London which, for historical reasons, provided criminal sanctuaries where those who broke the law could escape from it. 'Alsatia', an area just south of Frith's house, the old ecclesiastical sanctuary of Whitefriars between Fleet Street and the river, was one such 'liberty'. When malefactors were actually arrested, a great many of them were released from the legal process unscathed for a number of different reasons. Mary Carleton was unlucky; Mary Frith, dying peacefully in her bed, was more typical of a century when, according to John L. McMullan, 'Everyday enforcement and supervision practices suggest that legal censure was negotiable'.

Few people in the seventeenth century had much money in their houses in the form of coins, and even fewer would have carried much around on their persons, but there were certainly more consumer goods than there had been earlier, and their redistribution in various ways provided a living for many. According to McMullan, London had an invaluable 'network of fencing partners who helped thieves dispose of their goods. Often they functioned as patrons of crime, directing the organisation of thieving. Such brokers ran houses at which information, contacts, alibis, and shelter were provided. The risks of self-fencing were eliminated by this use of intermediaries. Many brokers of stolen property were themselves strategically placed to funnel the "takes" into wider legitimate markets'.[7] This certainly sounds like the world of Mary Frith, and Mary McIntosh[8] suggests a reason for the nature and importance of 'fencing' prior to the Industrial Revolution: 'Personal property still tended to be concentrated in the upper classes and to be of a distinct and highly individualised nature'. Before mass production, every watch, every piece of lace was slightly different from every other, making stolen goods difficult to sell, and this encouraged a system of offering rewards for recovery. But it was clearly dangerous for thieves to take goods direct to the owners themselves. McIntosh quotes Jenny Diver, a famous pickpocket of the 1730s: 'Suppose you go home with them and get the reward offered, here lies the case. The parties injured will, though they ask you no question, take particular notice of your person, and some time or other, you are out upon business, you may be smoked, then perhaps all may be blown. So my advice is that whatever things may be got, though we can fence them for but two-thirds of the value offered yet it is much the safer way and less dangerous.' Jonathan Wild did the same sort of thing as Frith – returned stolen goods to victims, with no questions asked; property was not so much stolen, as kidnapped and held until ransomed. This appears to have been Mary Frith's chief business for a number of years, though it seems likely that both she and others exaggerated the extent to which she, or anyone else, was actually in control of criminal activities.

One example of Frith at work, but encountering problems, survives in the form of the record of a suit of complaint of wrongful arrest and imprisonment heard in the Court of Star Chamber in 1621. The suit is against several people, including 'Mary Markham alias Frith, alias Thrift, alias "Malcutpurse"'. Frith's defence included the information that a man claiming to have been robbed

> ...became to this Defendant and desired her to doe her endeauour to try if she could by any meanes fynd out the pickpockett or helpe him to his monie, he being before of this defendant's acquaintance and hauinge heard how by this defendant's meanes many that had had theire pursses Cut or goods stollen had beene helped to theire goods againe and diuers of the offenders taken or discouered....

According to the evidence of Margaret Dell, the complainant, and her husband, a constable had taken this suspected pickpocket not before a magistrate, but straight to the house of

Mary Markham/Frith, and, when Dell insisted that his wife must be removed from the company of 'such a notorious infamous person', Moll angrily replied that 'she had a royal commission to examine all such persons, and advised Dell to go before he was beaten'. This certainly looks like an episode when Frith was trying to exert control. Towards the end of her defence in court, Moll's plea makes her sound very like the woman in the 'Diary', who is always quick and vigorous in exacting vengeance for any injury or slight: 'if...either of them gaue this Defendant any ill words or language she this Defendent might and did giue them some reply in some tart or angry manner agayne....'[9]

Modesty, silence and obedience were the passive virtues instilled into women; Frith constantly transgresses the traditional construction of femininity in early modern England. Her ability (and that of Mary Carleton) to speak up boldly and effectively in public is in marked contrast to the properly feminine behaviour which Margaret Cavendish, Duchess of Newcastle, describes in her account of herself. Driven back from exile by poverty, she attended Goldsmiths' Hall, where a parliamentary committee had been established in 1644 to negotiate with royalists who wished to regain their sequestered property. She hoped to get some of her husband's huge estates back, but when her petition was given an absolute negative, she 'whisperingly spoke to my brother[-in-law] to conduct me out of that ungentlemanly place, so without speaking to them one word good or bad, I returned to my Lodgings...'. She seemed to feel that it would have dishonoured her to have been more persistent and active. She saw the customs of England as having changed as well as the laws, 'where Women become Pleaders, Atturneys Petitioners and the like, running about with their severall Causes, complaining of their severall grievances, exclaming against their severall enemies...'. She was 'unpractised in publick Imployments, unlearned in their uncouth Ways, ignorant of the Humors, and Dispositions of those persons to whom I was to adress my suit, and not knowing where the power lay ... besides I am naturally Bashfull'.[10] This all makes the strongest possible contrast to Frith's attitude in the 'Diary'.

She was very ready to speak out in public or to join the 'honest matrons' who petitioned Parliament for peace in 1643, even, according to her own account, shouting back at those who were telling the women to go home. Above all, she was certainly unlike Margaret Cavendish in that she appears to have learnt where the power lay, or as much of it as she needed to make her way in the world in her chosen fashion.

Where Cavendish begins her autobiographical account by placing herself in a family and describing her upbringing, Frith's memoirs begin at the moment when she takes over her own life: 'I was hardly twenty from whence I date my self...'. That suddenly emerging 'self' was self-created, later to become a 'sweet self' focused in the mirrors in her house, and the greatest similarity between Mary Frith and Mary Carleton is that neither was willing to accept the role into which she had been born; each re-fashioned her self. Penniless and having rejected marriage, the external options open to Frith were not many and not attractive, as she herself realised: 'I had but very little choice'. It was precisely this 'little choice', this narrow margin of external possibility available to the ordinary woman, that led her to reshape herself as something extraordinary. McMullan writes that London was an economic magnet for single women seeking work, females outnumbering males by thirteen to ten. 'The refusal of guilds and of the city crafts to apprentice women narrowed occupation opportunities and confined many to "housewife trades" – brewers, bakers, and cooks – for which they were poorly paid. Women were particularly prominent in the victualing and vending trades; by far the greatest number worked as domestic servants for the wealthy, or at private inns. Many women drifted in and out of prostitution and thieving'.[11] Frith, however, does not seem so much to have drifted into a criminal life-style, as to have made a rational career-choice; with her dislike for domestic tasks (like Spenser's Britomart and George Eliot's Maggie Tulliver, she was a female child who hated sewing) and her reluctance to be controlled by others, her chosen *métier* must have suited her very well.

Her life was also a rejection of the enclosure that protected and constrained the female as traditionally constructed. In a period when a virtuous woman was supposed to remain at home, she was constantly 'abroad', transacting business at the Globe Inn near her house, sitting around in taverns recounting anecdotes, smoking, drinking (and getting drunk), galloping across London for a wager. A striking feature of her life as recounted in the 'Diary' and as mirrored in *The Consistory of London Correction Book* is that many of her activities are not in themselves illegal or even undesirable; they are simply activities which were firmly gendered as masculine. An image of the approved contemporary female could be constructed by negative inference from Frith's 'Diary', and not the least of her transgressions is that she takes a transgressive right in herself; she will not be married, sent to America, or put to a female trade by male 'friends'. Law-breaking itself was not just the only way a woman with no financial backing could earn a living without serving others in a feminine capacity, it was also a transgression of the patriarchal order which was the only order her contemporaries knew.

Yet the age in which Frith lived was apt for transgression. Living through the first half of the seventeenth century, she experienced one of the most turbulent periods of British history, a time when all boundaries seemed to have fallen or to be threatened. Unlike earlier civil wars, the struggle was not between two very similar powers, York or Lancaster, a white or a red rose. The whole traditional hierarchy of church and state, king, government and governed, was in a state of upheaval. The pyramid-shaped mountain of an originally feudal social structure had become an active volcano. The 1640s saw the demise of the Star Chamber, the Court of High Commission, the councils of Wales and of the North, episcopacy, the church courts, the House of Lords and censorship, and the executions of the Earl of Strafford, the Archbishop of Canterbury and the King. New administrative bodies included the county committees, which had the power to call errant ministers and politically suspect landlords before them. In this world where all categories, relationships and moral values were shifting and uncertain, the nature and position of women seems to have become a particularly sensitive issue. As Margaret Cavendish noted, women began 'running about with their severall Causes', and the exigencies of the time made them active in unaccustomed fields. Jonathan Dollimore notes that any disturbance of sexual identity was perceived as *socially* threatening:

> ...the early modern view of identity as constituted (metaphysically) was also, and quite explicitly, a powerful metaphysic of social integration. In other words, to be metaphysically identified was simultaneously to be socially positioned – the subject in relation to the prince, the woman in relation to the man, and so on...if (as was apparent in the early seventeenth century) identity is clearly constituted by the structures of power, of position, allegiance, and service, then any disturbance within, or of, identity could be as dangerous to that order as to the individual subject.[12]

The language used by the writer of the introductory material in *The Life and Death of Mrs. Mary Frith* betrays the fact that he sees assumption of male costume as assumption of power ('she resolved to usurp and invade the Doublet'), and that it was felt necessary to punish Frith and secure promises of amendment for behaviour which would have been thought innocuous in a man is apparent both from court records and from the evidence of her 'Diary'. When Frith perceives that she has earned a certain amount of status in the community, she feels she can relax somewhat and enjoy herself in the way which is natural to her, 'I was no way difficult or curiously cautelous in my Conversation, but with all freedome in a fair way...allowed my self in my humours'. This was a mistake, as she is arrested, taken to one of London's most unpleasant prisons for the rest of the night, then brought before the Lord Mayor and charged, not just with 'unseasonable and suspitious walking' but with 'the strange manner of my Life'. It is significant that, in order to be released with no more than a small fine, Frith has to counterfeit femininity; she pretends that she was out in the street late at night on the quintessentially female errand of going to support another woman in childbirth.

Mary Frith not only behaved like a man in various ways, she was also subversive in appearance. The picture of her on the title page of *The Roaring Girl* shows a fresh-faced figure wearing contemporary masculine costume, carrying a sword and smoking a pipe. Clothing has usually been the most immediate signifier of gender, and the failure to wear sufficiently gendered garments or the wearing of garments deemed by contemporaries to belong to the opposite sex had been condemned from the earliest times. Judaeo-Christian tradition explicitly forbids cross-dressing: 'The woman shall not wear that which pertaineth unto a man, neither shall a man put on a woman's garment; for all that do so are abomination unto the Lord thy God'.[13] In the seventeenth century transvestism was explicitly forbidden and Frith was not alone in receiving public punishment for this offence: John Taylor, for example, was indicted at Chester in 1608 'for wearinge weomen's apparel'; he received the sentence that 'his clothes to be cut and breeches to be made of them & to be whipped thorowe the citie tomorrowe'.[14] The portrait of Frith which has been bound in opposite the title page of a copy of the 1639 edition of *Amends for Ladies* in the Folger Library represents an older woman. Frith would have been in her early fifties by then, and this depiction of her with her pet animals looks very much as though it might originally have been taken from the life. Here again her upper garments are masculine; in this three-quarter portrait it is not apparent what nether garments she is wearing, but it could well be the skirts she says in the 'Diary' that she wears.

Earlier in the century, Frith had not been the only woman to wear such a costume; and garb that confused indications of one sex with those of the other may perhaps have been perceived as even more threatening than complete transvestism. In 1620, James I, a man whose sexual tastes may well have led him to feel an inner anxiety about how fixed gender identity actually was, railed against a new fashion: women wearing doublet and petticoat, with a masculine hat, and sometimes even a small dagger. Another of John Chamberlain's letters shows an attempt to mend matters:

Yesterday the bishop of London called together all his Cler-
gie about this towne, and told them he had expresse com-
maundment from the King to will them to inveigh vehemently
and bitterly in theyre sermons, against the insolencie of our
women, and theyre wearing of brode brimd hats, pointed
dublets, theyre haire cut short or shorne, and some of them
stillettaes or poinards, and such other trinckets of like moment;
adding withall that yf pulpit admonitions will not reforme them
he wold proceed by another course; the truth is the world is
very far out of order, but whether this will mend yt God
knowes.[15]

Frith may have represented what Marjorie Garber calls 'the
power of the transvestite to unsettle assumptions, structures
and hierarchies',[16] but she seems to have been singularly lacking
in that other transvestite power, 'the seduction emanating from
a person of uncertain or dissimulate sex'. The very existence of
such power is denied by the writer of the introductory material
in *The Life and Death of Mrs. Mary Frith* (who may well have grown
up in a period when the closing of London's theatres by a
puritan government denied young people the pleasures of
watching actors disguised as the opposite sex). He asserts, either
naively or disingenuously, that cross-dressing 'cannot but be
disgustful to mankind'. Frith tells the story of the joking rejection she received (she looked as if some Toad had ridden her)
when she made a joking offer of herself to a neighbour. She
claims that 'apathany and insensiblenesse of my carnal pleasure
even to stupidity possest me'; to judge by the 'Diary', she was
sociable and had many male friends, but the dominant tone of
these relationships appears to have been the camaraderie of male
bonding, with little hint of feminine seduction.

The character of Moll Cutpurse in *The Roaring Girl* may be
sympathetic to other women and sensitive to the disadvantage
under which they are placed by society's double standards, but
it would be difficult to see Mary Frith as a proto-feminist on the
evidence of her *Life and Death*, unless some of the remarks
ascribed to her are in fact interpolations of an 'editor'. If this
were so, it might support a reading of the final text with its two

presumably male-authored introductions as an attempt to subordinate female rebellion to male authority. The original presenter stresses that Frith is one-of-a-kind, thus turning her from a threat into an oddity, a monstrous peepshow exhibit, to be managed by and for men. But, whether it is the result of a male reading permeating any original material, or (as seems more likely) the subject's own attitudes conveyed in the alleged 'Diary', Frith shows little or no sympathy for other women, rather the reverse. We have already been told by the introducer of the 'Diary' that the 'Mag-pye Chat of the Wenches' was intolerable to her, and in her own words later she is more than once severe on other women, even siding with husbands against them. On the face of it, Frith can perceive having a voice and personal autonomy only in terms of becoming a male; she appears to be transgressing the homosocial system rather than rejecting it – moving over and redefining herself as (asexually) male.

An Epitaph for Mal Cutpurse

One more curious piece of seventeenth-century writing about Mary Frith remains; this is her supposed epitaph, which is reprinted in *The Uncollected Writings of John Milton*.[17] The editors quote Charles Johnson's *General History of...the Most Famous Highwaymen*[18], where it is also reprinted: 'When she was dead, she was interr'd in St. Bridget's [St. Bride's, Fleet Street] Churchyard, having...the following Epitaph, compos'd by the ingenious Mr. Milton, but destroy'd in the great Conflagration of *London*'. They suggest that, given the similarity to verses about Hobson, the Cambridge University carrier, and other verses which are doubtfully ascribed to Milton, 'there is some chance these verses are his'.

> Here lies, under this same Marble,
> Dust, for Time's last Sive to garble;
> Dust, to perplex a *Sadducee*,
> Whither it rise a He or She,

Or two in one, a single pair,
Natures sport and now her care;
For how she'l cloath it at last day,
(Unlesse she Sigh it all away)
Or where she'l place it, none can tell,
Some middle place 'twixt *Heaven* and *Hell*;
And well 'tis Purgatory's found,
Else she must Hide her under *Ground*.
These Reliques do deserve the Doom,
That cheat of *Mahomets* fine Tomb:
For no Communion She had,
Nor sorted with the Good or Bad;
That when the world shall be calcin'd,
And the mixd' Masse of humane kind
Shall separate by that melting Fire,
She'l stand alone and none come nigh her.
Reader, here she lies till then,
When (to say all) you'l see her agen.

THE CASE OF MADAM MARY CARLETON,
LATELY STILED THE GERMAN PRINCESS,
TRUELY STATED: WITH AN HISTORICAL RELATION OF
HER BIRTH, EDUCATION, AND FORTUNES

So to 'Kentish Moll', the 'German Princess', the most notorious female 'rogue' of her day. When the author of *The Sixth Part of the Wandring-whore revived*, published in 1663, wanted to make a point about the customers of a particular courtesan, he wrote: 'If our late Errant Female, high and low German Princess had such Suitors, she would ne'r have to do with Grooms, Coachmen and Footboys, and her husband might well be content to be the richest Cuckold in England'. Ten years later, when the author of the epilogue to Aphra Behn's *Dutch Lover* (1673) compared the female playwright and the famous 'German Princess' executed a month before, it was assumed that the audience would immediately understand the wit:

...sad Experience our Eyes convinces
That damn'd their Plays which hang'd the German Princess;
And we with Ornament set off a play,
Like her drest fine for Execution-day.

Unlike the German Princess, however, the playwright expects a 'Reprieve' from the execution of criticism:

Well, what the other mist, let our Scribe get,
A Pardon, for she swears she's the less Cheat.
She never gull'd you Gallants of the Town
Of Sum above four Shillings, or half a Crown.

The German Princess, hanged in 1673, was the famous Mary Carleton, alias Mary Moders alias Mary Steadman and possibly alias Mary Day. Despite what is alleged in *The Case*, in time the public came largely to believe her a wily and daring confidence trickster, a predecessor of Defoe's Moll Flanders and Roxana, who actually alludes to her real-life predecessor when she remarks at one point, 'I might as well have been the German Princess'.[19]

The following outline seems to emerge from the many texts. It may or may not be 'true'.

Mary was born Mary Moders on, she claimed, 22 January 1642, although others revised her birth back by about eight years; her father, possibly a chorister of Canterbury cathedral or a fiddler, died and her mother was remarried to either a fiddler or an inn-keeper in Canterbury. With her vitality and quick-wittedness Mary gained the interest of the well-to-do and began to mix with children of higher rank than herself. Thus she learnt genteel accomplishments and acquired an educated way of speaking above her station. Failing the grand alliance she craved, she married a shoemaker called Steadman from Canterbury with whom she had two children who both died. Trying to escape her marriage, she took the opposite route to Mary Frith and persuaded a master's mate to take her on board a ship bound for Barbados, but she was discovered and brought back by her husband. She then married a surgeon called Day from Dover, after which marriage she was indicted for bigamy, but the case was dropped because she claimed she had believed her first husband dead. She probably visited the Continent where she polished her languages and made a new identity for herself when by chance she was taken for another woman.

Decking herself out with jewels and finery and passing under the new name of Maria de Wolway, she descended on London where she claimed to be a noble German lady forced to flee incognito from an unwanted marriage. She impressed an inn-keeper with her display and he alerted his father-in-law of the rich pickings to be had by his son. Her appearance of wealth was aided by her ingenious planting of false letters supposedly from the Continent attesting to her estates. John Carleton, a young lawyer of eighteen, accoutred himself to match her finery, speedily won her consent, and the pair were married. Each believed the other to be rich.

A few days of display in Hyde Park and other public places followed and, after some irritation at the failure of her wealth to materialise, the appalled family of John Carleton was alerted by a letter from Canterbury discovering Mary's colourful past. They hastily called in the authorities and she was dragged to prison. There she was visited by people of rank and position including, on 29 May 1663, the diarist Samuel Pepys, highly susceptible to the charm that had, allegedly, procured three husbands. Just over a week later on 7 June he claimed that he was 'high in the defence of her wit and spirit'.

The trial of Mary Carleton for bigamy gripped the public. It was hastily opened at the Old Bailey, too hastily indeed for the prosecuting Carletons who bungled the case by managing to pro-duce only one witness to the earlier marriages, James Knot, who claimed to have given Mary away at her wedding to Steadman in Canterbury about nine years before. Steadman himself did not appear at court, apparently unable to afford the fare to London from Dover where he now lived. Considering that the Carletons were accused of trying to buy several other witnesses, this failure to advance his fare, if true, was an amazing oversight.

Mary Carleton spoke eloquently – more so in the pamphlets in support of her than in those against – and she declared that, though she was of high birth, her enormous wealth had been an invention of the greedy Carletons. Sensibly she made much of the absence both of a certificate of marriage to Steadman and of Steadman himself. She was thus easily acquitted. The public appeared jubilant and cheered her rousingly for 'so great Novelty had not been known or seen in our age'. Those who doubted her truth were as interested as those who did not, provoked by the daring impersonation of rank which was even more shocking than sexual impersonation; the Restoration was busy re-establishing rank and birth as of prime importance.

The public applause was heartening no doubt but it led to no money and, since the trial, Carleton had refused to support his wife. At the same time the Carletons would not return the jewels and clothes – as was their right since Mary remained legally married to John. In this situation a rather bizarre source of income presented itself.

During the furore of 1663, a mediocre playwright called Tom Porter had exploited events in a short piece entited *A Witty Combat; Or, The Female Victor* acted in Whitsun week. Despite the assertion on the printed form that it had been acted 'with great applause' it is hard to see how this could ever have been the case unless the actors themselves were independently popular, since the play managed to turn the comic events of the duping and the tension of the trial into as wooden a vehicle as the Restoration theatre had ever seen. Characterisation was on the level of repeated phrases such as 'yea verily' for the parson and 'd'ye see' for the innkeeper, while Mary was simply presented as calculating, feeding on the vices of others. In the following year when she was looking for income, Mary Carleton was persuaded to appear in the Duke's Theatre playing the part of herself in this play. Since it satirised both Mary and the Carletons as ridiculous and greedy, it was rather an extraordinary turn of events for a woman who elsewhere had tried to present herself with dignity. But she needed the money and, besides, she appears to have been an inveterate self-publicist. Perhaps she noted the comparison with Mal Cutpurse, remembering her brief appearance on the stage.

'She who had acted on the large Theatre of the World in publick, now came to act in a small Theatre', wrote Francis Kirkman who presented her life story in 1673. Of course many thronged to see the play including Pepys, but 'she did not perform so well as was expected', although she got 'great Applause' as she had at her acquittal, and it was agreed that she acted better 'in the wide World than in that Epitomie'. An epilogue spoken by her insisted that, since all the world was a cheat and everyone in it also, it was better to make a splash than not, 'to get a glorious name/ However got; then live by common Fame'. Pepys's view was recorded in his diary entry for April 15 1664: 'saw *The German Princess* acted by the woman herself....the whole play...is very simple, unless, here and there, a witty sprinkle or two'.

For seven years Mary Carleton was out of the public eye during which she apparently used her sexual attractions to gain lovers and her strategic abilities to fool them, sometimes two at a time. On each occasion she created a new identity for herself and a new life-story backed up with suitable clothing and supporting documents. But in 1670 she was caught for stealing a silver tankard and condemned to be hanged, a sentence which was changed to transportation to Jamaica in 1671. She seems to have travelled to the colony but in a short time she was prematurely back in England. There she engaged in further 'pranks' through working on men's desire for sex or money and presenting herself as 'quality', even managing one supreme fraud that netted her about £600 in goods and ready money.

Finally she was caught again and indicted for stealing a piece of plate. She was recognised by the old turnkey from Newgate as the German Princess he had had earlier in custody. Since she expected to get off, she did not see fit to tell any ingratiating truths which might have suggested a saving penitence; instead she answered her judges facetiously and wittily. It was a mistake. She was hanged at Tyburn on 22 January 1673, confessing her sins and dying piously and properly. Many people were condemned to be hanged, but not everyone was so; Mary Carleton's notoriety may well have contributed to her suffering of the penalty.

The Pamphlets of 1663

In 1663 before and after the acquittal and again in 1673 after her hanging Mary Carleton was the subject of a flurry of pamphlets, more numerous than those inspired by any other ordinary criminal of her time; indeed they went on appearing until well into the eighteenth century.[20] In these she not only starred in court room dramas, but also attracted to herself several extra stories of transvestism and trickery. The repetition of certain publishers' names at the ends of pamphlets suggests that there was much financial gain to be made by keeping up the interest. On the whole the pamphlets gave events in a rapid sequence; or, remaining short on facts, they vindicated one of the participants; or they mocked the event and everyone concerned with it, usually in doggerel verse. A list of the 1663 and 1673 pamphlets is given in Appendix 2 – there may well be more hiding under obscure names.

Several of the 1663 pamphlets were said to be by the participants, John and Mary Carleton: *The Case* printed here was delivered under Mary's name. To set the work in its controversial context of argument and scandal, then, some of the other pamphlets need outlining. Without them, a reader might appreciate *The Case* solely as a woman's self-fashioning of multiple and appealing identities; with them another possible reading is suggested: of *The Case* as a contribution to rogue literature. John Carleton, an interested party, warned readers not to be overcome by his wife's wiles and craft.

The Lawyer's Clarke Trappan'd by the Crafty Whore of Canterbury was published even before the outcome of the trial was known. It constructed a denigratory image of the whorish daughter of a Canterbury fiddler, married to one man in Dover and one in Canterbury. She cheated a vintner of £60 and was committed to

Newgate. She then cheated a French merchant of jewels and picked a Kentish lord's pocket at Gravesend, relieving him of watch and money. Once she had sold these she tried to take ship for Barbados but was caught.

This trickster's history had to be countered by the Mary Carleton camp and it was thus succeeded by the nobly toned *A Vindication Of a Distressed Lady* which declared *The Lawyer's Clarke* 'stufft so full of Lies and Forgeries, that it needs no other then a Denial to the whole'. In *A Vindication* Mary Carleton was descended from people of quality but she had 'some Reasons at the present' to conceal more about them. She could not be a 'Fidlers Daughter of *Canterbury*' for 'Her Accomplishments do demonstrate the contrary'. A fiddler could not have given his child an education in French, Dutch, Latin, Greek and Hebrew, as well as in music and singing, in all of which she demonstrated her skill. Her very 'Gestures and Carriage' suggested quality, the pamphlet averred. The story of the Carleton double fraud was presented as the preying of the man on the woman: she had spoken of her fortune only to gain respect but 'she observed that they as Fish greedily bit at [it], and intended to have made a Prey of her'. She was then kept more or less a prisoner by the Carletons who feared her being snapped up by an impecunious courtier. She was speedily married to John by a parson and a few days later she insisted on a proper marriage with a licence. During all this time the credulous greed of the Carletons increased her fortune and it rose to £5,000 and from £5,000 to £8,000.

On May day she was displayed in splendour in Hyde Park with Lady Bludsworth in attendance. But a few days later a letter deflated all splendid hopes by telling of her lowly birth in Canterbury. She was at once stripped of her finery, including even her stockings, and dragged to prison. There she was visited by John who blamed his parents for her treatment, claiming he could have lived with her without an estate – to which claim many witnesses could apparently testify. Mary Carleton 'never was a Whore to any man' concluded this pamphlet and a postscript declared that she never claimed her name to be

Henrietta Maria de Vulva. The name was both lewd and political since it mocked the unpopular French dowager queen who had visited her sons in England.

The performance stung the pro-John Carleton forces into action with *The Replication* which John Carleton claimed to have written himself. The pamphlet, intending to convey moderation and learning with its Latin quotations, gave a lofty sense of the myth-making going on around the events: 'the Various Rumours, Stories, Fancies, dayly encreasing Fables, and Proteus Shapes wherein the Different Humours, and Dispositions of the World bring forth the late acted Project, and Cheat'. Presenting himself as an honest dupe, the author scorned the 'scurrilous Scribler' of *The Distressed Lady* and would not begin to un-dress all his 'prodigious shapes'. None the less he told of the arrival of the 'unworthy Woman' and her speedy passion for him; in this account the Carleton clan were not involved until after John's engagement to Mary and so were not the prime movers in the enterprise. But he accepted his wife's 'Endowments', her wit and his duping by her apparent principles and religion. When she was discovered a fraud, he was, he declared, interested only in the charge of bigamy which the 'Miserable Creature' denied – had she been honest he would have forgiven her all. He was particularly aggrieved at the mention of the 'Worthy' Lady Bludsworth on whose 'Civility' Mary had played. There was no double marriage as averred and she was indeed wed as Henrietta Maria De Wollway. Loftily self-deprecating, John Carleton concluded, 'would She had less Wit, and I better fortune'.

An Historical Narrative of the German Princess was the first of the accounts said to be authored by Mary Carleton herself and responding both to the public appetite for scandal and her own need for vindication. Appearing a few days after her acquittal, it presented a distressed and heroic lady who should have aroused romantic and gallant but not sexual sentiment. Her learning, about which so much had been said, was displayed especially at the beginning in a sprinkling of sayings by philosophers and divines, but it was not explained as it would be later through stories of her early years in Germany. Wisely it remained vague about her birth and background since 'my Ambition never tempted me to write a History of my Life' and it concentrated mainly on the Carleton incidents. It took a high moral tone, discoursing abstractly about 'Truth' and reproducing actual documents such as the alleged letter from John to her in prison. It was preceded by an address to 'Most Noble, Generous, and Vertuous Ladies and Gentlewomen' dated June 12.

This performance seems to have incensed the John-camp which countered with *Ultimum Vale*, expanding on *The Replication* and also said to be written by John Carleton. In this he appeared a more tragic man than in the earlier text, inextricably married to the 'Out-landish *Canterbury-Monster*'. The work reads as a rant against the 'crafty Strumpet', with none of the narrative thrust of *An Historical Narrative* despite John's claims that he would show more passion and more truth than ever before and counter the 'thick Mists of some persons Imaginations, other Narrations, other wilful Additions, other Jealousies, other Suppositions, other Suspicions, other Inquisitions...' and disabuse all those won by Mary's 'Charmeing tongue and Sycophantick stile'.

Unfortunately for John he had the problem of giving a plausible impression of his wife's verbal performance to explain his own gullibility, but thereby risking the reader's divided sympathies. Consequently he often entered the text to point to his moral and indicate the lady's baseness, always urging readers to imagine themselves in his place. At intervals he broke into some dismal verse and the text was not enlivened by his occasional efforts at irony.

John Carleton was eager to reveal the events of the earlier Mary-text as stratagems: so for example she was described as placing agents to cry her up where he might hear them; she managed to burn the incriminating evidence of the letters that had been sent as from Germany to fool the Carletons; she pretended suicidal fits when cornered; and her fear of Newgate derived not from feminine weakness but from her anxiety that she would be recognised from her former stay as a common prisoner.

The non-appearance of Mr Steadman on the crucial day of the trial was explained by his being at this time a soldier in Dover and unable to get leave. This was partly because Mary, facing the death penalty if convicted, had threatened to haunt those who let him come. To the witness James Knott, who had, John claimed, proved her marriage to Steadman in the previous trial for bigamy, he added several others who remembered Mary as the shoemaker's wife from Canterbury; and to the list of her husbands he added a Mr Billing the bricklayer. To make her the more outrageous John also claimed that, once freed, she took up with a lawyer and began studying the law and that, shadowing Mal Cutpurse, she went to the Lord Mayor's to thank him for her release 'in mans Apparel, as this Hermaphrodite told me her self on Sunday 14th of June last, when I happened to see her...'.

After writing *Ultimum Vale* but before publishing it, John Carleton came across his wife's new defence, *The Case of Madam Mary Carleton* which appeared a few weeks after the *Historical Narrative*. It infuriated him and he appended a final attack on it as one more of Mary's 'untrue and abusive Prints'. He was particularly irritated by the new portrait illustrating the work and appalled that she had the 'unparallel'd confidence' to use her 'Counterfeit Effigies of her ill-shapen painted face to be inserted as Prologue'. The performance was the more amazing now that it was 'generally known that she is the Production of an infamous brood' and he was angry that, since their marriage had not been disproved by bigamy, she could use his name of Carleton. He was also annoyed at her effrontery in dedicating her work to Prince Rupert whom, he claimed, she did not know at all. Towards the end of this attack he worked himself up to such abuse of the 'defiled Creature' that he wished he could offload her onto anyone who would have her. Oddly, however, although he declared she had not written the pamphlets that went under her name, he was upset that she had not believed he had written his.

As can be gauged from John's furious response to it, *The Case* was a skilful performance which much expanded the account in the *Historical Narrative*. For example the first forty pages of *The*

Case described what the *Historical Narrative* presented in one and many details were added from published versions of the trial, as well as some information from *A Vindication of a Distressed Lady*. There was also a richer texture of life with mentions of such fashionable accoutrements as glass coaches and lackeys, which made the central action more credible. The issue in the work became one of counterfeiting: Mary Carleton had been robbed of her real jewels which were then said to be counterfeit but were not returned to her. She had to prove her jewels and herself authentic through her written work since no person or thing had arrived from Germany to validate her story.

To do this she had to flaunt herself and show her worth without her jewels and without corroboration, to go public in a way that might have argued against her ladylike status, for there was always some sexualising of the public woman in the Restoration. But, to try to avoid this outcome, she refused overt sexual labelling: she was not an adventuress, for example, or a rollicking whore, although others 'prefer my Wit and Artful Carriage to my Honesty, and take this untoward passage of my life for some festivous and merry accident'. Although, as this quotation suggests, there might be some titillation in the text, on the whole *The Case* passed up opportunities of arousing sexual interest, as for example in the description of Mary's disrobing. The rude handling she received was crude, but she presented herself as both ambiguous and dignified when she asserted that such treatment would be inappropriate even if she had been the whore they claimed her to be.

Despite many opportunities of pathos, too, there was relatively little of the damsel in distress, although the writer was well aware of the romantic appeal of the story. Like her appearance at the trial, success in *The Case* depended on Mary's ability to make a suitable subject of herself, to present an image that was appropriate as well as convincing. So she in part used the conventions of the female subject popularised by French romance writers, with which the female readership was familiar and with which female self-imaging was so intimately bound. That she had struck the right note in this was apparent from John Carleton's dismissal of her story as a 'pretty Romance'.

Mary Carleton was not overtly transgressive in her text because it was still possible that she could convince the world of her authenticity – in which, to an extent, she herself might well have believed by now. Despite her dedication to Prince Rupert and the hints of seduction which the address of a beautiful woman to a libertine man implied, she provided an image of injured innocence wounded by scandal. She was thus worthy of a champion while showing herself her own best champion through her skill at languages and writing.[21] She was worth fighting for because she could fight for herself, not because she was helpless.

The ability to write and to plead suggested a breeding which the tongue-tied Carletons of the trial and John in his clogged pamphlets could not match. That he bought the connection of breeding and linguistic skill was evident from *Ultimum Vale* in which he noted her 'handsome and noble deportment as a person of quality, and good languages as being well bred' – which led to his belief in her being 'what she pretended and represented her self'.

In *The Case* Mary enclosed other documents in her text such as the libels of *The Lawyer's Clark* and the transcript of the trial, to nullify them. She could, she implied, afford to be honest. These enclosures revealed other people as hidden, secretive and venal where she was open and honourable. She clung to her loftiness of tone and tried not to be thrown off-course by the material she quoted. Although at one point she insisted that she could not tell all she knew and that secrecy was necessarily part of a lady's repertoire, as the narrative progressed she moved towards openness. By the time she arrived at the history of the Carletons, she had nothing to hide and took them on with gusto. So confident did she become that she even risked shadowing her own story with a real fraud perpetrated by her enemies: they had set up a man to claim to be her husband, but he proved so ignorant of her person that he was in the event prepared to go off with Grizel Hudson, one of the other prisoners, in her place.

While John and Mary or their surrogates battled it out in print, other pamphlets appeared purporting to give details of the actual charges and trial. Usually they claimed 'to stand neuter', but in fact they frequently took sides, as can be observed from part of the title of *The Great Trial and Arraignment of the late Distressed Lady* and of *The Articles and Charge of Impeachment* which described Mary and John Carleton as 'This Rare Inchantress and That Worthy Gentleman'.

Among these accounts, *The Arraignment, Triall and Examination of Mary Moders* has a certain status because it was later included in Howell and Cobbett's *Collection of State Trials* as presumably the most impartial of the accounts. It added this convincing detail: that, once the imposture was known, Mary addressed John: 'You cheated me, and I you. You told me you were a Lord, and I told you I was a Princess'. Details of the witnesses were provided: of James Knot who claimed he had given Mary away in marriage to Steadman in Canterbury and of Sarah Williams who declared she had known Mary when she had been bound for Barbados and intercepted by her husband. Mary's spirited responses were also given fully, together with her reasonable assertion that the accusing letter from Canterbury, which described her as fat, full-breasted and speaking several languages, could have referred to many women beside herself. In this account Mary also alleged that witnesses had been offered bribes to identify her as the fiddler's stepdaughter.

The Arraignment tended to reveal Mary as spirited and resourceful certainly, but not entirely distressed and honest – consequently it was followed by *A True Account of the Tryal of Mrs Mary Carlton* 'Published for her Vindication, at Her Own Request' which gave the events described in the Arraignment a more sympathetic inflection.

While the romantic, distressed but self-reliant lady opposed the rogue and crafty whore for primary possession of the image of Mary Carleton, several comic pamphlets and poems appeared to amuse the public with more humorous pictures. The author of *Vercingetorixa: or, the Germane Princess Reduc'd to an English Habit* mocked both John and Mary Carleton and caught the high comedy of the whole incident. Written in rollicking, doggerel, Hudibrastic style, the verses presented Mary Carleton as a trickster and John Carleton as a dupe and fool. Among the various commendatory poems that prefaced it was one supposedly by J.C. or John Carleton to the author lamenting that he was a much mocked man and would like now to sell his princess – he had been prepared to give her away in *Ultimum Vale*.

In the *Vercingetorixa* version of the story, John Carleton, who had hired various elaborate props including a silver sword, was spied in his finery by Mary who declared him to be her 'fate'. He was fetched by a vintner's wife who encouraged him: 'Sh'ath Gems in plenty: / Pray enter on her; Room is empty.' Mary was soon eager for a wedding and even stated that she would not check his finances: 'my Dear, / ...I have thousands by the year.' John was quickly won:

> Most lovely witty German,
> Fairer then Negro, strong as Carmen,
> I do consent, and from this Toe
> To Ivory Belly I will go;
> And enter with thy Arched Cloyster....

She was, she claimed, called Vulva.

The Carleton parents were apprised of their son's good fortune : 'Quoth Mother to her aged Husband, / Rejoyce with me, and put on clean Band' to visit her, and the father announced that his son had 'snatcht [her] away by Ink and Pen, / Like Chick by Kits from wary Hen'. Momentarily the household was set into a 'Chitty Chatty' on hearing that someone from Germany had come to rescue the 'princess' and quickly a wedding licence was procured to head off the threat.

But soon Mary was discovered to have a past: she had been married to a shoemaker and a surgeon. She was stripped by the Carletons and bundled off to prison. The writer was left promising a second part to his poem giving an equally rollicking version of the trial and her defence.

The Female-Hector, or, The Germane Lady turn'd Mounsieur was in similar vein to *Vercingetorixa*, but, unlike the latter, it strayed a good deal from the presumed facts set out in the accounts of the trial, assuming presumably that a trangression of class might well include a transgression of gender. It exploited the sexual side of the story which, as the title indicates, included transvestism – this providing a further link between the images of Mary Carleton and Mal Cutpurse. Her gallant deportment suggested that 'instead of the Germane Lady, she may well now be called the Germane Lord...doubtlesse she would make a stout General att the head of an Army of *Amazonian* Ladies'. Much was inevitably made of the stripping. During it Mary Carleton was reduced to her old weeds: the distressed lady became the whore.

The Pamphlets of 1673 and Kirkman's 'Counterfeit Lady Unveiled'

Another rash of pamphlets occurred in 1673. These were at pains to explain the phenomenon of national credulity in 1663, as well as to capitalise on the scandalous life of Mary Carleton. With her unhappy end, the authors could be surer than before of her image and, instead of allowing the ambiguity of 1663, they presented the whole life as a kind of morality tale. Her success at her fraud was partly a matter of her abilities and partly a matter of English gallantry, especially towards supposedly foreign females.

The Deportment and Carriage of the German Princess was an example of the later trial-narrative. In this Mary Carleton was indicted for stealing a piece of plate from someone in Chancery Lane, found guilty and, to avoid her sentence, pleaded her belly. A jury of women was empannelled and they decided 'after long and serious Consultation and Debate' – no physical examination was mentioned – that she was not pregnant. Mary was sentenced to death. The night before her execution she was agitated but was quiet and calm on the day itself and ready to embrace her 'deserved dissolution'. She gave instructions for her burial to a relative who, with her sister, was attending her before she set out to the place of execution. Her patience and pious exclamations were recorded, contrasting with her 'enormous and criminal life'.

Before her death she confessed to general wickedness but desired those around her not to credit all the stories she had inspired. She was prepared to die well and would be hanged on the very day of her baptism, 22 January. She would die, she claimed, a Roman Catholic. When in the cart at the place of hanging she wanted to give a last speech to the crowd, she found her voice too low, and so someone relayed her words for her. She had been a vain woman and she warned others against 'ill Company'. Begging God and her husband to forgive her, she was dying 'in perfect Charity...with all the World'. So, exclaimed the writer with satisfaction, 'this vitious Woman, guilty of such gross Immoralities, did dye well satisfied and unconcern'd, with a Resolution and Courage beyond the weakness of her frail Sex'.

Satiric verses were inevitable. *Some Luck, Some Wit, Being a Sonnet upon the Merry Life and Untimely Death of MIstriss Mary Carlton* appeared before her death, not a sonnet but a nine stanza satire concentrating on her trickeries, and *An Elegie on the Famous and Renowned Lady*, a mock-elegy in heroic couplets. More interesting were the fuller pamphlets which often tried to give some unity to the life and its episodes

The Life and Character of Mrs. Mary Moders, alias Mary Stedman, alias Mary Carleton, alias—— exploited the new publicity generated through the hanging by reprinting *The Case*, simply correcting errors and adding the year 1663 since the dates were not as self-evident as they had been in the first printing. It stopped reproducing the text at the point when the author expressed irritation at the publication of mocking pamphlets and turned to specific points of contention between herself and the Carletons. There then followed a new *Appendix* which addressed the reader: 'Thus have you read her Case, as she relates it' and gave the opinion that the Carletons were as covetous as the lady was cunning. There followed a description of her life since 1663, occasionally with sympathy as when her predicament, after the furore had died down, became her reliance 'upon the cold Bleak of the World'. Some details were added: how she was born in 1642 the daughter of a chorister of Canterbury Cathedral and how, when she failed on the stage, friends suggested she set up a coffee house, but 'her running Brain made it out of the question; always she craved some notable Action'.

Memories of the Life of the Famous Madam Charlton was another short pamphlet which took up the refrain associated with Mary and her images in 1663: that all the world was a cheat and one should not therefore wonder at impostors. It again saw her deceit as a manifestation of her desire to enter a higher sphere than her birth had allowed. It concentrated on her early life, which it claimed had been described to the author by her in prison, and it provided some alternative details, for example that she had been born on 10 April 1639, and some touches of apparent realism: that she read English perfectly and played the virginal and violin at the age of five, that she intruded herself

> into the company of the best Children in the City, with whose Relations, her winning Deportment, and ingenious answers on all occasions, soon did ingratiate her, insomuch that several persons of good quality frequently took her home as a Play-mate for their little ones for a week together.

From these patrons she stole as many pretty things as she could; she saw no other way to come by them for, like Moll Flanders after her, she loathed any notion of 'laborious drudgery'. At thirteen, now nicknamed 'Confident Mall' and expert in writing, dancing, singing and fancy needlework, she begged to accompany a young lady to France where during four years she acquired the language and 'French assurance'. She had begun using her appearance – she was 'a plump succulent Girl' – to cheat men and her lady noted 'her extravangancies'; so they parted. 'Our Lady Errant' returned to Canterbury where, after many pranks and sorties elsewhere, she 'lays the Plot of a Nobler Comedy': the cheating of the Carletons. After this there followed the tricking of an apothecary and the work abruptly ended with a wretched epitaph.

Finally and magisterially after the sequence of short pamphlets came Francis Kirkman's *The Counterfeit Lady Unveiled* which declared itself to be the last and best of all the accounts, a controlling narrative that rose above faction and scandal into history. It was, claimed its author, based on careful intelligence from informants (including 'her unfortunate Husband') and on all previous texts. Indeed the uncharitable might find an over-dependence on certain previous works such as the *Appendix* to *The Life and Character of Mrs. Mary Moders* and *The Memories of the Life of the Famous Madam Charlton*, thus suggesting *The Counterfeit Lady Unveiled* as counterfeit as its subject. But Kirkman also openly quoted a great deal of *The Case* and *The Westminster Wedding*: this 'Book' therefore contained Mary Carleton as no others had. In it she would serve 'as a Looking-glass, wherein we may see the Vices of this Age Epitomized'.

Kirkman took up the image of the lady knight errant from *The Case* but now reminded the reader what such a figure really was: an errant lady. Although she was accepted as the writer of *The Case*, Mary Carleton was presented not primarily as an author but as an actor, a careful and cunning operator who let others make her image while she herself refused to be caught in a single narrative. She was the object not the subject of dis-course. When she was forced to speak, it was defensively so as to confound rather than enlighten the listener; she never answered charges directly but always exaggerated what had been claimed.

Kirkman gave validity to his narrative when he declared himself an eye-witness – and when he occasionally suggested the limits of his first-hand knowledge. So he noted that the picture in front of *The Case* was very like Mary, but that she had actually become thinner in the face during the subsequent nine years. At her final trial, which he allegedly attended, she had worn her hair fashionably dressed and frizzled on top of her head, and she had been clothed in an Indian striped gown, silk petticoat, and white shoes laced with green. In this dress she was hanged. Kirkman had been thus careful to describe her outside; the rest of his book would acquaint the reader with her inside in similar careful detail.

And yet his claim to truth was necessarily unsettled by his anxiety over the nature of truth itself. What was real and what was counterfeit? The jewels with which she had captured Carleton had been true in her narratives and false in John's, but Kirkman declared them neither counterfeit nor worth what she claimed. 'How,' he asked 'can Truth be discovered of her who was wholly composed of Falsehood?' He described Mary Carleton as composed of lies which he would expose, but, at the same time, he allowed that she had told the story of her high birth in Germany so often that she herself had come to believe in it. It was, he thought, the very self-deception of the counterfeit that made the acting so natural.

Despite much condemnation of fraud and some heavy moralising at his subject's expense, the work was also somewhat disturbed by Kirkman's own identification with Mary Carleton. Both seem to have craved a higher social status than that in which they were born and both appear to have found some satisfaction in reading romance and in creating fictions of themselves. In his own autobiographical account *The Unlucky Citizen* (1673) he called himself 'unlucky', the same epithet he used for Mary Carleton at the end of her tale. Although he did not draw attention to it in *The Counterfeit Lady Unveiled*, both also tried to rectify the accident of their birth by writing fantastic accounts of themselves.

Kirkman's Mary Carleton had to be a trickster since her hanging had eliminated the extremes of the 1663 representation: the devilish whore or the distressed lady. The accomplishments which the naive John Carleton had allowed her in 1663 were denied by Kirkman in 1673: she had only a smattering of languages amd she knew no more of Latin and Greek 'then *Jack Adams* the Town Fool'. But in their place he provided a detailed background of French romance, coincidentally rather like that which had inspired his own boyhood.

The tricks which she performed before 1663 and between 1663 and 1673 were filled out. Throughout the narrative she was always on the move, always changing her identity and her story, stealing indiscriminately from anywhere she stayed: silver tankards, bowls and drinking cups from inns and taverns for example. In Cologne she had been mistaken for a person called

Maria Van Wolway by an old and wealthy soldier – the suitor of
The Case – and, with the help of her landlady whom she
subsequently cheated, she had gained jewels and money from
him before bolting with them to England. She had therefore
arrived in London with a name and riches. There she fooled the
Carletons, was tried and acquitted, played herself in the theatre,
and became mistress to a man from whom she finally stole
money and jewels. As with the Carletons, she again used a
'counterfeit Letter' to gain the trust of another man whom she
then relieved of his money. In even more imaginative or folktale
mode, she pretended to bury a friend; by this trick she acquired
'a Pall of Velvet and several pieces of Plate for the Solemnity'
with which she inevitably ran off, leaving 'a Coffin with Hay and
Brickbats'. Kirkman referred to this trick as 'one of her Master-
pieces'.

To deck herself as a rich lady, necessary for the success of her
confidence tricks, Mary easily cheated a mercer, weaver and
laceman of their commodities and she made a tailor supply her
with the clothes without payment. Gloves, ribbons, hoods and
scarves were lifted from an Exchange shop. With such a show
she could even manage to cheat a lawyer of £100. She worked
mainly by appealing to the desire of gain in others but she also
played on her sexual allure or her ladylike appearance once
decked in her stolen finery.

When caught for one of her tankard thefts, she was condemned to transportation to Jamaica. On the voyage she heard
of a planned mutiny; this she betrayed to the captain, thus
gaining his favour and, when she arrived, that of the governor.
But she found Jamaica not to her taste, with few opportunities
of amusement and tricking. So she returned to London where
she 'falls into her old Trade of Pilfering and Cheating'. But she
also tried another fraud reminiscent of the Carleton one: pretending to be a rich citizen's niece, she cheated an apothecary of
£100.

Through her tricks, Kirkman presented a portrait of utter
selfishness, almost perversity. Even when financially comfort-
able, Mary Carleton, like Defoe's Moll Flanders, had to be active

and cheating. When she had money she could not bring herself to part with it 'where Wit would serve the turn'. She took pride in her stratagems and even entered competitions at cheating with other rogues she met. So she presented a kind of masquerade of identities both for gain and for psychological pleasure: after some time, the reader is told, she tired of her 'splendid gallant Garb' and for no immediate pecuniary reason desired to dress in mourning (stolen of course). In this attire she stopped to think whether she should appear as bereaved daughter or widow.

Throughout the later anecdotes recorded of her, Mary Carleton used letters and documents to create persuasive images. She enjoyed the challenge of masquerade and she could become so flushed with success at being able to pass herself off as whatever she wished that she simply cheated automatically 'any body friend or foe, rich or poor, all was fish that came to net whether Salmons or Sprats', as Kirkman put it.

But finally she was caught. She was sent to the Marshalsea prison and then to Newgate. Clearly she had learnt nothing from her previous trials when she had erroneously answered her charges in a merry style for she continued in the same mode. But, when she understood that she had indeed been sentenced to hanging and that no reprieve was likely, she fell into the other extreme of melancholy, in which mood Kirkman himself visited her. Despite his chronicling of her acting and counterfeiting, he declared his belief in her true repentance; he added that she was now 'fit to receive any impression' as if her defensive layers of counterfeit had been stripped from her. So, since she was influenced by Roman Catholic priests at the end, she died in that faith. Kirkman might have seen such protestation in a presumably Protestant woman from Kent as the last attempt to die as the 'German princess'. But, at this crucial time, he was eager to downplay the multiplicity of protean shapes, roles and guises she had assumed and present her as single. The veil must be removed and the counterfeit become the true.

Throughout his work Kirkman showed himself aware of the publicity side of Mary Carleton. He appeared almost sad at a wasted opportunity when he followed the *Appendix* in stating that, after her trial for bigamy in 1663, she was a great celebrity: 'I never heard of her Parallel in every thing, and I believe had she been exposed to publique shew for profit, she might have raised 500l. of those that would have given 6d. and 12d. a peece to see her; It was the only talk of all the Coffee-houses in and near London'.

The Case of Madam Mary Carleton

Did Mary Carleton write *The Case*? In his discussion of the various narratives, Ernest Bernbaum assumed that Mary had not authored the work.[21] He found in it evidence of more education that the allegedly low-born Mary Moders could have achieved.[22] John Carleton earlier claimed that Mary had not written the *Historical Narrative* and that it was actually composed by her Machiavellian companion with whose name he would not sully his pages. When *The Case* appeared, he was quick to insist that it again was 'not by her composed, though by her means' and that its main author was a 'mercinary Pedant' who also assisted her in contriving it; it was, he asserted, 'better worded then beleived...'. None the less he repeatedly attacked both works as if they had indeed been written by his unwanted wife.

Certainly *The Case* did have a mercenary motive as John Carleton implied, but it would have had one whether or not written entirely by Mary herself since, without her husband's support, she had had nothing to live on. It must also be remembered that Mary had stung John by stating that he could not have written the works ascribed to him; he might, then, simply be retaliating, despite his acceptance elsewhere of her verbal skills.

Although he had not known Mary Carleton during 1663, Kirkman may have had some cause when in *The Counterfeit Lady Unveiled* he stated that in 1663 Mary Carleton 'was so Confident as to write, print, and publish a Book, calling it the Case of *Mary Carleton*'. The picture he used as his frontispiece was, he wrote, the same that adorned *The Case* and he declared that it was 'taken by her own order'. Indeed Kirkman was so impressed by the performance of *The Case* that, when he placed the work by John's alleged accounts, he could not 'find it or her guilty of any considerable untruth'; thus he felt free to quote a great part of *The Case* as if it were indeed Mary Carleton's work and views.

The truth, as so often, may lie in the middle. Both Mary and John Carleton may not have written all of the texts ascribed to them but they may well have written parts and presented material for another to inscribe. If one considers her contemporary Aphra Behn, probably from a similar background and education in Canterbury, who so clearly achieved a great degree of literary skill and learning, it does seem possible that Mary could have written some of what she alleged.

But there are problems as well. Given the huge stylistic differences between the *Historical Narrative* and *The Case* it seems unlikely that she (or anyone else) would have been entirely responsible for the two works; otherwise she would have had to have enhanced her skills quite radically within a few weeks – unless one credits her with a desire to present a cruder work at one time and a more polished one at another. Also there are breaks in the text of *The Case* that might suggest multiple authoring. Clarity is promised in one place, narrative obscurity claimed as a right in another. Much information is given at the beginning, but then there appears to be a new start in a less specific and more elevated tone. The result of the change is some ambiguity: did Mary come to England to avoid the menacing marriages or to seek her fortune? If she were helped, then Mary Carleton's ghostwriter was skilful in marketing an image since *The Case*, whatever its inconsistencies, is remarkably convincing.

There is a literary quality to both the images of trickster and distressed lady constructed in 1663, though neither is entirely determined generically. The John Carleton defenders tried to place Mary within the line of rogues such as Guzman and Lazarillo. These were mainly male but the appearance in 1662 of the *The Life and Death of Mrs. Mary Frith* gave one female model of rollicking roguery to which Mary occasionally seems close. But the differences are always stark. Moll Cutpurse trangresses gender, Mary Carleton trangresses sex.

In opposition to the image set out in *The Female Hector*, in *The Case* transvestism is confined to discourse and romance, and Mary expressly denies the vulgar charge of literally dressing as a man. She is writing herself in romantic not bawdy mode: she can imagine herself as a knight errant on adventure certainly, but not as an adventuress in breeches. Masculinity inheres in bravery and daring and these, as a foreign lady, she assumes; cross-dressing she avoids. If she wished to be a man it was not for the sexual licence allowed to men but because she covets their legal and social advantages. Throughout her work she is eager to illustrate her performative ability and yet to de-fang it. Her skill at acting should not be associated with the whorishness of the Restoration actress, but with good birth. Those with breeding can act and control themselves on the stage of life. Hence she comports herself well and wittily before the audience who visited her in prison before her trial. The Carletons, however, have no manners and no wit and cannot act nobly.

In the description of the mutual deception with the Carletons, she hints at lewdness in the metamorphosis of De Wolway into 'De Vulva'. She cannot be ignorant of a pun and this is not the sort which a lady could easily record. Her technique here is to separate herself from the lewdness, while suggesting a sophisticated attitude that could allow the repetition and avoid involvement and embarrassment. So too with the old suitor in Cologne: he claims that his sexual wounds are in fact martial. A hint suggests that the confounding of military and sexual could have allowed a reading of campaigns as a blazon of the female body. But Mary simply retreats from this and instead uses the incident to teach that women as well as men would do well to have weapons of some sort.

The curious equivocal effect of *The Case* can well be seen in the treatment of Mary Carleton's wit. It is amply demonstrated but it is allied to a certain innocence, as when she admits that she was foolish to indulge in a flippant reply to the magistrate. She further uses the incident to the advantage of her story by pointing out that her mistake was due to her foreignness and ignorance of English institutions.

Clearly she is aware of the effect of wit in women and insistent that hers is not the wit of knowingness. Wit may suggest dissembling and she knows the connection made between truth and female virtue. So she works to avoid letting her clever answers argue her skill. Later, however, she admits that she displayed her wit to the visitors who came to see her in prison as if she were a theatrical show. She cannot, then, pretend not to know her effect. But again she suggests that her high spirits do not falsify her innocence and that she has a kind of natural humour that cannot easily be suppressed. She uses her concept of wit to undercut the admission she almost makes, that there is design in all her acts; she insists that her counterfeiting has been wit not crime.

Although it was not especially acceptable for a woman to be writing herself so clearly, the insistence on her foreignness mitigates the affront. She has ingested the classical and romance languages and even added the exotic 'oriental Tongues', and this arcane knowledge separates her from the company of English spinsters. It also draws attention to her probable skill in authorship.

At the beginning of *The Case*, especially in her dedication 'To the Ladies', she bolsters her image with a feminist plea for more female power within law. By insisting on her foreignness she can make herself into the satiric stranger who regards English customs with open-eyed amazement. So the practice of *feme covert* which makes the law no defender of woman except through a man becomes absurd. (To those who doubted her identity, however, her statement of this view would seem equally absurd since she had voluntarily run into several simultaneous marriages.) Her own self-assertion further ridicules it. The woman who can create herself as her own subject of discourse should be a legal subject as well. Indeed she comes near to being so through her knowledge of the law – a knowledge that makes a link with the play *The Roaring Girl* in which the Moll Cutpurse character defends herself against charges of being a thief and an hermaphrodite.

The Case in general gives a ferocious picture of sex warfare, rather in the manner of Aphra Behn's comedies. As in her creation of a writing self, the consciousness of inadequate rights seems a legacy of the Interregnum when women played an enhanced legal and political role. It became a theme in Restoration drama though frequently expressed to be mocked, as, for example, in Wycherley's Widow Blackacre in *The Plain Dealer*. The difficulty for women after the Restoration is well caught in Mary Carleton's vacillation between criticism of marriage and her need to portray herself as a proper and loving wife.

The baldness of the assertion in the accusing letter from Canterbury – that Mary was an absolute cheat, to be known by her skill at languages, her fatness and her high breasts – suggests a reduction of the clever woman that almost justifies any pretence. The self-reliance, embodied in the writing of *The Case* itself, is a response, as well as a proof of rank. Despite her enemies' attempts to label her self-reliance and her discourse as mimicry and so criminal weapons, both argue breeding. Indeed they are the only proofs available to her.

Since it appears likely that in a literal way Mary was indeed a 'Cheat', *The Case* cannot be described as autobiography. But the whole age was reinventing itself; puritans were being rewritten as firm royalists and, in the colonies, criminals and paupers were repackaging themselves as justices and soldiers. *The Case* does not simply contain a fake identity staged for the public, but rather conveys a mingling of fiction and fact, desire and some fulfilment, romance and reality. In this context she rightly allows the ambiguity which the John Carleton camp, seeing her always as rogue and whore, explicitly refused her.

NOTES

[1] *Crime in Early Modern England: 1550–1750* (London: Longman, 1984); *Early Modern England* (London: Edward Arnold, 1987).

[2] *The Mary Carleton Narratives 1663–1673: A Missing Chapter in the History of the English Novel* (Cambridge, Mass.: Harvard University Press, 1914), p. 43.

[3] Until recently it was only possible to read *The Life and Death of Mrs. Mary Frith* in this copy (Wing 2005, BL c.127.a.25) or a microfilm of it, but a new edition, including a facsimile of the original text, has recently been edited by Randall S. Nakayama (New York: Garland, 1993). This is based on a photocopy rather than on the original print, which Nakayama believed to be lost, possibly because of a change of shelfmark; it contains some errors of transcription, and is somewhat sparsely annotated.

[4] *Travels and Works of Captain John Smith*, II, ed. Arber and Bradley (Edinburgh: J. Grant, 1910), pp. 498–99.

[5] *The Roaring Girl*, ed. Paul Mulholland (Manchester: Manchester University Press, 1987), pp. 262–63.

[6] *The Letters of John Chamberlain*, ed. Norman Egbert McClure (Philadelphia: American Philosophical Society, 1939), vol. I, p. 334.

[7] *The Canting Crew: London's Criminal Underworld 1550–1700* (New Brunswick, N.J.: Rutgers University Press, 1984), pp. 24, 45.

[8] 'Thieves and fences: markets and power in professional crime', *British Journal of Criminology* 16 (1976), 256–66.

[9] Cited Margaret Dowling, 'A Note on Moll Cutpurse – "The Roaring Girl"', *RES* 10 (1934), 67–71.

[10] *Natures pictvres drawn by fancies pencil to the life...* (London, 1656).

[11] *The Canting Crew*, p. 33.

[12] *Sexual Dissidence: Augustine to Wilde, Freud to Foucault* (Oxford: Clarendon Press, 1991), pp. 280–82.

[13] Deuteronomy 22:5

[14] *Crime in Early Modern England*, p. 178.

[15] Cited by Linda Woodbridge, *Women and the English Renaissance: Literature and the Nature of Womankind, 1540–1620* (Urbana and Chicago: University of Illinois Press, 1984).

[16] *Vested Interests: Cross-Dressing and Cultural Anxiety* (London: Routledge, 1992).

[17] Ed. Thomas Olive Mabbott and J. Milton French (New York: Columbia University Press, 1938).

[18] (London, 1734), p. 192.

[19] *Roxana, The Fortunate Mistress* (New York: Penguin, 1982), p. 317. Moll Flanders draws a similar analogy with an earlier Moll, saying that she is as 'impudent a Thief, and as dexterous as ever Moll Cut-Purse was' (*The Fortunes and Misfortunes of the Famous Moll Flanders*, ed. G.A. Starr [London: Oxford University Press, 1971], p. 201.

[20] See the bibliographic essay by C.F. Main, 'The German Princess; or Mary Carleton in Fact and Fiction', *Harvard Library Bulletin,* 10 (1956), 166–85.

[21] In *Virtue of Necessity: English Women's Writing, 1649–88* (Ann Arbor: University of Michigan Press: 1989), pp. 95–96, Elaine Hobby argues against attempts to deny authorship to Carleton.

[22] Like John Carleton before him Bernbaum had his own agenda in alleging *The Case* to be written by someone other than Mary Carleton. He was eager to disprove a theory of Sir Walter Raleigh's, that realist fiction in England was written in imitation of truthful record and began with Defoe. Bernbaum wanted to find fiction not fact in the Carleton works. Similarly he was eager to prove that Aphra Behn did not go to Surinam; *Oroonoko* had to be pure fiction. For a fuller discussion of Bernbaum and Carleton see Mihoto Suzuki, "The Case of Mary Carleton: Representing the Female Subject, 1663–73" *Tulsa Studies in Women's Literature* 12 (1993), 61–83.

NOTE ON THE TEXTS

The texts have been reproduced with minimal alterations. Long Ss have been changed and 'than' has been changed to 'then' and 'whither' to 'whether' where appropriate. In some cases of words with two current spellings in the seventeenth century, the one more comprehensible to modern readers has been substituted. Such emendations, and any others that are more than corrections of obvious printers' errors, have been included in the endnotes. Additions to the texts have been noted in square brackets. Passages of capitalisation or gothic script have been rendered into italics.

The text of *The Life and Death of Mal Cutpurse* is primarily edited and annotated by Elizabeth Spearing; that of *The Case of Mary Carleton* is primarily edited and annotated by Janet Todd.

MOLL CUT = PURSE.

See here the Presidesse o'th pilfring Trade
Mercuryes second Venus's onely May'd
Doublet and breeches in a Uniform dresse
The female Humurrist a Kickshaw messe
Here no attraction that your fancy greets
But if her FEATURES please not read her FEATS

Pub? by W. Richardson, Castle Street, Leicester Fields.

Mal Cutpurse, from a portrait bound into Nathan Field's *Amends for Ladies* (1639).
By permission of the Folger Shakespeare Library.

THE
LIFE
AND
DEATH
OF
Mrs. MARY FRITH.

Commonly Called

MAL CUTPURSE.

Exactly *Collected* and
now Published for the
Delight and Recreation
of all Merry dispo-
sed Persons.

LONDON,

Printed for *W. Gilbertson* at the Bible in
Giltspur-street without Newgate, 1662.

TO THE

READER.

See here an account of this Sybilla Tiburnia,[1] the Oracle of Felony, whose deep diving[2] secrets are offered to the World entire, without the envy of that vain price, and more fond sullenness, which lost the Roman Emperour[3] the happy knowledge of those fam'd Divinations.

For he that looks not upon Mall Cutpurse with the same admiration, and thinks not her Nymphship as venerable as any of that mysterious sisterhood, is not fit to carry Guts[4] to a Beare, nor officiate in the rites of those Games consecrated to this Bona Roba,[5] and goodly Matron.

Such people shall yet give us liberty to take her for a Prodigy of those Times she lived in, and to be altogether as presagious in her Habit and Manners, as they[6] were in their ambiguous and doubtfull sentences.

We are not always bound to look upward in the Air, as Hoggs doe against windy weather for prognosticks and revelations of Future Occurrences and Events: Our angry Fates doe sometimes dispence and afford us more familiar and near Hints and Omens of their displeasure (like pitylesse Judges that Laugh before they give sentence) in the strange yet ridiculous corruptions and indispositions of humours, which they perspicuously manifested in this Epicoene[7] Wonder.

One might as easily have guessed, there were some Caprichios[8] in the State, (which appeared afterwards in the Jealousies, Whimsies, and odd conceits of the whole Masse of the Multitude) by this persons, and other her Cotemporaries, Odd and Fanatick[9] and unheard of Tenour and Manner of life; as the people of Jerusalem[10] might have imagined the Destruction of their City, by the severall Arrands[11] and wofull Proclamations thereof, from the Mouths of those Mad Men that ran up and down roaring forth that Approaching Calamity.

This is it which indeed makes her remarkable (and may we never see her *Successour or such a Mad* Cassandra)[12] *beyond all other considerations, which yet are not in themselves regardlesse; nothing appertaining to her, being to be matcht throughout the whole Course of History or Romance; so unlike her selfe, and of so difficult a mixture, that it is no wonder she was like no body, nor could not be* Sorted[13] *by any* Comparison, *or* Suited *with any Antick* Companion.

She *was the Living Discription and Port[r]aiture of a Schism and Separation, her* Doublet *and* Petticoate, *understanding one another, no better than* Presbytery *and* Independency;[14] *and it was wondred by some, that in*[15] *imitation of the latter, and in honour of the* Rump[16] *she wore not the Breeches; but it seems she was Loath to innovate in her Old Years.*

So much may suffice for her person; *there is something due to be said of her* Practise, *and to this part I must invite none but* Mercuriallists[17] *and the* Procuratresses *of the* Colledge *of* Venus, *who have long desired and expected the* Works *and* Memorialls *of this* Virago,[18] *as deserving a place in the* Rationale *and* Account *of Time, as well as* Oliver,[19] *but farre beyond* Prince Crispine[20] *and his* Lady, *and the rest of that Leud Rout, and band of Knight Errantry.*

Know ye therefore, O all ye Pick-pockets, Lifters,[21] Heavers,[22] Rumpads,[23] Bawds, &c. *that as far as with preservation of Honesty and Credit, we might (not to be endangered by your Converse out of design of more perfect intelligence)*[24] *we have prosecuted the discovery of all those Arts and Artifices, for which your* Governesse[25] *was Famous, and your Government under her* Discipline *no lesse reputable for it's due regulation. Read therefore if you can spare time from your businesse, the sad decayes of your Trade, in the losse of this Monopolizing Improver thereof, and begin hereafter to Thieve with Discretion and Judgement, that your Incomes be weighed and ballanced with the issues; and remember that a composition*[26] *is better, than the whole principal upon the score of Totring.*[27]

There is a word due also to the Venerable Matrons, that broak in Petticoats;[28] *be not you so impudently immodest and shameless in your* Profession, *in venturing upon all chastities and innocence, to the debauch of unwary and unarmed pudicity;*[29] *For be assured* Mal *was no such open and common offender in this kind, but was very heedfull where she layed her Baits and Temptations; though her Bribes were High, and* those that employed her very Potent, who yet would descend to the lures of poor and naked Beauty: Such she most generously scorned to betray, if they had magnanimity to resist. The Town abounds with you, and therefore this caution from so great an Example, to which you owe respect and observance, may be very necessarily and civilly Welcome.

Her other more indifferent Pranks and Feats will be good diversion to the honest and ingenious, [30] and to him they are commended, desiring him to Excuse the Abruptnesse and Discontinuance of the Matter, and the severall independencies [31] thereof; for that it was impossible to make one piece of so various a Subject, as she was both to her self and others, being forced to take her as we found her though at disadvantage; which we pray you to consider and accept of this Endeavour as it is.

VALE. [32]

The *Life* and *Death* of

M^{ris} MARY FRITH,

ALIAS

Mal Cutpurse

To write this Womans History (a Task for the Clerk of *Newgate*,[33] if he had no worser thing to do) many strong and sufficient reasons and impulses there are, and those partly from the strangeness and newness of the subject, and Her unparalleld practises and courses, and manner of Life and Livelihood (which in their time were the Talk and Discourse of the Town, and therefore may not be unworthy of a reducing them to Memory) and partly out of a pleasant officiousnesse to the publique good, which hath been advantaged (according to information) by such kind of Essayes.

Equally distant it is from the purport and intent of this piece, to favour her Ashes, or to rake her in her Grave; but as she lived in a kind of mean betwixt open, profest dishonesty, and fair and civil deportment, being an *Hermaphrodite* in Manners as well as in Habit; with the same indifferency shall she be used here, by avoiding all Partiality.

She was indeed a perfect *Ambodexter*,[34] being Mistresse of that thriving Art: no doubt *Mercury*[35] was Lord of the Ascendant at her Birth, and with his influences did so endow her, that from her very Cradle she gave signes of a very towardly and pregnant[36] Wench, manifested by several petty Stratagems and designes as oft as occasion and opportunity presented, at her Neighbours as well as at Home.

She was Born *Anno Domini*, 1589,[37] in *Barbican*, at the upper
end of *Aldersgate* street[38] (a very ancient street, and probably of
as ancient a House, and from thence she may challenge
Gentility,[39]) This place was formerly a Defence or Bulwork of
the City: such Rampires and Fortifications in our Ancestors days
being called *Barbicans*. It is since a Magazine, but of Pawns
altogether, being a Brokery,[40] which made her extraction so
well sute with her condition of life afterward. Plants and Trees
do relish in their fruit, of the Ground and Earth they grow in, as
we see in Wines and Tobacco: and our *Mal* had a very great
smack and tincture (which lasted throughout the whole Course
of her Life) of that most laudable quality and profession exer-
cised in the place of her Nativity; though to give her her due,
she was not altogether so unconscionable and cruel as those
Vulturs, Harpies[41] and Wolfes, which follow that Trade; and it
is wonder they are allowed to have any other signes, and that in
order thereunto it is not publiquely decreed. But some few
honest men, and rare they are, keep off that brand from the
other. But this hath another place herein, where it will be
properly resumed.

I do not find, that any remarkable thing happned at her
Nativity: such as the flattering southsayers pretend in Ecclipses,
and other the like motions above, or Tides, and Whales, and
great Fires, adjusted and timed to the genitures of great States-
men: though for a she politick,[42] she be not much inferiour to
Pope *Joan*;[43] for she was in her time the great Cabal[44] and
Oracle of the mystery of diving into Pockets, and was very well
read and skilled in the Affairs of the Placket[45] too among the
great Ones. There being no such notable Accidents falling out
then as aforesaid, I cannot ascertain the Week nor Moneth of
her Nativity.

She was born of Honest Parentage, her Father being by his
Trade a *Shoemaker*, living in good esteem and repute in the
world, and in love and friendly familiarity with his Neighbours,
a fair and square conditioned Man, that loved a good Fellow
next to Himself, which made his issue be so sociable: we do not
here dispute the Company; for she kept of all sorts.

Both of her Parents were very tender of this Daughter, but especially the Mother, according to the tendernesse of that Sex, which is naturally more indulgent than the Male; most affectionate she was to her in her Infancy, most careful of her in her Youth, manifested especially in her Education, which was the stricter and diligentlier attended, by reason of her boysterous and masculine spirit, which then shewed it self, and soon after became praedominant above all breeding and instruction.

A very *Tomrig*[46] or *Rumpscuttle*[47] she was, and delighted and sported only in Boys play and pastime, not minding or companying with the Girls: many a bang and blow this Hoyting[48] procured her, but she was not so to be tamed or taken off from her rude inclinations; she could not endure that sedentary life of sewing or stitching, a Sampler was as grievous as a Winding-sheet, her Needle, Bodkin and Thimble, she could not think on quietly, wishing them changed into Sword and Dagger for a bout at Cudgels. For any such Exercise, who but she! where she would not fail, tide what would, if she heard of any such thing, to be a busie Spectator: so that she was very well known, by most of the rougher sort of people thereabouts, when she was yet very young and little.

Her Head-gear and Handkerchief[49] (or what the fashion of those times were for Girls to be drest in,) was alike tedious to her, wearing them as handsomely as a Dog would a Doublet, and so cleanly, that the driven Pot-hooks[50] would have blusht at the comparison, and alwayes standing the Bear-garden way, or some other Rabble-rout Assemblies.

This perplexed her Friends,[51] who had only this Proverb favourable to their Hope, *That an unhappy*[52] *Girl may make a good Woman*; but they lived not to the length of that expectation, dying in her minority, and leaving her to the swing and sway of her own unruly temper and disposition.

She would fight with boyes, and couragiously beat them, run, jump, leap or hop with any of them, or any other play whatsoever: in this she delighted, this was all she cared for, and had she not very young, being of a pregnant docible wit, been taught to read perfectly, she might well through her over addiction to this loose and licentious sporting have forgot and blotted out any easie impression. But this Learning stood her much in stead afterwards.

She had an Uncle, brother to her Father who was a Minister, and of him she stood in some awe, but not so powerful, as to restraine her in these courses; so that seeing he could not effectually remedy that inveterating evil in her manners, he resigned her to Time, which bringing with it discretion and judgement would certainly at last reclaim her, and bring her to right sense and reason.

This Uncle the Parson, had a whimsey too, (for I am not informed that it was out of any settled serious perswasion, or non-conformity to the Church or it's Customes) which few of the Priests have ever been troubled with; that is, he refused to take Tyth[53] of his Parishioners, but received his maintenance from them under the notion of Contribution; and yet a Jolly Fat fellow he was, and would take off his Cup merrily: but it seems it ran in a blood, each of the Family had his particular Freak, and so had our *Mary*. But in her Trade afterward, she would not be contented with the Tyth, but commonly a full half, or such large composition; for *to give the Devill his due*, was one of her chief Maximes improved beyond the bare letter of a Proverb.

I have thus traced her from her Originals, to shew in what proportions she differed from, and approached to them: and that neither the derivations of the same blood, the assimilation and resemblance of parts, can conform the mind and the faculties thereof, or indue it with the like qualities: but that there is a prevalent power of our Stars which over rules all, and resists and subdues the additionall and auxiliary strength, and reserves of Education: and this I have said to be *Mercury* in conjunction with, or rather in the house of *Venus*[54] at her Nativity.

This Planet *Mercury* you must know (if you have not well studied *Lily*)[55] is of a Thievish, Cheating, Deceitful Influence, which is not so powerful in Citizens Shops, Warehouses, Bargains and Sales, Merchandizing and bartering; nevertheless some little finger it hath as with a ray to point at them: so that seldome but some Couzenage[56] or lying at the least, intervenes in those affairs. In great Fairs and Markets this Planet Operates exceedingly, but it violently rages in great throngs and concorses of people at any great shew, Pomp or Solemnity, as Coronations, my Lord Mayors day[57] and the like; where it doth so whet and set such an edge on the knives and cutting instruments, so quicken and expedite their fingers, and lastly, so vigorously incite and stir up the minds of those whose genitures[58] have relation thereunto, and with such conveyance too, that it were impossible to be done without the connivance of this Star, under the position whereof *Turnmill* street[59] is directly sited.

For the other of *Venus*, most Men and Women know without teaching what are her properties. She hath Dominion over all *Whores*, *Bauds*, *Pimps*, &c. and joyned with *Mercury* over all Trapanners[60] and Hectors,[61] She hath indeed a more general influence than all the other Six put together; for no place nor person is exempted from it, invading alike both sacred and prophane; Nunneries and Monasteries, as well as the common places of Prostitution; *Cheapside*[62] and *Cornhill*,[63] as well as *Bloomsbury*[64] or *Covent-Garden*.[65]

Under these benevolent and kind Stars, she grew up to some Maturity of years, seasoned all along with such rudiments as these, to be put in use[66] as soon as occasion should present; She was now a lusty and sturdy Wench, and fit to put out to service, having not a competency of her own left her by Friends to maintain her of her self; but this went against the Grain and the Hair as we use to say: She was too great a Libertine,[67] and lived too much in common to be enclosed in the limits of a private Domestique Life.

A Quarter staffe[68] was fitter to her hand than a Distaffe, *stave and tayle*[69] instead of spinning and realing; she would go to the Ale-house when she had made shift for some little stock, and spend her penny, and come into any ones company, and club[70] another till[71] she had any left, and then she was fit for any Enterprize.

She could not endure the Bake-house, nor that Mag-pye Chat of the Wenches; she was not for mincing obscenity, but would

talk freely what ever came uppermost; a spice she had even
then, of prophane dissolute language, which in her old dayes
amounted to down-right Swearing, which was in her not so
malicious as customary.

Washing, Wringing, and Starching were as welcome as fast-
ing dayes unto her; or in short, any Houshold work; but above
all she had a natural abhorrence to the tending of Children, to
whom she ever had an aversness in her mind, equall to the
sterility and barrenness in her womb, never being made a
Mother to our best information.

At this Age we spake of before, she was not much taxed with
any Loosenesse or Debauchery in that kind; whether the virility
and manliness of her face and aspect took of any mans desires
that way (which may be very rational and probable) or that
besides her uncomplyable and rougher temper of body and
mind also, which in the female Sex is usually perswasive and
winning, not daring or peremptory (though her Disposition can
hardly find a suitable term for an indifferent expression of the
manage of her life)[72] she her self also from the more importunate and prevailing sway of her inclinations, which were masculine and robust, could not intend those venereal impurities,
and pleasures: as stronger meats are more palatable and nutri-
tive to strong bodies than *Quelque choses*[73] and things of variety,
which may perchance move an appetite, provoke a longing; but
are easily refrained from by any considerate *good Fellow*, that
knows what is the lastingst Friend to *good Drink* and *good
Company*; her *Motto*.

She could not but know moreover (for I suppose her of a
very competent discretion and sagacity of mind as well as
maturity and sutable growth at those years) that such Prostitu-
tions were the most unsatisfactory, that like an accidental scuffle
or broyl might end in danger, but never in Love, to which she
was no way so happily formed; nor was so much a woman as
vainly to expect it.

Several *Romances* there are of many Knights who carried their
Ladies away in disguise from their Parents and Native Coun-
tries, most commonly in the habits of a Page or some such Man-

servant; Certainly it must be a stupified and far advanced affection which can admire, or fancy, or but admit the view of so unnatural a shape, the reverse of Sexes in the most famed Beauties, and to whose excellencies and lustre the world were devoted. How unsightly and dreadful is the hinder region of the air in the sable breeches of a dropping cloud? what an uncomely mantle is that heap of waters which covers the ground, and deluges and invades the dry land? That which so much offends us in the boysterousnesse of the Elements, cannot but be disgustful to mankind in the immodesty of either Sexes attire and dresse.

Hercules,[74] *Nero*[75] and *Sardanapalus*,[76] how are they laught at and exploded,[77] for their effeminacy and degenerated dissolutenesse in this extravagant debauchery; The first is portraited with a Distaff in his hand, the other recorded to be married as a wife and all the Conjugal and Matrimonial Rites performed at the solemnity of the Marriage; the other lacks the luxury of a Pen as loose as his female riots to describe them. These were all Monsters or Monster Killers, and have no parallels either in old or modern Histories, till such time as our *Mal Cutpurse* approached this Example; but her heroick impudence hath quite undone every *Romance* ——— For never was any woman so like her in her cloaths.

Generally we are so much acquainted with our selves and so often do dislike the effect of too much familiarity, that though we cannot alter the inside yet we diversifie the outside with all the borrowed pomp of Art in our Habits; no doubt *Mals* converse with her self (whose disinviting eyes and look sank inwards to her breast, when they could have no regard abroad,) informed her of her defects; and that she was not made for the pleasure or delight of Man; and therefore since she could not be honoured with him she would be honoured by him in that garb and manner of rayment He wore ——— Some Wenches have been got with Child with the onely shaking of the breeches, whereof having no great hopes, she resolved to usurp and invade the Doublet, and vye and brave manhood, which she could not tempt nor allure.

I have the rather insisted on this, because it was the chief remarque of her life, as beginning and ending it; for from the first entrance into a competency of age she would wear it, and to her dying day she would not leave it off, till the infirmity and weaknesse of nature had brought her a bed to her last travail, changed it for a Wastcoat and her Pettycoats for a Winding Sheet.

These were no amiable or obliging vests,[78] thay wanted of a mutuel correspondence and agreement with themselves, so unlikely were they to beget it abroad and from others: they served properly as a fit Covering, not any disguise of her, (according to the Primitive invention of apparel) wherein every man might see the true dimensions and proportions of body, onely hers shewed the mind too.

So that by this odd dresse it came, that no man can say or affirm that ever she had a Sweet-heart, or any such fond thing to dally with her. A good Mastiffe was the onely thing she then affected and joyed in, in whose fawnings and familiarity, she took as much delight as the proudest she ever gloried in the *Courtship*, admiration, attraction and flatteries of her adored beauty. She was not wooed nor sollicited by any man, and therefore she was Honest,[79] though still in a reserved obedience and future service either personally or by Proxy to *Venus*.

Her Nuptials and Wedding grew to be such a Proverb, as the Kisses of *Jack Adams*,[80] any one he could light upon, that is to say, as much design of love, in one as in the other: all the *Matches* she ever intended was at Bear-baiting, whose pastimes afforded not leisure or admittance to the weak recreations and impertinencies of Lust.

She never had the Green sickness,[81] that Epidemical Disease of Maidens after they have once past their puberty; she never eat Lime, Oatmeal, Coales or such like Trash, nor never changed Complexion; a great Felicity for her Vocation afterwards that was not to be afraid nor ashamed of any thing, neither to wax pale or to blush.

No Sighs or Dejected Looks, or Melancholly clouded her vigorous Spirit, or supprest her Joviality in the retired thoughts and despair of a Husband; she was troubled with none of those longings which poor Maidens are subject to: she had a power and strength (if not the will) to command her own pleasure of any person of reasonable ability of body, and therefore she needed not whine for it as long as she was able to beat a fellow to a complyance without the unnecessary trouble of Entreaties. Nor in all her life time was it ever known, that by meer request, and precariously she ever designed or obtained any favour whatsoever, but by a strong hand carried and performed all her Enterprises.

She made much of for a while, and was very often in company with a *Shoomaker*, (a profession for her Fathers sake she alwayes favoured) to whose expences she contributed all she could *wrap and run* (which is a term of Art belonging to that trade, whose Factor[82] afterwards she was) until she found the fellow made an absolute prey of her Friendship, and squandered away the money she with difficulty enough provided.

This and some such other like chouses[83] and tricks, to which a freenesse of nature subjected her, not only took her off from the consideration or thought of Wedlock, but reduced her to some advisement[84] which way she might maintain her self single.

She cast about therefore what course of life she should betake her self to, and long she was not in the determination, chusing that which was the most easie, and by a good management would prove also the most profitable; called living by the quick. As you may perceive by what is already said, she had a numerous acquaintance, and amongst others, her company was known to some of the *Fortune Tellers* of the Town (from whom she then learned some smatch[85] and relish of that Cheat) and by their Schemes and Figure-flinging,[86] was further encouraged in that her hopeful Occupation.

For a while therefore she gave law to her former open Licentiousness, and seemingly betook her self to a civiller life; that is, to a closer and cunninger way of living, not being so much in the eye of all people, by whom she was already defamed beyond remedy. But there is nothing so bad which

thinks not by showes and pretences to impose upon and deceive
the Vulgar.

This her sudden reclaimednesse was more admired[87] than
credited by her Neighbours, who mused what it would turn to,
or what strange effect it would have. She had learned to
Curchee,[88] and some other such beginning of Manners, but yet
very abrupt, which shewed they were troublesome to her, and
her new designes; however she framed and formed her self to
them for their better accomplishment.

She continued in this sort for some space of time, having
entred and initiated her self into a private crue of some loose
Women, who had undertaken to manage the promptnesse and
dexterity of her wit to some notable advantage. Their Trade
being to receive Goods which were lifted: that is to say, Stollen
by Thieves, and so in a fair way sell them again; *Mal Cutpurse's*
insight was very little at first in this kind of Dealing, and before
she came to practise for her selfe, or do the like businesse for
those Pilfering Customers, most of that Gang were either
Hanged or Runne away: so that it was high Time for *Mary* to
leave that dangerous and uncertain course.

But being thus seasoned, she was fit for any employment, and
indeed she did but for a while forbear from entring into some
such like occupation. Doing still she was, though never so little,
otherwise it were impossible she should have ever attained and
arrived to that eminence and extraordinary faculty, having an
absolute incontroleable power, more than ever the Law or
Justice had over that Mercureal Tribe, they being entirely at her
beck and command; submitting themselves and their stollen
purchases to her onely Order, Will and Pleasure.

It will be high time now to recount to you the many notable
passages of her Life, which from this *Foundation* rose to these
ensuing *Stories*.

The Remaining Varieties and shapes of her Life, which were
no way so constant as her Habit (the beloved disguise of her
strange Humours) are here presented according to that tract of
her own Genius, with which she pleasured her self and her
discourses in all company, fitted and suited to the gust[89] and

palate of her different Converses; and shall therefore re-assume her person for the better grace of this discourse in the ensuing account of her manner of Livelyhood, from the time of her Woman-hood.

Which estate having seriously considered of, and duely weighed her propensity and inclinations to the inordinacies and unruliness of her mind; not to be guided either by the reservedness and modesty of her own Sex, or the more imperious command of the other; she resolved to set up in a neutral or Hermaphrodite way of Profession, and stand upon her own leggs, fixed on the basis of both Concerns and Relations; like the *Colossus*[90] of *Female* subtlety in the wily Arts and *ruses* of that Sex; and of manly resolution in the bold and regardlesse Rudenesses of the other, so blended and mixed together, that it was hard to say whether she were more cunning, or more impudent. — As you may see in this Diary of her own here following.

MAL CUTPURSE'S *Diary*.

All people do justly owe to the world an account of their Lives passed; and therefore mine being a greater debt than any other, as I have drawn more observation by unknown practises upon me, I shall dispense with reputation and credit, and following the laudable example of others, who have in part preceded me as *Seignior Gusman*,[91] and the Spanish Tribe of Cheaters, I will freely declare my self to all my loving Neighbours, and whomsoever this relation of mine shall happen to meet with, intreating them with all Fairness and Candor, and the pity of a *Sessions*[92] *House Jury*, to hear me in this my Defence and Apology, which my faults do not exceed.

I beheld my self more Obnoxious to my Fate, and to have a greater quarrel with that, than the world can have against me; the Universe consists and is made up of Cheaters and Cheatees, saith the Learned *Albumazer*,[93] and there is no great difference below between them; To be excellent and happy in Villany, hath been alwayes reputed equal with a good Fame,[94] whose wings being short, and reaching not beyond the memory of a person, can little prejudice the Fortunate Atchievments of new undertakers. My Devices were all of my own spinning, nor was I beholding to any Stale-Artifice whatsoever of any Woman preceding me, which I have not bettered, and so far forth as became the principles of such mysteries, facilitated and accomodated to the more ingenious Moderns.

I will not therefore reckon my Childish ignorances, and those extravagant Sallies of an undisciplined Wench for any thing; for it is no matter to know how I grew up to this, since I have laid it as a Maxime, that 'twas my Fate not Me; I doe more wonder at my self than others can do, and dare assure them that Nature doth sometimes disport her self not only in the carelesse Nativities of Dwarfs, Changelings, and such Naturals, but also in her more considerate productions; for I am confident I can boast of as much humane policy,[95] in acquisitions, revenges, dissemblings &c. as any of the Grandees of the world, if proportionably considered.

I was hardly twenty from whence I date my self; when viewing the Manners and Customes of the Age, I see my selfe so wholy distempered, and so estranged from them, as if I had been born and bred in the Antipodes; but yet such was the kindnesse of my Stars, that for all the noyse of the New World, and the Plantations and incredibly Rich Mines of Gold and Silver said to be found there, which seemed to have been allotted for me, the discovery so patly then happening, and my friends very willing to humour it so they might have been rid of me, yet neverthelesse I escaped the Voyage,[96] alike hating *Virginia* (the first Land possessed by the *English* in *America*) and my Virginity, the manner thus.

My Friends perceiving my untoward dispositions designed me* thither, where there was no doubt of such manly work and sport I affected, and where the necessity of Women be they what they would, could not but commend me to some *Jack* as good as my self, whose Dominion over me might subdue that

---

* *Mal Cutpurse* spirited[97] for *New England*.

violence of my spirit, or else I should be so brok
labour, that I would of my own accord return to a wor
civil behaviour. There was then no noyse or talk of *Spi*
was so generally known that I thought there could be
tricks shewed me; but poor silly Wench as I was, being under
pretence of a Fair, and some Matches[98] at *Gravesend*[99] trayned[100]
down and invited thither by Water, I was carried aboard a *New
England* man[101] to drink strong Waters, which were nothing else
but the distillation of mine eyes boyling with Fury and impatience; for in my grief there was nothing womanly.

I was left sitting upon a Chest under Decks blessing my self
from the Company I see hasling[102] and stowing their Goods,
(who ever and anon would laugh at me) but no way dreaming, I
was to be part of the venture or to be concerned in their voyage,
till the Boatswayn came to me; and half mild half sowre, askt me
what Provision I had aboard, and where I would bestow my self;
I replyed as roughly, I would give him no account, but straight-
with suspecting the manner of the question called for my
Company; when the whole Crew of these *Cannibals* fell into such
a passion of laughter, that I began to consult of an Escape but
was presently prevented and put in the *Hold*, where I found
some others in the like miserable Condition.

This sudden misfortune being the first check and controul-
ment of all my proceedings, did not so much for the present
stupifie me as it did soon after quicken me to the thoughts of
my Deliverance, which having understood could not be effected
without the Captain's privity[103] or permission, being sold to a
private Merchant, the first beginner of this inhumane way of
Merchandize, (whom I afterwards when he came to a miserable
distresse for requital helpt unto a *Beadle*)[104] I was forced to await
his coming on board, when having the liberty of the Deck, I
very observantly and with a submissive gesture presented my
self before him, and with many a briny tear told him of this
injury done me and my Friends (of whom God knows I had few
who were not privy to the Design) which would not fail to be
severely revenged on those Complices of this Treachery, and
with such protestations of my Parentage and their certain

lamentations over me, together with my own innocence and civil behaviour, I at last won upon this good natured Master, who was not yet hardned this way, to suffer my Escape, having promised Him very fair and largely when I should rencounter him at *London*.

Thither, by the help of the mony I had otherwise intended,[105] and which I now gave to the Coxon,[106] I hyed, very exceedingly blith that I thus got off, musing of nothing but revenge for this disgrace upon my Companions, but such occasion seldome proffers it self to forlorn people without great disadvantage; and I was not so well recovered of my former fright as to venture upon such desperate and dangerous Enemies, who might have other as subtle devices against me, being alone, and as I said friendless. Therefore abandoning those Hot-spur[107] Meditations, to which I was very prone, I resolved to betake my self to some *santuary* from the like attempts, whose priviledges might secure me, while I could better provide for my self.

I had but very little choice, so I listed my self of another Colony or Plantation (but who neither sow nor reap) of the *Divers* or *File-clyers*.[108] A cunning Nation being a kind of Land *Pyrats*, trading altogether in other mens *Bottoms*,[109] for no other Merchandizes than *Bullion* and ready Coine, and keep most of the great Fairs and Marts[110] of the world. They are very expert Mathematicians, but excellently good at Dyalling;[111] as also they are rare Figure Flingers,[112] and most dexterous at the Tacticks;[113] they had been long incorporated, and had their Governours and Assistants as other Worshipful Companies; and had a good stock for the maintenance of their Trade. At my admission among them, I was examined to several questions, relating to my fitnesse and capacity of being a Member; to which I gave such satisfactory answers, as rendred me very acceptable to be one of their Community. I remember they viewed my Hands, not only to see whether I had not been manumitted[114] at Sessions, but if they were not naturally fitted and made convenient for the Exercise of the Trade, being indeed the neatest *Manufacture*[115] of the world. The best Signes and Marks of a happy and industrious hand, is a long middle Finger, equally suited with that they

call the fools or first Finger; nor can any Surgeon or Doctor of
Physick read a learneder Anatomy Lecture of the *Nerves, Fibræ*[116]
and *Arteries* of the same; than these secant[117] and cutting
Empericks[118] as justly challenging the name of Chirurgy[119] as
they. Above all things they abhor a Clumsy Fat Finger, as apt to
slip the Cole[120] which they put for[121] money, and not carry it
cleverly; and they hate a Bungler as much as a Dunce. They have
several Forms or sorts of Pick-pockets, they have one fellow
alwayes in company when they go about this Employment,
whom they call a Bulk, that is to make some quarrel in the
streets, or else obstruct the passage while the Whipsters do the
Feat; and then there is another ready whom they call the Rub,
into whose Hands the prey is conveyed, and he clearly carries it
away. But of these I shall speak more at large hereafter.

I had no great promising symptomes of a lucky Mercureal in
my Fingers, for they had not been used to any slight and fine
work;[122] but I was judged by these Palmisters from the hardnesse
and largenesse of the Table of my Hand, to be very well qualified
for a receiver and entertainer of their fortunate Atchievments,
and was thereupon with the usual Customs and Ceremonies
admitted. Now I bethought my self how I should govern my self
in this Condition of Life; I could not but foresee the danger, but
was loath to relinquish the profit; every snip or share I got as
accessary to the theft, was like green fruit to me, sowre and *sweet*,
not did I ever *disgest* it, but with a conceited[123] sore throat; yet I
could not forsake my Company though I was very wary how far I
engaged, till a years impunity or more had so stocked me, that I
resolved to run no longer the desperate hazard of these Courses
(which I see so many of my Comrades monthly expiate with their
Lives, &c. at least by whipping and the satisfaction of *Bridewell*[124]
Work-house) but to address my self to a very fair expedient,
whereby I might live, if not Honestly, yet Safely; a mean betwixt
the strokes of Justice, and the Torments of Poverty.

I was well known to all the Gang, and by my good dealing with
them not a little in their favour; I never wrangled for a share, or
when I had the dividend to make, did I ever with-hold any of their
Dues; so that I was commonly an Umpire in their Quarrels, and

thereby did save them from the malicious discovery[125] of one another, which they were sensible of, and did therefore look upon me with more than[126] ordinary respect. I would now and then too out of my own Pocket, lend some of the most desperate of them a Crown[127] or two, to keep them from apparant hazards of doing such Robberies which fatall necessity prompted them to, whereby I saved them often out of the Hangmans Clutches; so that among all the Thieveries they did, my name was never heard of; for they made it the chiefest of their Religion to Conceale me and to Conceal nothing of their designes from me; nor did I ever openly accompany with them, save at our own retreats and places of meeting, where we had all possible privacy and security.

I held very good Correspondence now also with those Grandees[128] of this function of Thievery, the Blades and Hacks[129] of the High-way; who having heard from their inferiour Tribe this repute of my equitable dealing, did deposite in my hands some of their Coine against a Rainy day. Money was a portable and as partable Commodity, but the luggage and lumber of goods purchased by Burglary, I was shy to deale withal; for they serve commonly as the traces and sents to the owners to recover them; and I thank my Fates, I had still the luck to avoid that inconvenience, though I have been enticed with Moveables of good value, which I abandoned to other Receptories.

Nay, I never harboured any *Fellon* under my Roof, which from a private Chamber at first, was now converted into a publique dwelling, well stored and well accomodated; the difficulty of entrance[130] which was much scrupled at first by my Landlord, I removed with the all powerful charm of Silver; and there are few of those in City or Town, who for the like advantages will not admit of any Tenants, be they of what report or Trade they will; Houses were not built to stand empty, nor I Born to stand idle. However I did no way abuse his House, but made it rather an Exchange and place of Entercourse, than prostituted it by any unseemly or lewd action; by this means I kept my self free from all manner of suspicion, save that I was taken for a Woman of a single and strange Humour, and lookt upon as one of the conceits of the Times which laboured under very new and Exotick Fashions.

Among the rest *Tobacco* was grown to be the great *Mode*, and much in use, and a sect of Swaggerers there were which from thence were denominated the *Puffers* and high *Huffers*; I was mightily taken with this vanity, because of its affected singularity; and no Woman before me ever smoakt any, though I had a great many to follow my example, how commendably I know not. I had nothing or would have nothing to do, but what might better be left undone; all easie and proffering deceit was my businesse, and my recreations or pastime was suiteable and like it; for I grew to be more reserved in my boysterous exercises of bayting, &c. and could content to be a spectator and a better onely, where a Pipe of Tobacco did much accomodate me.

One time, an unlucky knave, at a Grocers shop where I used to sit and talk in the intervals of my Trade, which I could not patiently awayt at Home; at my demand of a Pipe of smoak, presented me with a Pipe full of *Gunpowder*, covered at Top with *Tobacco*; which little suspecting I *took* and suddenly it fired in my mouth with such a blast and stench, belching and throwing out the Ashes, that it was a little resemblance of mount *Ætna*.[131] I was all agast at present, but perceiving it was a Boyes Roguery, I restrained my passion further than flinging the pipe at his Head, but forsook the Shop, resolving of no less satisfaction than *blowing up* both of Master and Man by *Engines* and *Devices*[132] in convenient time.

In my house I should have told you, I set up a kind of *Brokery* or a distinct factory[133] for *Jewels*, *Rings* and *Watches*, which had been pinched or stolen any manner of way, at never so great distances from any person; I might properly enough call it the *Insurance Office* for such Merchandize, for the Losers were sure upon Composition[134] to recover their Goods again, and the Pyrates were as sure to have good ransome, and I so much in the Grosse for Brokage[135] without any more danger; the *Hue and Cry* being alwayes directed to me for the Discovery of the Goods not the *Takers*.

A Lawless Vocation yet bordering between illicit and convenient, more advantagious by far to the injured, than the
Courts of Justice and benefits of the Law, and more equal to the
wrong-doers, who by such an hazardous seisure have as themselves think, an equal propriety[136] in their Spoyl, by yielding and
restoring it upon such indifferent[137] Terms as my Markets and
Prizes usually were.

Sometimes I met with obstinate Thieves, who would by no
means part with their Purchases,[138] but would stand to their
Possession as stifly as if it had by right accrued to them, yet such
a hank[139] I had upon them, by working with their Partakers,[140]
and using my Authority, that I alwayes prevailed, and made
them stand to my agreement and arbitrement.[141] Nor could
ever your *Thief-catchers* do any good upon these sort of people.
My House was the *Algiers*[142] where they traffiqued in safety
without the Bribes to those *Fellows*, and publiquely exposed
what they had got without the danger of Inquisition or Examination or Fees of silence. I could have told in what quarter of the
Town a Robbery was done the Evening before by very early day
next morning, and had a perfect Inventory of what they had
taken as soon as it came to the *Dividend*;[143] Nor were ever the
Custom-House Bills shewing what Goods and from whence
they are imported more duely published for the advantage of
Trade, than was the Account of those Robberies entred with me
for the satisfaction of the *Owners*.

So that I may be said to have made a perfect regulation of this
thievish Mystery,[144] and reduced it to certain rules and orders,
which during my administration of the Mistressship and Government thereof, was far better managed than afterwards it was;
nor were the Robberies so frequent nor so grievous then as
when my Discipline was cast off, and this sort of Cattel[145] left
to themselves, when I became obnoxious to these *reforming
Times*[146] just before the more licentious and legaller way of
stealing, called *Plunder*, who needed no body to sell their *stollen
Goods*, having Authority (though little better than mine) to
countenance them therein. For my part I profess I held it
lawfuller to take a Pound by the Old than a Pin by the New

way, and the *guilty persons* concerned therein to stand in need of
a *Pardon*, and to make *ample restitution*, more than any *Newgate-
Bird.*[147]

Insomuch that I very well remember a *Coyner* that was
hanged at *Tyburn* in the beginning of the War for Counterfeiting
and Clipping[148] of *half* Crowns, out of a just indignation of the
partial Fates, who had singled him out of so many Offenders to
be sacrificed to the Lawes, then more impudently and publickly
affronted in his last words, used this Expression, *That he was
adjudged to die but for Counterfeiting of a* half Crown, *but those that
Usurped the* whole Crown *and stole away its* Revenue,[149] *and had
Counterfeited its* Seal, *were above justice and escap'd unpunished.* ———
I sympathized with the poor man; for I was well acquainted
with him, and knew he did it out of Necessity, and that
mistaken unhappy Maxime, *That it was no deceit, to deceive the
Deceivers*, such were the Grandees of those wretched Times.

I had forgot to tell you the place of this my *dwelling* which
slipt me the rather, because few men need to be told where the
Exchange[150] or *Cheapside* Standard[151] stands, since my Habitation
was little lesse Famous; but since that particular is very
requirable,[152] and to shew you I was no *Lady Errant* or this Story
a *Romance*, know ye that I lived within 2 doors of the *Globe*
Tavern[153] in *Fleetstreet*[154] over against the Conduit,[155] where I
dispensed justice likewise among the wrangling Tankard-
bearers, exchanging often their burden of Water for their
burden of Beer as far the lighter, though not so well portable;
for which kindness I had the Command of those Waterworks,
being Admirallesse of the Vessels that sayl upon Folks backs (as
they have Ships in *China* which sayl over dry Land) and unlade
themselves in Kitchins.

Being thus seated and lookt upon by my Neighbours with a
civil though wondring respect, I was no way difficult or curiously
cautelous[156] in my Conversation, but with all freedome in a fair
way (as they term it) allowed[157] my self in my humours. In one
of which comming home late through *Ludgate*,[158] with a Lant-
horne carried before me; a *Shoomaker* or (as his due) a
Traslatour,[159] being then Constable,[160] very well known of me;

was pleased for all my faire Words and Account to send me to the *Counter*[161] for a *Rat*;[162] I made many reluctancies to the contrary, and when I see I must go, did seriously threaten him with being resolved of satisfaction from him; the Watch[163] were very unwilling (for I had alwaies some of them retained to my service) to carry me; but a Constable in his Watch is a Prince, and there was no dispute of his will. So away they carried me, and put me into the Hole,[164] for I was determined to see the worst of that Prison, and to learn at this cheap experience (for I cared not a *Fart* Sir *Reverence*[165] what this fellow could do) the tricks and devices of the place of which I have heard such strange Tales.

It was neer One a Clock when I came in, but I found the *Turnkey*[166] and the Prisoners in such a readinesse to entertaine me and other Commers, as industrous people are about Six in the morning to betake themselves to their businesse. For in this little *Round House*,[167] and *Epitome* of the world (which is but a large Prison) the Sun never sets, but twincleth and slumbereth a while under some Cloud of drowsiness, and ariseth again out of the Ocean of Drink, just about the time as we fancy and calculate the morning. The first salute they gave me was their demand of *Garnish*,[168] which I stubbornly refusing to pay, they called their Constable, the chief *Officer* in this Garrison of the Law, to make seizure of some thing equivalent to their due, which by inevitable Custome amounted to half a Crown. This Constable who had not see other light, nor breathed other Air for Thirty years, and had renounced the world out of quarrel for it's neglect of him; having seconded the demand with an imperious look, which is the sad prognostick of a stripping; laid hold on my Cloaths, and called to the *Chamberlaine*, another of his Officers, to fetch in the drink, who recoyling from me, startled with the new guise of a Doublet and Pettycoat, he began to conjure[169] and ask who I was, being very willing to come to a composition, not knowing how to lumber[170] or engage my Rayment which would fit no body else. I laught at this puzzle, and drew forth a Crown and bid them drink on; in all which time I heard not a word of other concern, than the depth of the

Can, and Two or Three hearty prayers for more of my Condition; to help out the tediousnesse of time, which lay upon their hands and could not be disposed of, but in the clack and din of the Pots, and rules of Tipling.

Next morning came the Constable and had me before my Lord Mayor, and there laid to my charge my unseasonable and suspitious walking; aggravating that offence with the strange manner of my Life. I never wanted confidence so much as I did now to defend my self; but having excused the necessity of my being abroad so late, by a good Plea of a Womans labour, (at which indeed nor no other, I was ever present) I humbly prayed his Lordship to passe by those other accidents, and new matter to this offence, and remit me to my good behaviour, which at last he was contented to do; and upon a small fine discharged me of this Constable, but not the Constable of me.

I could never digest this disgrace, though I computed with my self that I was not born to live without them; but I heard it frequently reported, here; this Headborough[171] vapoured[172] what a trick he had served me, and it galled me to the very Heart to be abused and to be jeered of it; besides by such a Widgeon,[173] who had nothing tolerable in him but his Wealth, which in truth made him the rather intolerable. I studied Twenty wayes how to effect my revenge, which I would have to draw as little envy or trouble upon me as possible; nor would I gratifie my spleen with any thing but what should tickle nor vex it; at last this project came in my Head; I knew the fellow to be Vain-glorious, and altogether as covetous; having so understood from his Neighbours how he used to boast of his Friends in the Countrey, and his Wealth at Home; by some narrower inspection of my Emissaries, I found him to have some relations after his report about *Ludlow*, in the Confines of *Hereford* and *Shropshire*; whereupon I procured one of my Imps, of whom I was furnished with store and variety to put this trick upon my Gentleman.

In a Summer Evening something late, all Booted and Spurred with a Horse in his hand, and covered with Dust, my *Mercury*[174] comes to the *Old Baily*,[175] and very solicitously and hastily

enquires out Mr. *Wall* (so was this fellow called) and by the
Neighbours was informed which was his House; The fellow
followes their directions, yet like an ignorant Countrey-man
that dared not to go one step without new directions in this
wood of the City, kept the same gawping inquiry in his Country
Tone, where Mr. *Wall* dwelt: The people thought the fellow
mad, but it prepared Mr. *Wall* with very great solemnity to
receive this importunate Visitant. Being come to his Door he
with the same earnestnesse and elevation of voice demands
which is his House, he gravely answers beyond the question, *for
want of a better*, *He was the Master of it*; the fellow seeming not to
understand that City phrase, interrogates again whether Mr.
William Wall lives there or no; to which he replies in some doubt
and softly, what would he have with him? The Chouce,[176] to
put him out of his dumps,[177] tells him, that if he be the
Gentleman, He hath some News out of the Country which most
nearly concerned him to impart to him, having come a purpose
to be the first Messenger of such glad tydings; pray Sir come in
quoth *Wall*, you are very heartily welcome, pray how do all our
Friends in the Country? very well quoth this *Spirit*[178] except
your Uncle that is Dead, but yet we hope he is best of all; a little
before his Death he made his *Will* and Sir, hath made you his
Heir, and left you all his personal Estate besides, save a few
Legacies: As today he is buried by some of his Kindred; but
before I came away, knowing my Deceased Master your Uncles
mind; I have inventoried all the Goods, and lockt up his
Evidences and Bonds, and the Money and Plate in one of the
great Chests, and have brought the Key along with me, which I
here present you.

To have seen the perplext looks of this *Cobler*, which he
laboured to frame to a Countenance of grief, but could not for
his more prevalent joyes which appeared in the better half of his
Mouth, and made him to grin as if he were a Shitting; would
have made a man to Spew. At length after a deep Sigh and
Ejaculation of the certainty of Death; he unridled his Face,[179]
and very heartily welcomed the Fellow; brought him into his
Kitchen, sent for strong Beer and a Glass of Sack,[180] and a hot

Joint from *Pye Corner*;[181] commanded his wife to make him what cheer she could: and since there was no recalling of the Dead, though he was a Dear *Uncle* of his, (Ah Wife quoth he, I have lost a Friend, and a Friend) to pluck up their hearts and be merry. During this preparation, the Fellow stands at some distance, plucks off his Hat and so keeps it, and much ado there was to perswade him to be covered; when he made bold he sayd to desire his new Masters favour that he might continue the Bayliffe and Steward of his Lands; to which *Cob*[182] readily assented, fore-praysing his Honesty and Faithfulnesse.

After Supper they resumed the discourse, with which *Wall* being as much delighted as assured; they began to consider of their journey, the expedition whereof this fellow very much urged, in regard of those poor Kinred of his *Uncles*, who no doubt would make Havock of those household Goods which were left about the house, and perchance might venture on the Locks, and seize the rest; whereupon all hast was used to begin the Journey, but the *Cobler* would not disgrace himself among his Kinred, and therefore would stay till he had provided himself and his Wife with new Mourning Cloaths and things sutable to his new Fortunes, with a Black Cloak for the Man, who was to attend them down into the Countrey, and bring them to this Inheritance.

Accordingly they sate forward, (the *Cobler* having discharged his Mans Horse-hire, and other expenses besides Diet and Lodging during his stay in *London*) and in his Inns on the way was very officiously waited on by this new Servant the 4 first dayes Journey; lodging the last night as this Impostor said, within Ten miles of the place whither they were to go: but early in the morning up gets my Youth, saddles his Horse with the Portmanteau and his Cloak in it, and away Gallops another Road, leaving his Master to find out the *Eutopia*[183] of his great Wind-fall; who arising and missing his Guide and Servant, that was lost beyond enquiry, began to suspect the Cheat; but covetousnesse prevailing against reason, he resolved to pursue the adventure: and having the Town in mind, which he was informed was no further than Ten Miles off; he rode thither where he could hear of no such man, nor no such matter.

Vext and yet ashamed to enquire any further, or to make a discovery of his own folly the old Sinkater[184] and his *Joan*[185] turn'd their Horse head and sorrowfully depart, cursing the hour they ever saw this Cheating Rogue, and to add to their misfortunes, their Money (expecting a full Treasure and Recruit out of the aforesaid Chest) was drawn very low, so that they were forced to make long Journeys[186] and short Meals in their way homewards; and yet notwithstanding to *keep* themselves, were faine to *part* with their Horse at St. *Albans*, whom his hard Travel and harder Feeding had brought down to a third of the price he cost them in *London*; where on Foot wearied and wasted with vexation, they at last arrived, and in the Evening crept into their House to avoid the laughter of their Neighbours, among whom before their setting forth, they had noised their sudden Wealth; the defeat whereof at length coming to their knowledge, never was poor Old Cuckold so Flouted and Jeered at; but time and shame wear out all things.

Though I knew not of his Arrival, yet I had notice how farre my project was prosecuted by my *Sancho Panca*,[187] whom I ordered to spread the report thereof abroad; which being made publique, I one day as I passed by his dore on purpose, took occasion to gratulate him with his great good Fortune: and askt him how he lik't the Air of his Lands, and whether his Mannor House were conveniently seated; he replyed little, but with some merriness retorted the Counter to my better remembrance; I have discharged my memory already said I, and have quit scores with you, be you now pleased to remember it, which I gave him constant occasion of till his dying day.

I now followed my Vocation, which in a full and silent streame flowed in upon me; the clack of my dealing bringing other Grist to my Mill than it was first erected for; so that my House was become the onely Office of *Addresse*, whereunto all people resorted for all manner of businesse. The *Astrologers Figure Flingers* were not so universally practised; nor had the Cunning man any open Trade since the Ominous end of Dr. *Lamb*[188] stoned by the Apprentices in the streets; no curiosity of a Love-sick Maid invited her to the remedy of their helplesse Art, In

Revealing, a Person whose properties, qualities, and features they had hinted before to the *wise Master* whose skill like a true Looking-glasse should represent the *Idæa* of their Fancy. People were not so fond of the Stars and their cheating Secretaries,[189] as to consult their advice to be solved of those Oracles which their Folly and Dotage had made, untill the world was mad and the angry unsollicited *Planets* in their late miserable revolution set folkes a gadding after the riddling Prognosticks and hab-nab[190] events of *Lilly*[191] and his ignorant Gang. Nothing but Losses and the certainty of the recovery of them engaged them to my Office, where without the fallacy and pretended opera-tions of a *Scheme*,[192] or any Familiar save a constant Correspond-ence with my Imps, I always satisfied them.

Once a Gentleman that had lost his Watch out of his Pocket by the busie fingers of a *Pick-pocket*, came very anxiously to me, enquiring if I could help him to it again, I demanded of him the Marks and Signs with the time when and where he lost it, or by what Croud or other accident; he replyed, that coming through *Shoolane*,[193] there was a quarrel betwixt two men, one of whom as he afterwards heard was a *Grasier*, whom they had set in *Smithfield*;[194] having seen him receive the summe of 200*l.* or thereabouts in Gold, and it being a hazardous and great purchase; the choice and most excellent of the Art were assembled to do this Master piece; there was one *Bat Rud* as He was since informed, who was the Bulk;[195] who observing the man held his Hand in the Pocket where his Gold was, just in the middle of the Lane whitherto they dogged him, overthrew a Barrel trimming[196] at an *Alehouse* door, while one behind the *Grasier* pusht him over, who withall throws down *Bat* who was ready for the fall; betwixt these two, in the ground arose a quarrel, the *Pick-pocket* demanding satisfaction, while his Comrades interposing (after two or three blowes) in favour of the Countrey-man (who had drawn his hands out of this Fob[197] to defend himself,) soon drew out his Treasure; and while he was looking, on the scuffle, some of them had lent him a hand too and Fingered out his Watch.

I smiled at the adventure, and told him he should hear within a day or two at the furthest; to enhance my Market, perceiving the Gentleman very earnest to recover it: but I knew not by what ill fortune, the Gentleman perceiving amongst my Magazine of Watches, whereof I had always good store in my Window; his own as he confidently presumed, pretended to come to me againe according to my appointment, but suddenly returned with a *Constable*, who bolted in upon me, and made seizure of the said Watch, and withall had me before a Justice.

This was the first Criminal Fact[198] I ever was judicially taxed with, wherefore I requested two of my Neighbours, (for I bore much upon my Honesty and Innocence) to accompany me thither, where notwithstanding my protestations that I had had the Watch so many years, and that there might be such a similitude in the Watch as was not easily discernable, and that hitherto I had lived untainted; yet notwithstanding my *Mittimus*[199] was made, yet by my Friends request, and upon their security I was bayled, to answer it the next *Sessions*, and the Constable commanded to keep the Watch in his Custody in the *Interim*, and to have it produceable at my Tryal: which being come, I was Arraigned and held up my hand at the Sessions House, the Court being full thronged to see and hear my Defence. I had before offered to take up[200] the businesse, but they stood upon such unreasonable terms, thinking I would never hazard my life,[201] or indeed my name at that Tribunal (where I could not but be suspected) that I resolved to stand the Issue,[202] having concluded on an expedient to bring me off, if Fortune should favour the boldnesse of the attempt. When I had pleaded not Guilty, it came to this Issue, whether that Watch for which I was indicted, was the Gentlemans Watch or no; whereupon the Constable was called, to deliver the Watch, that the Gentleman upon his Oath might declare the truth; when, as the Constable was crouding into the Court, one of my small Officers[203] dived into his Pocket, and sought out the evidence against me and departed invisible.

My Lord Mayor was very much incensed at this affront, and concluded it was my designe: but in spight of all their anger, the Jury could not but acquit me for the present; with the Courts terrible threatnings of me, and Menaces to look to my future deportment, which I took very good heed of, resolving to come no more into their Clutches, and to be more reserved and wary in my way and practise.

But this did no way discourage my Continuance therein, I was grown of late acquainted with a new sort of Thieves called the *Heavers*, more fitly *Plagiaries*, whose Employment was stealing of *Shop Books*,[204] the manner thus; They would cruse up and down a Stall when the Master was at Dinner or other way absent, about *Drapers* or *Mercers* especiall, whose Books lie commonly neer the Door upon a Desk; and upon the turning of the backs of the Servants, who are commonly walking to and fro, snatch it off and be gone, with an intent only of some redemptory Money upon its Delivery, for which they had the Convenience of my Mediation, which was ordinarily no less than three or four Pieces[205] award, for the pains the Thief had taken, for I proceeded alwayes by a *quantum Meruit*:[206] the Apprentices willing to give any thing rather than their selves and their Parents should be liable to make satisfaction for so great a damage happned by their Carelessnesse.

I had another sort called the *Kings Takers*, these were men as much of their Heels as their Hands: in the dusk of the Evening or at high Noon when few people were ready for the race, they would run by a Shop and catch up any of the Wares or Goods lying upon a Stall and away with it; sometimes they got Prizes of good Value, and such as by no means might be lost, being either sold, or some remarkable Commodity or other, which the Losers were sure upon trucking with me to have back again.

While I thus raigned, free from the danger of the Common Law, some promooting[207] Apparator[208] set on by an adversary of mine, whom I could never punctually know,[209] cited me to appear in the Court of the *Arches*,[210] where was an Accusation exhibited against me for wearing undecent and manly apparel. I was advised by my Proctor[211] to demur to the Jurisdiction of the Court, as for a Crime, if such, not cognizable there or elsewhere; but he did it to spin out my Cause, and get my Mony; for in the conclusion, I was sentenced there to stand and

do Penance in a White Sheet at *Pauls* Cross[212] during morning
Sermon on a Sunday.

They might as soon have shamed a Black Dog as Me, with any
kind of such punishment; for saving the reverence due to those
who enjoyned it, for a halfe-penny I would have Travelled to all
the Market Towns in *England* with it, and been as proud of it as
that Citizen who rode down to his Friends in his Livery-Gown
and Hood:[213] or that Parson who being enjoyned to wear the
Surplice[214] contrary to his will, when he had once put it on,
wore it constantly in his own and other Towns, while he was
complained of, for his abusing that decent Ministerial Garment.
I am sure there were some few who had no cause to be merry
or sport themselves at the sight; for my Emissaries were very
busie without any regard to the sacrednesse of the place, but in
revenge of this disgrace intended me, spoyled a good many
Cloaths by cutting of part of their Cloaks and Gowns, and
sending them home as naked behind as an Apes Tayle; which
espying, I remembered that story of another Crue of these *Pick-
pockets*, who coming to a Market Town where there was next
day a Fair to be kept; fearing to be discovered in that concourse
of so many people, resolved to do their businesse that very
evening, the people being very busie in fitting their stalls, and
some little Trading stirring besides. Their first consultation was
how to draw the Folks together to make one job of it, which
was agreed on in this manner; one of them (the worst at the
knife) pretending to be an ignorant Clown, got himself into the
Pillory,[215] at the bruit[216] whereof the whole Town ran together
to see the Spectacle, where those Cutters so plyed their work,
while they gazed, laugh'd and stared, that they left not any of
them either Purse or Money; the very keeper of the Pillory who
frolickt at this curious fetch,[217] being served in the same manner
as he stood neer the fellow: who seeing the work done and the
signe given him that they were departed, having continued an
hour in that Condition, and then at his desire released; told the
Spectators that he hoped they could not lay any thing to his
charge if they had suffered any losse, for he was in no capacity
to do it: when clapping their hands to their Side, and then to

their Heart, they cryed out with one voyce, their Purses were Cut, while in this Confusion he slunk away to his Companions, who were out of the reach of apprehension.[218]

I did not say as much whatever I thought when my penance was over; but this dealing with me therefore was so far from reclaiming me to the sobriety of decent apparrel, that I was [   ][219] offended with it, or others [   ]sex, I could by no means indure at any time before the Finicall and Modish Excesses of attire, into which Women were then, as in all Ages very curious,[220] to the wasting and impoverishing their Husbands, beyond what they are able to afford towards such lavish and Prodigall Gallantry.

There was a pleasant story which I used to prate of, of a Neighbour of mine that was given this way; being on a time in her Bravery, her Husband liking and not liking the riches and Gaudery of her Cloaths, by way of Droll[221] accosted her in this manner; sweet-heart quoth he, you are very fine, but you never think of the charge, there is never a time I have anything to do with you, but it stands me in a Crown towards this very superfluity. Husband replyed the Dame, it is your own fault that you pay so dear: for if you would do it oftner, it would not be above a Groat[222] a time: for I would rather take my Money in such Quids and Parcells,[223] than in Sums and in Gross, provided the Coine be as Currant, neither clipt, washt,[224] nor Counterfeit.

There was also a fellow a cotemporary of mine, as remarkable as my self, called *Anniseed-water Robin*: who was cloathed very near my Antick[225] Mode, being an Hermaphrodite, a person of both Sexes; him I could by no means endure, being the very derision of natures impotency, whose redundancy in making him Man and Woman, had in effect made him neither, having not the strength nor reason of the Male, nor the fineness nor subtlety of the Female: being but one step removed from a Natural Changling, a kind of mockery (as I was upbraided) of me, who was then Counted for an Artificial one. And indeed I think nature owed me a spight in sending that thing into the world to Mate and Match me, that nothing might be without a

peer; and the vacuum of Society be replenished, which is done
by the likeness and similitude of manners: but contrariwise it
begot in me a naturall abhorrence of him with so strange an
Antipathy, that what by threats and my private instigating of the
Boyes to fall upon, and throw Durt at him, I made him quit my
Walk and Habitation, that I might have no further scandall
among my Neighbours, who used to say, *here comes Malls Husband.*

I shall never forget my fellow Humourist *Banks*[226] the Vintner
in *Cheapside* who taught his Horse to dance, and shooed him
with Silver. Among other fantastick discourse, one day he would
needs engage me in a frolick upon a wager of 20*l.* which was
that I should ride from *Charing-Crosse* to *Shoreditch*[227] a straddle
on Horseback in Breeches and Doublet, Boots and Spurs, all like
a man *cap a pe.*[228] I was all for such sudden whims (as old *Noy*[229]
said when the Shepherd laid him on his Head with a Crook,
which he being surlily askt called a whim; who returning to his
Company from whom just before he had in great hast parted;
and being demanded by them the reason thereof, replyed that a
whim took him in his Head.) Just so it took me, I accepted the
Condition and prepared me with all the before named particulars against the day, and to doe something more than my
Bargain; I got a Trumpet and Banner and threw it behind my
back as Trumpeters use to wear it.

The day appointed being come I set forward, none suspecting
me, yet every body gazing on me, because a Trumpeter in those
dayes was as rare as a Swallow in Winter, every body wondring
what it meant, and taking it for a Prodigy. I proceeded in this
manner undiscovered till I came as far as *Bishopsgate*,[230] where
passing under the Gate a plaguy Orange Wench knew me, and
no sooner let me passe her, but she cried out! *Mal Cutpurse* on
Horseback, which set the people that were passing by, and the
Folks in their Shops a hooting and hollowing as if they had been
mad; winding their cries to this deep note, *Come down thou shame
of Women or we will pull thee down:* I knew not well what to doe,
but remembering a Friend I had, that kept a Victualling House a
little further, I spurred my Horse on and recovered the place,

but was hastily followed by the rabble, who never ceased cursing of me, the more soberer of them laughing and merrily chatting of the Adventure. In my own thoughts I was quite another thing: that I was Squiresse[231] to *Dulcinea* of *Tobosso* the most incomparably beloved Lady of *Don Quixot*,[232] and was sent of a Message to him from my Mistress in the Formalities of *Knight Errantry*, that I might not offend against any *punctilio* thereof which he so strictly required; and also to be the more acceptable to my lovely *Sancho Pancha*, that was trained up by this time in Chivalry, whom I would surprize in this disguise. These quirks and quillets[233] at that instant possest my fancy, but presently I had other representations. Methought those about the door were the very people that gazed at *Jane Shore*[234] in her scornful and unpitied misery when she laid her self down to die in one of the adjacent Ditches. The undeserved lamentable Fate of that noble Dame and the penance she had formerly underwent, wherein I was something like her, awakened me out of these imaginations which way I should be rid of the people; for I did not like that rudeness which manifested it self in their Speeches: when by chance came by a great Wedding on foot, at the instant that five or six Bayliffs had arrested a man, whom the multitude endeavoured to rescue; so while part was scuffling and part gazing at the Bride and Bridegroom, they had forgot me and gave me an opportunity of getting out the back way riding clear for *Newington*,[235] where I rested my self in my Chamber not daring to come out till toward Evening, and so came late into *Shoreditch*, where I paced the same way back again to the winning of my Wager, and my great Content, to see my self thus out of danger, which I would never tempt again in that nature.

This was so famed and noised all about Town that I durst not appear for the Boyes: I therefore betook my self to the instruction of my Parrets and tutoring my Dogs, whereof I had nine of a most lovely sort of Shocks,[236] who were trimmed and looked to with the same Care as other folks did their Children. I alwayes laid them in Trundle Beds, with Sheets and Blankets, and was as choice in their Diet, boyling as Gentlemen doe for their Hunting

Dogs a Pot on purpose for them with Broth and meat, and they well shewed their breeding and education, never bewraying[237] the Chambers, nor any part of the House: In the exact and curious cleannesse whereof I alwayes much delighted, none of my Neighbours equalling me in the neatness thereof: which was the onely part of womanhood I did.

Nor were the Ornaments of my house less curious and pleasing in Pictures, than in the delight of Looking Glasses, so that I could see my sweet self all over in any part of my rooms. This gave occasion to folks to say that I used Magical Glasses, wherein I could show the Querists (those that resorted to me for Information) those that stole their Goods in the resemblance of their proper persons; as likewise to others, curious to know the Features and shapes of their Husbands that should be, the very true and perfect Idæa of them, as is very credibly and consistently enough reported of your *African* Sorcerers; and we have a Tradition of it in the Story of *Jane Shores* Husband, who by one of the like Glasses saw the unchast embraces of his Wife and *Edward* the 4th. But this was a Fable as to mine, though I could have wished it had been true or have known which way to make it so; for I should have needed no other means to make me rich; seeing the very report of it did me some benefit by bringing folks thither upon that score, whom I could satisfie without the help of *Old Nick*;[238] and my *Cheats* not so *transparent*.

There was a shameless Jade, as noted in this Town as my self at this time, but for far more enormous Actions; she was called *Abigail*, her way of living (she being a kind of Natural)[239] was by ringing the Bells with her Coats for a Farthing, and coming behind any Gentleman for the same hire, and clapping him on the back as he turned his Head, to kisse him, to the enraging of some Gentlemen so far as to cause them to draw their Swords and threaten to kill her. This stinking Slut, who was never known to have done so to any woman; by some body's setting her on to affront me, served me in the same manner. I got hold of her and being neer at home, drag'd her to the Conduit, where I washt her polluted *lips* for her, and wrencht her leud Petticoats to some purpose, tumbling her under a Cock,[240] and letting the

water run, till she had not a dry thred about her, and had her
soundly kickt to boot.

Give me leave to remember other my Cotemporaries very
remarkable for their tricks,[241] and my boon and pleasant companions, *Mulsack* the *Chimney-Sweeper*, and *Cottington* the Cheat,
who made up the Pack of our *English Gypsies*. *Mul* I think was
Honest, but *Cottington* could cheat me, and I durst scarce
venture my self in his company; for he pawn'd me once in a
Tavern even to the shaming of me, though I think I was even
with him at the long run: having light upon him drunk, and
enticed him Home, I brought him to a Constable and charged
him with him, who had him to a Justice, by whose Warrant he
was set in the Stocks till he was sober. But he was grown
confident in such wooden punishments, having stood in the
Pillory at *Charing-Crosse* a little while before with a *Tinker*, whose
Kettle he wore on his Head all the time: the *Tinker* was put in
before him on his right Hand, which he *Spaniard*-like quarrelled
at, saying, *he was a person of more reputation than the Tinker*, and
made the Officers remove him to make place for his *worship*. I
visited my Gentleman in his Yoke, but I could not tell whether
his Face or his Kettle were the better Brass.

I shall often mention my Bull dogs though I had almost forgot
this pleasant[242] Story. Among other of my Bull-dogs I kept, I
had one whom I constantly fed my self, and by a *trick* I used
(which was to offer him Meat in my left Hand, and if he snapt
at it, to give him five or six Cuffs of the ear) I had learnt him to
take no meat but out of my right Hand, which howsoever I
stood, and whether he came to me behind or before at my
feeding of him he exactly knew. There was a Wench a Servant
to an Alehouse, I used to resort to, whom one time I overheard
to call me *Mal Cutpurse*, which I could by no means endure, and
resolved to revenge with this device upon her. I came thither
one morning with some Company, and as my Custome was, I
brought what cold Meat I had in the House for a *Breakfast*: we
sate in the Kitchin and fell to, while the Maid was busie up and
down, and my Dog lying in her way she took occasion to rate
him and gave him a kick; I laid hold on the opportunity which

would otherwise have put me to a shift to make one, and askt her the reason of her so doing; telling her withall that it may be she had a spight to the Dog for his good qualities; Marry Gup[243] quoth she, to be scabby is one of them; yes said I, I will lay a Wager of ten shillings as much as your Quarters service comes to, the Dog shall discover whether you be a Maid or no; agreed quoth the Wench, with that I stept to her and caught hold of her right Hand, as making sure the bargain, saying, *Give him this bit of Meat that lyeth on my Trencher, and if he taketh it from you and eat it, you are a perfect Maid*; *otherwise not:* she was very unwilling to make an essay or refer her virginity or rather impudicity to the Dog, but in a careless manner held the Morsel to him in her left Hand, which he refused, but instantly took it out of my right Hand which was free; she was all abashed (for she had seen the Dog roving up and down the House and gnawing of Bones, and it could not be imputed to his repletion) and would fain have slunk away, but I forced her, holding her hand still, to stay and make another Tryal; the Dog continued in the same care-lesse obstinacy which made the Wench stark mad: Well said I, before all the Company, it is apparent you have lost your Maidenhead, and if you will venture further, Ile tell you how often you have gone awry in your shoo;[244] for here's twice already. Thereat she was so surprized, that she blushed exceed-ingly and had not the confidence to deny it, but sculkt out of the Kitchin and came in no more to us; when her fellow servant coming in we told her the Story, and would likewise wager with her upon the same bargain: the Gypsie either knew her self tardy or else was a wag; for she merrily replied, Do you think me such a Fool to be tried by Dogs? I was fully satisfied from the other for the affront she did me; for she was forced to leave her place the boyes made such a Town Talk of her. Other the like pranks I plaid with this Dog which made me very careful of him, because he yielded me sport and pastime every way, so that I never suffered him to be abused at the Bull; for I made nothing to crack any mans head with a good Battoon[245] I had alwayes in my hand if they played foul play; which gives me occasion to add (that I may not misse any of my good qualities) that I could

use a Backsord[246] as well as the best of them. Once I challenged
a fellow to fight with me in a School at that Weapon, whom I so
soundly beat that he was forced to lay it down and confesse me
the Conquerour.

I will tell you also of a drunken rencounter of mine as
festivous[247] and unhappy[248] as any of my other, and something
of kin to this. I had been quaffing one night late at the *Devil*
Tavern,[249] and had got my Load[250] with some of my acquaintance, who being loth to stir I slunk away from them, and
making hast out of doors, in the Dark reeled or stumbled at a
great black Sow that was rousting[251] of a Dunghil neer the
Kennel,[252] where into I fell and most lamentably bemired my
self with the dirt, and turning about to see who gave me this
abuse, I perceived by its grunting 'twas a Swine; thought I to my
self I can have no better satisfaction than by driving of it home,
and the pounding[253] of it, and so make the owner pay for the
Trespasse. I then fell a driving the Sow, for so she proved; but I
know not whether I reeled or she wallowed the more; for she
was full of Pigs.[254] This pleased me so much the better, and
invited me to that entertainment of her beyond the impulses of
my present humour; I knockt at Door, and it being opened I put
in my Lodger before me. My Maids began to scold and to tell me
they had new washt the House, the fitter said I for my Guest;
you do not know my meaning, get you to your Distaffe and lend
me a Candle. So I gently drove her up to my best Chamber,
which was matted, and with a Mat made her a Bed; and a little
after made her a Drench[255] to hasten her farrowing. It pleased
the Hogs next morning she brought me Eleven curious sandy
Coloured Pigs spotted like the *Guynny*[256] ones, very fat and tydy
to my no little rejoycement.

I made a shift to eat them merrily inviting my Gossips and
Compeers[257] severally to them, till I had spent them all, and
then I very fairly turned the Sow out of Doors, who presently
repaired to her old Master a *Bumkin* that lived at *Islington*,[258] who
with wonderment received her again, and having given her some
Grains turned her out of his Gates, watching what Course she
would take, and intending to have satisfaction for his Pigs

wheresoever he should find her to have laid them. The Sow naturally mindful of her squeaking brood, came directly to my Doors, and there kept a lamentable quarter[259] to be admitted; this was Evidence enough for the Whorson that there his Sow had laid her Belly; when with a clear Confidence he knocks at my door and demands to speak with me: I wonder'd what rustick Visitant I had got, and suspected him come out of *Smithfield* from a bad Market, among my Harvesters there; but it proved quite another Story. He tells me a Tale of a Sow and her Litter: I reply he is mad. He swears he knows his *Sows* meaning by her grunting, and that he would give me Sauce to my Pigs if I made no better answer. *Goodman Coxcomb* said I, come in and see if this House look like a *Hog-stie* (which though I say it, was kept as neat and clean as any Lords in *London*, my Lord Mayor not excepted) He came through the Parlour into my Kitchin and Yard: do you think said I she is here? thence up Stairs into my Bed-chambers and Dining Room, where he saw his nown[260] face in the boards, do you think she Pig'd here? no quoth the Fellow: lastly I carried him into my Matted Room, What think you of this? Oh no, quoth the *Hogherd*, I wonder you think me to have so little manners! yfaith said I, if she pig'd not here she pig'd no where in my House you may believe me. The Fellow was Convinced, beyond my pardon, for this trouble, and went home cursing his Sow.

About this time happened that memorable Story of the five *Women-Shavers* in *Drury-lane*,[261] which I was very glad to hear; for it was a most impudent debaucht piece of malice and lessened the envy of my Actions; these five Furies had got a poor Woman, (whom they suspected the principal'st Shavers Husband had to doe with) and having stript her, whipt her with rods most terribly, and shaved off all the Hair about her, and then souced her in suds till they had almost killed the poor Wretch, whose tears, cries and protestations prevailed not a rush. They were afterward prosecuted for the riot, and condemned to the Pillory, which one or two of them suffered, and the rest fled to *Barbadoes*; but all of them ruined their poor Husbands.

I was now declining in my years, but my Trade as flourishing as ever, so that I lived in great plenty, and took the swing of[262] my delights and pleasures, which way soever they invited me. I was always a good *Fellow*, and loved good *Liquor*, especially good *Wine*, and growing into years such *Cordials* were not amiss: once sitting chirping[263] a Glass or two in a Tavern at one of my Neighbours where I used to resort, (though the *Globe* was my principal Mansion, whence I issued out my Processes and Warrants to bring the Offendors and the Thieves before me and usually determined the wrong) my Company began to suspect, that the *Vintner* deceived us, and dasht our white Wine with Water: I had long before suspected him for the like sophistication,[264] but he had alwayes stoutly denyed it, but this time I was resolved to make tryal; I went home and got some Green Seg,[265] such as grows in your clearest Fountains, and returned presently again, and calling for a fresh Quart, I put some of it into the Pot, and then called for the *Vintner*, who all agast and amazed at the surprizal, had not the Confidence utterly to deny it, but runs out and pretends to examine his Boy in the Kitchen, beyond which I had planted one of our Company to hear the Result, which was no more than this: the Master fell a beating the Vinegar-drawer or Pot-boy for not looking to the clearness of the water that was set aside for this use of mixture, which I hearing run in on the Gods speed,[266] and to part the Fray fell with the like fury upon the Master, for his cheating couzening practices upon his Neighbours; and thence forward utterly forsook the Fellow and his Drink. This was a small and inconsiderate[267] passage, but it serves to usher in a more famous and notable One, on this very Subject, onely turned and altered to the better.

After that unnatural and destestable Rebellion of the *Scots*[268] in 1638: upon His *Majesties* return home to *London*, where preparation was made for his Magnificent Entry, I also resolved to show my Loyal and Dutiful Respects to the *King* in as ample manner as I could or might be permitted. 'Twas usual with the *Roman* and modernly the *Italian* Courtezans to be very splendid in publique Works, as erecting of Bridges or Aqueducts, Causewayes, making of Moles,[269] or cutting Passages; and this they

doe either tributarily and by Order of the State, who set such an
annual or other Rate upon them, or else Testamentarily, when
at their Death they bequeath proportionable Sums of Money,
which they have got by their unlawful Trade, to such good and
laudable uses.

And memorable is that Story of *Phryne*[270] the great Harlot of
Greece (as you must know I am well read in all such kind of
Learning) who when the Walls of *Thebes* lay demolished, she
being a Citizen thereof, offered to build them up and Rear them
again, on Condition and Proviso, that on the Gates which were
to be a Hundred, there should be engraven in *Greek* these words,
Alexander overthrew them, and Phryne the Courtesan rebuilt them;
which they disdainfully refusing, she to preserve the memory of
her wealth (procured by the prostitution of her body) caused a
Massie Image of *Venus* to be made all of Gold, which she
Consecrated and gave to the Temple of *Apollo*, where it stood
the wonder of succeeding Ages, till Sacriledge and Covetousness, and the *ruine* and *destruction* of the place reduced it to one
and the same Nothing.

But to return from this not unpleasant digression, I was
resolved in my own account to beare a part in the charge of this
Solemnity; and therefore undertook to supply *Fleet-street* Conduit adjacent to my House with Wine, to run continually for
that triumphal Day, which I performed with no less Expence
than Credit and Delight, and the satisfaction of all Comers and
Spectators. And as the *King* passed by me, I put out my Hand
and caught Him by His, and grasped it very hard, saying,
Welcome Home CHARLES! His *Majesty* smiled, and I beleeve took
me for some Mad Bold *Beatrice*[271] or other, while the people
shouted and made a noyse, in part at my Confidence and
presumption, and in part for joy of the *Kings* Return. The rest of
that Day I spent in jollity and carousing, and concluded the
night with Fireworks and Drink.

This celebrated Action of mine it being the Town talk, made
people look upon me at another rate than formerly. 'Twas no
more *Mal Cutpurse* but Mrs. *Mary Thrift*, my neighbours using me
with new respect and civility. If I interposed in any Tumults,

which happned frequently, and I would be sure to Concern my self; if the Constable were called he followed alwayes my Direction; for I was lookt upon as the onely *Umpire* in such businesse! I had also a Custome which was duely observed to be charitable on *Sundayes* to the Prisoners of *Ludgate* and *Newgate*, so that I grew well acquainted with the Keepers, and could Command any Favour from them that lay in their power, which most an end[272] I used in procuring of Bayl and getting them accepted for Felons, and those of my Tribe and Family,[273] though I was never nice[274] or weary of doing the like Courtesies for poor Debtors when they made their Addresses to me.

Among these Keepers I had Contracted a firm and close Friendship with *Ralph Briscoe* the Clerk of *Newgate*, a notable and famous Person, and the best and ablest to go through that place, they ever had or are like to have. He was right for my Tooth[275] and made to my mind in every part of him; insomuch that had not the apathy[276] and insensiblenesse of my carnal pleasure even to stupidity[277] possest me. I should have hired him to my Embraces. I had known him a Child, bred up most an end in the same Exercises of Bull-bayting, wherein I presided. I alwayes praised his towardliness and believed he would come to preferment; For he was bred at *Grays Inne*[278] which made him to write and read so perfectly in his youth, and I knew also he had good Parents; yet I know not that ever I mist him at any Match in my life: Besides, ever since he came to know himself, he alwayes deported himself to me with abundance of regard, calling me his *Aunt*;[279] keeping close by me and engaging with me in the Broyl. I once brought him off when his venturousnesse had like to have cost him his life, the Bull having made a heave at his breeches which broke and gave way, and me the opportunity of pulling him back. Ever after we two were both one, he never failing of any duty, nor any service I required of him, which he was capable to do in that place and quality.

Having such sure Cards at every Sessions, and having recovered and gained such an estimation, I did constantly interpose my self at all the Gaol Deliveries in and about *London*, and having gotten the ears and favour of some great Lords of the

Court, by what artifices Ile tell you presently, I made it no
difficulty to Reprieve any one Felon that could either make
most Money for me, or had deserved well, or was like by his
dexterity to deserve well of me, so that in process of Time I had
as many Tenants for Life belonging to me as any Nobleman
whatsoever. These I had always ready at my Devotion, and the
power and willingnesse I shewed to save some, brought other
Thieves to my obedience, so that I was as good as *Queen Regent*
of *Misrule*,[280] being obeyed from the two great Principles of
Subjection, *Love* and *Fear*, being alike able to preserve from, and
to deliver to the Gallowes, upon any the least spleen or conceived displeasure: the load whereof some untractable Rogues
felt in their deceived hopes of a *burnt Hand*,[281] when (like the
Turkish Emperour of late, who gave a private Sign for the cutting
off a Malefactors Head for Coyning when the punishment of the
Law was but the Losse of his Hand) I gave them over to
themselves and the Law, and left their Heads in a Noose and
their Lives in the Lurch.

But to abrupt a while the thred of this Thievish Discourses, I
will tell you some other of my Pranks and devices, which were
far more innocent and civil, being a fair Negotiation betwixt
Man and Man, upon honest and equitable grounds. I had made
many Friends, and some of them monied Men, with whom
(having quickly got an inside into the Scriveners way of lending
other Folks money,) I did now and then pleasure a Friend;
among other of the courtesies, when Money was very scarce for
a Courtier to find in the City without very good security,
(though they have had the luck to bite them of their wares and
goods to the *disparagement* of *Inprimis* and *Items*)[282] I did upon the
earnest entreaty of one of those gay Cavelleiros[283] endeavour to
take up a 100*l.* for him of one of my *Dons*,[284] who was very rich;
acquainting him with the quality and fortunes of my Brave,[285]
and that there could not possibly be any danger in crediting him
with that summe; he smiled, and replyed he knew the Gentleman very well, that his Uncle was yet living his very good
Friend, and therefore should be loath to displease him, by
supplying his Nephew in any extravagant courses; but yet if I

thought there was no danger, or that the young man was civilized, he would venture such a summe if he would be bound. I undertook both these considerations, as sure of a good snip and share, when my youngster should have the Money, but the Old Rogue intended no such matter; for when my Friend came to receive the Money, he very punctually told it him out and suffered him to bag it up, when according to agreement he asked him to be Bound,[286] with all my heart replyed the other, when straight wayes rusheth in a couple of Fellowes with a double Cord, and make the Gallant fast to a great bed, and throwing him his Money at his Feet, leave him to consider of the disposal of it: in which consultation he was not long before he knocked very hard, desiring the Old Gentleman to come up and receive his Money again, but there was no body would hear, while he was even tyred with hooping and the impatience of his restraint; at last up comes the Grave Seignior with his two security men, and release the Gentleman, making him count over the Mony again, and pay it in due form of Law, and with some hints to him of his Uncle, and his own ill Husbandry,[287] gave him leave to depart.

Immediately he repayres to me and tells me his disgrace: I furthered his passion by being as mad at it as himself, but how to help it I knew not; yet see the Invention of disappointed and frustrated expectation. I presently mustered my Wits and set him upon this project; go you, said I, to such another *Veilliago*,[288] which I named to him, a great Friend and Familiar of the others, and tell him you come from me; and if I see him before, which I afterwards did, I will tell him as much, that you want a 100*l.* upon your own bond, and if he shall scruple it, tell him you were bound to such a Man and you paid him very honestly at the day; he knows your Family likewise, and no doubt the plot will take effect.

My advice was followed, the Usurer, as I supposed before, comes to be resolved of the other, whether what was told was true? he answered, yes, I had him bound and he pay'd me very honestly; whereupon the dotard no way doubting of just dealing, lent the 100*l.* upon his bond, but to this day never saw a

Farthing again; but came constantly to his dying day rayling at me, though to the same purpose as pissing at the Conduit. He was a kind of a turn'd out[289] Lawyer, who having got his Estate by broyls, thought it requisite to spend the rest of his dayes in ease and plenty; I thought it contrariwise no way fit or just, that such Tormenters should have their *Quietus est*[290] either in this Life or the next; for I alwaies hated cruelty and oppression, but of all people I affected not a Lawyer.

I had tasted of their covetousnesse and dilatorinesse so much, that I never advised any person upon any misusing whatsoever to have recourse to them for remedy or redresse. I knew their quirks and quillets and how they could and did wrest the Law to any thing for their own advantage; and therefore I alwaies by my self or Friends composed all differencies that came to my cognizance. I was never better pleased with any thing justly done by them than I was with that story of Mr. *Atturney Noy*[291] (which relating to my Trade, was of good use and direction to me in such like Causes) concerning the 200*l.* left by two Cheaters in an Inn-keepers hand by them both, to be delivered to them both again; which the man forgetting, pay'd it to one of them, and the other brought his Action; when the Court and the Defendants Counsell were Non-plust, *Noy* strikes in, and being Feed,[292] acquaints the Judge if the person would come and receive it, the 200*l.* was ready, and since they could not help it would pay it twice: but the Cheater durst not venture upon that score, and so the Court was satisfied of the Trick. In like manner, a Countrey Dealer had lost a 100*l.*[293] with Cloak-bag and all upon the Road, it having dropt from him, and a good honest poor man had the Fortune to find it at the Townes End. The looser cryes it, offering to give Twenty pound to any that should informe him of it; the Countryman hearing of my practise, comes to me and acquaints me with it; I expecting a little consideration also, gave the man notice, who came and told out the Money, and when he had told it, threw the poor man Twenty Shillings, saying, that indeed there was neer 120*l.* and that the founder had taken out the odd Money, and had more than satisfied himself; the Man denyed it, the other persisted in it, why then said I, there is no other way of decision but by your Oaths; and if either of you dare forswear himself for the Money, at his peril be it. The Covetous *Londoner* accepts of the condition, the other desires his Purgation; so they made two Affidavits[294] the loser swears he lost 120*l.* the other swears there was all he ever found; so that upon reference of it to me, I ordered the Money to remaine still with the honest finder, it appearing by both their Oaths that this was not the Money that was lost, but another summe, and might possibly by a favourable construction be another mans.

THE *Seeds* of that Unnaturall War,[295] which not long after grew up to be the *Harvest* of *Death* in the numerous Slaughter of many Brave and Gallant Persons, some of them of my acquaint-ance, began now to appear, when the popular Artifices and Cheats of some Grandees of those Times upon the multitude, by their specious pretences of *Liberty* and *Religion*, so farre outdid all the wayes and methods of my Imps, and their most Jugling impostures, and Hocus Pocusses,[296] that I was at a losse and had nothing at all to do.

The publique[297] was all the Noyse, and all the Trade and Resort was to Mr. *Pyms*[298] Chamber; poor City Guls,[299] that came thither to have their Pockets Pickt, and to learn how to throw away their Money.

This new invention I say, very much troubled me, for, besides that I had a tincture of Religion and good Nature, both which made me affectionately Loyal to my Prince, whose Honour and Saftety was principally endangered; I plainly perceived that there would be no living for me in those precise[300] times that I boded would ensue; which would endure none but holy Cheats and sanctified Delusions, where another guesse[301] *spirit* than of *Mephistophilus*[302] was pretended in their Godly Legerdemain[303] and most zealous operations.

But they soon resolved me, that it was indeed *Old Nick* who actuated them by his principles of Malice, Lying and Murther, Vices and Impieties I can proudly say, thanked be my good innocent Stars, I never was the least tainted with; (for if I had

any thing of the Divel within me, I had of the *Merry* one, not
having through all my Life done any harm to the Life or Limb of
any Person) when I perceived them engaged in that desperate
Fatal conspiracy against that renowned States-man, the Earl of
Strafford,[304] Lord Deputy of *Ireland*.

That bloody Prosecution, most implacable revenge, and im-
potent rage of the Rabble, did very much move alike my
indignation and compassion, which I was not afraid for all the
mad Prentices ran down almost every day crying, *Justice* and
Execution (and a casting glancing blow at me might have been
feared) publiquely to resent and declare my abhorrence.

Nay to make that Unfortunate Earls Enemies appear equally
Cruel and Ridiculous to that sort of people I conversed with; I
published a solemne *Bull baiting*, where in the hearing of them
all, I named a generous and cunning *Bull* that threw off all the
Dogs that made at him, *Strafford*; and my Dogs that played at
him, *I named Pym* and St. *John*'s[305] and so forth; This is *Pym* cryed
I, he bawls and makes a noyse but bites not: but this is St. *John*'s,
he fastneth shrewdly, but yet he playes not any fair play, and so
Allegorized the whole story.

There were some *Phanaticks*[306] there who caught hold of my
words, and began to question me; but oh my sides! I cannot but
laugh to think I see those *Rascalls* beaten. My Crue without any
command of mine, fell upon them, calling them all the Saucy
Rogues in the World, for daring to question me that was the
uncontroulable Mistresse of the Game, and at whose service
they all were; and having kickt and banged them to some
purpose, turned them out of the *Bear-Garden* to relate to their
Complices how like a stage they had seen there to that at
Westminster-hall,[307] which they failed not to doe, with many
Aggravations of my impudent (as they were pleased to call it)
Behaviour and Language, to the Dishonour of the Parliament
and those famous Patriots and Assertors of its Priviledges and
the Liberty of the Subject, when I could have said more truth in
behalf of my *Pick-pockets*.

The Blowes these Roundheaded sneak-noses had received,
stuck so close to their skins, that they could not forget me the

occasion thereof, which made them uncessantly diligent in procuring an order of Commitment of me to the Sergeant at Arms[308] attending the House of Commons. I had timely notice hereof and prepared to avoid the Storm, by running for shelter under the protection of a Nobleman my Neighbour,[309] who interposed his Power and Authority, and superseded the Warrant for seizing me.

I know people will be inquisitive from whence and upon what occasion came this kindnesse, and therefore I will passe from this Noble occurrence to another lepid[310] and pleasant Story forbearing only the Name and Place, because its yet recent in Memory. You must know therefore that among other my large acquaintance I had some familiarity with the mad Girls and the venerable Matrons of the kind Motion,[311] among the rest, I was very intimate with the Abbesse[312] of the *Holland* Leagure[313] on the Bank side, and with *Damaris* Page,[314] newly then from a *whore Rampant* separated to the Office of a Procurer or Provider, and some other notable and the ancientest Traders in that Profession. Now seeing how little hopes there were of my interlooping[315] in stollen Goods, I thought it the best Course to keep me in my old Age which grew apace upon me, to deal altogether in prohibited Wares, not doubting but that pleasure would invite as many Comers as Profit, there being alwayes, which I considered both in War and Peace, good Vent[316] of such Commodities. The voluptuous Bed is never the lesse frequented for those hard and painful Lodgings in the Camp.

I saw also, that the former Traffiquers this way were very straightlaced and too narrow in their practise, as Confining their industry in this Negotiation to one Sex, like Women Taylors,[317] that if they were to be hanged cannot make a Doublet for themselves. In this I was a little prosperous, though to make good the Simile, I could never fit my self. One time (you may spare me this digression; for since there was nothing serious in the whole course of my life, save the very anticknesse thereof which alwayes kept the same tenour, it is no great matter how I place my words and matter) as I was going down *Fleetbridge*[318]

I espied one of my Neighbours Mr. *Drake*, a Taylor *God bless him*, and to my purpose, he was altogether for the women; quoth I in Droll, Mr. *Drake* when shall you and I make *Ducklings?* he *quackt* again, and told me, that I lookt as if some Toad had ridden me and poysoned me into that shape, that he was altogether for a dainty *Duck*, that I was not like that Feather, and that my Egs were addle. I contented my self with the repulse and walkt quietly homeward.

To return, I had new and strange faces now frequenting and haunting my House quite contrary from those before, I began to think my self a *Generalissima* or some great Military Officer, such a Troop of Gallants and Souldier-like Men using to me for employment and preferment; Among the rest I was cruelly troubled with *Frenchmen*, who were very sollicitous with me for Orders, with such confidence that I could not any way be rid of them; one of them whom I ventured upon a finical[319] Madam, I saw afterwards in a splendid Condition, and generally all whom I set at work were ever afterwards very seldome idle or needed my assistance. I never well knew the knack of it (for they were very sordid and ingrateful, and courted not (when they were served) my acquaintance that advanced them) but if I should modestly forbear it; for I love it not my self; and therefore will restrain others so, through their forced ignorance thereof. But without great wrong to Civility it is imputable chiefly to the Mignardises,[320] and more Effeminate Wantonnesse of the *Mousieur*; whose soft dalliances and Courtships, and impudent bold Flatteries are in that preferrible, before the rude and downright attempts of the *English*; and I remember a leud story of *Vavasour Powell*,[321] inveighing in his Pulpit against the *Cavaliers*, and taxing the violence of their lust to this very purpose; but it is well known, and his Authority not worth a rush; and so I passe it least I foul my Paper.

Generally, I therefore chose the sprucest Fellows the Town afforded, for they did me reputation at home and service abroad; my Neighbours admiring what this retinue and attendance meant, nor would I now discover it but to unburden my conscience, and shame the private practices of some great

Women; who to this very purpose keep Emissaries and Agents to procure Stallions to satiate their desires, as confidently as they entertain Grooms and Laundries. I will stirre this Puddle no longer, nor dive into the depth of it any further, least I pollute and inquinate[322] the Reader with the Filth hereof.

This was Fortunes right hand to me in this new undertaking, by which I got good store of Money, being pay'd on both sides: I had also a bountiful one of her left, in my trucking with the other Sex: I told you my acquantance there, [among whom I ought to have reckoned Mrs. *Pike*, one of Mrs. *Turners*[323] breeding up, and of the like fate with her, for they were both hanged at *Tyburne*: the latter for dealing unskilfully in my Vocation, having received stollen goods from the hands of one *Crowder* (a notable High Way Man who used to Rob people in the Habit of a Bishop, attended by Four or Five in the quality of his Servants, and was very famous for the great prizes he took) I did much regret the fortune of both these, having parallelled and compared them with my Condition, which as to the future resembled Mrs. *Turners*, whose unhappinesse it was to have to do with great Personages; my present way, and as to my past Life, was neer a piece with Mrs. *Pikes* as I was *Receiver Generall* of the Thieves Revenue. I did all I could to save her, but the Notoriety of her Crime prevayled against all endeavours that way; and so I resigned her to her cruel destiny.] Now I will tell you what good use I made of it; I had my Purveyors continually abroad, who had alwaies the prime of the Market: whatever Maidens came to Town there was none durst or might see them till my turn was served, my Sisters of the Tribe must wait for my leavings; very frequently I have had notice of some, even from those persons and places that *retailed* them themselves, it being counted a piacular[324] fault to conceal any such thing from me, and which they were sure to satisfie me for by one revenge or another, which the proudest she of them all durst never think to retaliate upon me.

This was the Common road, but these were other private ways, which were chalkt out to me by the particular Fancy of some great persons, whose eyes had lighted upon some difficult love, which lay not in their Knight Errantry to atchieve. Herein my service was Courted, who by reason of my general knowledge and the Confidence of addresse had access every where. I sometimes on such Errands delivered Letters, sometimes a *Complement* and *how do' ye* and the proxy of a visit, when I would be sure to have the servants at my devotion: In these Affairs as in all other I was no less dexterous than lucky, which made me very acceptable to those who stood in need of such an Instrument.

So that my House was become a Double Temple of *Priapus* and *Venus*, frequented by Votaries of both sorts,[325] to whose desires my answers (the Oracles of a Couch chair where I sate as chief Priestesse) were always favourably accommodated; some of my Proselytes, for their good *omen* of their initiation by my predisposal of them (but to their thinking occasionally)[326] rencountring one another at my threshold, to the ravishing wonder of those mutual desirers, who little expected such sudden Fruition, which always enhanced my price to the defraying of my liberal Expences in wine and good Cheer.

With others I lingred, delaying their Impatience by laying before them the difficult but certain attainment of their wishes, which served as a Spur to the dulnesse of their Purses; for my Lady *Pecunia*[327] and I kept the same pace; but still in the Conclusion I did the Feat. There was a noted Lasse a married Wife of this time, whose Story shall serve to conclude all the amorous tricks and pranks that were wrought by me; for indeed it sums up all that belongs or attends to such doings, and the account I promised; want and shame never failing to bring up the rear of Lust and wantonnesse.

She was in her youth a very curious Piece indeed, but wanting a Fortune Competent and proportion able to it, arrived no higher at her Marriage than an ordinary Citizen, yet of good Fame and Reputation. For a while in the beginning of this state she lived continently at *home*, but the Flies buzzing about her as they resort alwayes to sweets, soon Corrupted and Tainted her: this was not unknown to me, and thereupon I resolved that she was as free for my turn as for any bodies, and forthwith I

accosted her, using such Caresses, promises and invitations as I
knew the Market would bear, so that I made her entirely mine,
and gratified a friend with her first acquaintance, who in short,
was that Noble Friend,[328] that preserved me out of the hands of
the People at *Westminster* who had resolved on my mind: He had
not long after occasion to leave *London*, and then I bestowed her
on another, and so to a Third, Fourth and Fifth, &c. according
to my best advantage, till such time she had Contracted those
distempers, which not long after brought her to her Grave; her
sickness having first buried those quick and lively Colours in her
Face under the cold Earth of a dead and lurid palenesse, that
enviously triumpht in the spoyls of so proud a Beauty. Being in
this plight, and judging her self both by the glasse of her face
and that unerring mirrour of her Conscience unworthy to live,
since the first told her she could be in no *favour* with Men, and
the other more surely told her, she was out of *favour* with
Heaven, she addrest her to Late but serious Repentance, beginning at the right place with Confession, unbosoming her self to
her Husband, and craving first his pardon and forgivenesse;
which being granted, she desires him to call up all her Children,
which were in number Twelve, that she might take her leave of
them, and say something of them to him which concerned him.

When they were come, she begins, This Eldest Boy is truly
yours, no Man ever having to doe with me untill after his Birth;
but this next to him is such a Knights Son, that such a
merchants that such a Noblemans, that such a Doctors, and so
forward (naming men of all good quality and Estate) till she came
to the youngest, who was carelesly biting on a piece of Bread
and Butter, when just as she was pronouncing his Parentage, the
Boy broke out into this Language; hold Mother, pray bethink
your Self; for Gods-sake let me have a Father that's Rich and
Gentile,[329] as well as the rest of my Brothers and Sisters: which
proving to his wish, the Boy was over-joyed; but the poor
Cuckold dismai'd; till after her Decease, (for I durst not come
neer her, as well loath to give her any occasion of regret and
imbitter her sad Condition as indeed ashamed of my selfe, being
toucht with the like, though not so through Convictions of the

evil I had done) coming to condole with him for the losse of my
Gossip: he roundly taxed me with inveagling his Wife into such
lewd Courses, to his no lesse shame than Ruine, by such a
numerous Train of *Bastards*. I bid him be quiet, and if he would
follow my advice I would make him a gainer by his hard
Fortunes; which I effected by procuring him round summs of
Money from his respective Rivals, to the maintenance of their
Illigitimate Issue, which they honestly paid; and all was husht up
in a contented secrecy, and he and I as good Friends and
Companions as ever.

The *sweets* of this sinne are not so *luscious*, but the *sowre* of it is
altogether as *tart* and *piercing*; and usually those pricks are
applyed to the Conscience, when there is no outward comfort
left to intervene and rebate[330] their Keennesse, when Pleasures,
Friends and Health have forsaken them and exposed them in the
Loathsome dresse of their own impurities, to the contempt of
the world, and the abhorrence of themselves.

For I do not know of those many I was acquainted with, that
ever parted hence as others do: but either they died the pity and
scorn of people, or else they ranted away their lives in a
desperate and carelesse manner, to no lesse scandal and ignom-
iny, than if they had perished through want and distresse. I
speak of Common and Continuall Strumpets, who live by the
Divels pay, and are constantly in his Service; Yet is death in
what shape soever a Felicity, if it comes seasonably, and nicks
them in the very critical time of their decay; but if they chance
to survive that, who can reckon those numberlesse miseries that
attend them? what old sinner is she who thinks not of Calami-
tous *Shrove Tuesday*,[331] with Dread and Horrour? who skips not
out of her Bed if she have any, or else off a Dresser every night
with Fear and Affrightment at the Apparition of a Beadle at a
Whipping Post or Carts Tayle? who Dreams not of that Terrible
Tempest of *Turnip Tops*, *Garbage*, *Dirt*, and *Brick-bracks*, and of a
Hog in Armour to ride through it? who trembles not at those
dire Execrations, and Curses of the Prentices, during that
Martydome?[332] Damming all Bauds to Hell, and the Sharpest
inflictions of punishment there, yet the very day before smiling

in her Face, calling her Mother, Aunt &c. and sending for *Mull-Sack*,[333] or *Strong-waters*,[334] to assist them in the prosecution of their Lusts, and to deal Honestly and civilly with them. Oh this Contradiction and Unagreablenesse between Twenty and Forty years! the longest distance betwixt the temperate and horrid[335] Zone of Woman-hood; In which last Climes, what Fætid Exhialations, what Putrid Breaths, what Parched Skins, what Withered and Dryed Faces are there? As for those real Fires hereafter, the terrour of that were insupportable; but that they have a device to quench those Flames by continual pouring in strong liquor, which swimms their brain into a *Lethe*[336] of all future misery.

But I love not to dwell long on this subject, having other passages of my Life (which were down-right honest) to r'account, that so my Reputation may be like my Habit and Mind, equally Good and Evil; a kind of indifference or neutrality, as to generals of either, but in particulars especially as to the Times I am now speaking of, I think I was the onely declared person in our street against the Parliament; For I well remember when the King came to *Branford*,[337] and the City was in a great Fright by his neer advance, (which I wished were to my Doors, where I would have made his Majesty a great deal welcomer than at his return from the *North*). The whole force of Trained Bands and Auxiliaries marched out to oppose him, and Carts came door by door for Victuals to follow them to their Camp which was thrown into baskets, which I having warning of, prepared two Ox Livers, which I just Perboyled,[338] and wrapping it up with broken Brick-bats for Bread, threw into the Basket: it fell very heavy and plump in, which made the *Virago* that was set in the Cart to stow the Guttage, a zealous voluntary Wench, of which there were numbers, to intend an inquiry; but there were so many Disloyal Hands heaving in Provant,[339] that she had not the present opportunity: but he whom I sent to Dog the Cart, for the pleasure of the discovery was all; told me, that about the Church she unpin'd the Clout,[340] spying the Dainties, fell a raving[341] as if she had been inspired by *Hugh Peters*;[342] wishing she knew the Cavalier Dog that did it; but I valued not such unskilful Conjurers, giving the Rebels Muskiditchee with my Currish Fair.

Of all the Zani's and Jack Puddings[343] of this sad Reformation: I never abhorred any man more than that *Hugh Peters* and *William Lilly*, the very disgrace of our Art and Profession; who with their lying wonders and jugling deceits, and impudent falshoods, did very much prejudice the King's Cause. I wonder'd to see fellowes so expert in the Mystery, of whom I never had any intelligence before I see them at work; and therefore no doubt they were of Old Nicks own planting, who fitted them to that work in an instant, to which my Imps rose by degrees.

These Forrainers and Interlopers had all the Trade, while the Natives, those *Burgesses* of *Turnmill-street*[344] had nothing to do: unlesse they would learn their hands to Fight in a fair Field, or against Walls and Bullworks (to which they were highly urged, by their necessity; for as to the vehement preachments that way, they had the grace and happinesse never to come within a Church, which is one of their principles) instead of cutting a Purse in a Crowd.

The Money was all got into *Guildhall*[345] *London*, and a pick-aron[346] might have sooner rob'd a Wench of her Maiden Head, than of her Bodkin and Thimble;[347] for there were some hopes she might happily have preserved that, but the other were gone without Redemption.

Many an untoward look I gave to that *Corban*,[348] that Treasury and Exchequer of the Cause, about which I would willingly have employed some of my *Janizaries*;[349] but there were so many Thieves hankering over it, for the whole was but a great Robbery, that my puny ones could not tell where to creep in. And oh how I laught when I heard the Folks parted with their Gold and Silver, upon the warrant of the Publique Faith; to which my Trade was an *Amsterdam* Bank, and a safe sanctuary. Some jeered at the term and said it was the Punick Faith,[350] infamous for all manner of Treachery and Perfidiousnesse; others that it was the Publike prostituted Faith, all, that the Publique was Mad; and would need double the sums to recover it. I lived to see all of it verified, when it became a by Word and a term of Art, used by my *Mercurialls*, when they would signifie the unlikely-hood of restoring their purchases.

Now they began to raise and Lift their *Militia*,[351] and the division and ward of *Fleet-street*, making one entire Regiment; because of the vicinity and nearnesse to their Generals, the Earl of *Essex*[352] his house; they were graced with his Colours, which were *Orange* or *Tawney*: whereupon I fell upon my former imitation, and instead of *White*, *Green*, *Red*, and *Blew* Colours used to be put into my Doggs Heads, at Matches for distinction; I set on *Orange* and *White*; and with the usual stile given that Earle by the Cavaliers, I called the *Bull* his Oxcellency. These apposite pat words and whimsies could not escape notice, though they escaped punishment; my Neighbours hearing of the danger and interceeding for me as one of crackt reason and judgement.

One time as they were drawing up in *Fleet-street*, on a Generall Training-day, I could not forbear upbraiding them with their Fighting against the King; whereat one of the Officers a great Zealot, gave me a wrap on my back with a little Cain he had in his Hand; Sirrah said I, I'le make you repent this blow you gave me; 'tis not your *Turd Coloured* Scarf shall excuse you. The fellow was very wroth, and cryed out to seize me, and have me before his Colonel; but I withdrew through the presse, and got to my House, meditating on revenge for this affront.

Now the Women and Maids of every Parish, with Drums, Mattocks,[353] Shovels and Baskets, went Rank and File to cast up the line and make the Fortifications round the City; I was invited to be one of the number, and for Honours sake should carry a Flag, as was then used, in the Head of a Company; as the custome is with the Fencers when they play their Prizes. I refused the motion, returning to them that Dichery, tuned to the beat of the Drum on those Occasions — Round-Heads and Cuckolds go Dig, go Dig — your Wives *Aprons*, grow short and their bellies big; and that they need not send their Wives to make works, for they could make *Horn-works* enough at home; where the Embraces of their Gallants would serve for a better *line* of communication, without the help or direction of Captain *Bulmer*, or rather *Bull-maker*, the principal Engineer[354] of the Parliament.

But I mingled my self among those Honest Matrons, that went down and Petitioned at *Westminster* for Peace, when we were *bade to go home and to wash our Dishes*; which answer so moved my patience, that I could not forbear to cry out aloud, *Rather wash you your Mouths from such foul Language, and your hands from that blood which is already shed*; which begat such a fuming in their Guards, who were commanded to fall on and drive us away, that some of the company for hast lost their Hats and Petticoats, beyond my Art of retriving and recovering them; for I had no acquaintance, nor would I hold any correspondence with those Modern Thieves, who plundered every day one honest man or other without any controul.

I never thereafter could abide the Earl of *Essex*, for that he, that was no Womans Man,[355] and therefore very obnoxious to me, yet could adulterate the affections of the Kings Subjects; and out of a sort of revenge for the disgrace he received in being repudiated by his Wife, did divorce them from their Allegience to their Prince, who had no way merited at his hands any such demeanour, which made me resolve never to Contribute a Farthing or pay any of the *Assessments* for the maintenance of the War, but what was levyed by distresse or composition made by my Neighbours, who preserved me from the violence of those miserable Times. I had a Finger likewise in the Commission of Array;[356] that was set on foot in *London*, and had it proceeded, could have brought a hundred of as stout fellowes to assist the Enterprize, as any were in the City; being my Companions at Bull-baiting who were ready to serve me or my designes in any thing.

But all things coming to confusion by the carrying on the Rebellion; I betook my self to a Contemplative Life, and retired my self at home despayring to see good day again: lamenting the sad and miserable distractions into which we were reduced. Let no person think I had no sence thereof, for though I say it my self, I had as much English Nature in me as any body, and suffered as much in my way as any one whatsover. But that which more nearly grieved me, was the absence and losse also of many of my great Friends, who were of the other side. In this solitary Condition, to alleviate and lighten the tediousness thereof; I played with those my several sorts of Creatures of pleasure and imitation; such as my Baboons Apes, Squirrels, and Parrots, with them, and the Recreation of their Tricks to passe away the time, and supply the defect of better Converse.[357]

I likewise got me three Maids, intending now at last to play the good House-wife, whom I set to Card, Reel and Spin, and other such Domestick imployment; keeping them to their Task, and overseeing their work, and hearing them sing which I much delighted in: though my voice was the untuneablest thing that ever was heard, and as gratefull to the Ears of people, as the squeeks of a Mandrake[358] at it's Revulsion; with these Creatures and Wenches, and a Strange Cat I had which would follow me into the Streets, I passed the day, but the nights were long and irksome: whereupon I set my rooms out to Lodgers, such as I liked, and well understood. Among the rest of those that came to enquire for a Chamber of me, there came one bonny blade[359] whom I well knew by his Name to be a Gentleman, and askt me the question, I told him I was well contented, but my price was Seven Shillings a Week; contented quoth he, I like my Lodging and my Land-lady so well, that I value not the Rent; Sir quoth I, I have another Article then to make with you, that you keep good hours (which I very constantly observed) for I shut my doors presently after Nine a Clock at Night; saith he, I shall do well enough for that, you may shut your doors as you please; but where I use to lie, I never trouble the Doors, for I alwaies come in at the Windowes, or through the Wall, or down into the Cellar.

I lookt upon the Gentleman very seriously, wondring how any of my Tribe, as I had cause to conceive of him by his discourse, durst use that boldnesse and quicknesse with me; but recollecting my self, I thought he might be a merry wag[360] and ingenious, and therefore resolved to try him; he proved to be a person of good Worth and Estate, and of very great Civility: to whose courteous Friendship and good Company, I was for a long time after much beholden.

In this privacy I lived till the then War expired, whose event mightily discontented me: but was however a little Comforted at the sight and enjoyment of my Friend, the Old *Cavy*'s,[361] who survived those Extremities meerly to be engaged in new ones; particularly that Noble Lord my Neighbour[362] returned to his house, whose very sight did much solace me. His pleasures and my other Friends businesses invited me again into the publique. I undertook their Compositions,[363] and frequented their Committees of Sequestration at *Haberdashers-Hall* and *Goldsmiths-Hall*,[364] untill the Hobgoblin Tyrants routed me away, charging their Ushers to keep me out; and to terrifie me the more, to Shoot me if I presumed to Enter.

About this time, one *Walker* a notable *Pick-pocket*, had got a rich Gold Watch set with Diamonds from my Lady *Fairfax*,[365] the Generals Wife; the manner thus. My Lady used to go a Lecture[366] on a week day to *Ludgate* Church, called St. *Martins*, where one Mr. *Jacomy*[367] Preached, being much followed by the precisians;[368] *Walker* perceiving this, and that she constantly wore her Watch hanging by a Chain from her middle; against the next time she came thither, he drest himself like a Commander in the Army, and having his Comrades attending him like Troopers, one of them takes off a Pin of a Coach Wheel that was going downwards through the Gate, by which means the passage was obstructed, so that my Lady could not alight at the Church door, but was forced to leave her Coach without; which *Walker* taking occasion of, readily presented him self to her; and taking her from her Gentleman Usher, who attended her alighting, led her by the Arm into the *Church*, and by the way with a pair of Keen Scissors for the purpose, cut the Chain in two, and got the Watch clear away: she not missing it till Sermon was done when she was going to see the time of the day. Presently I was sent to, and any thing I would ask offered me, if I would discover or recover the Watch. I never had any intention to do her that Courtesie for her Husbands Sake; but indeed then could not tell. For the Fellow and his Complices suspecting a strict Search, were presently fled, and I could not tell whither; at last *Walker* was taken for another Fact,[369] in the same manner and Condemned; when to save his Neck, he presently sent to me, knowing he might safely trust me with a thing of that value, of Two Hundred Pounds; and desired me to go my Lady and offer her the Watch if she would get him a Reprieve, and some other small consideration. I effected my Reprieve, but he failed of continuing it; for he was the Prime of the Profession, the Master of them all: and therefore the Court would by no means spare him but the next Sessions delivered him to *Gregory*:[370] who shewed him a flight worth Twenty of his, and sent him swinging into the other world.

There were then the rarest pack of them, some whereof I left, who would lay a wager to pick a Mans Pocket, though he was warned of it but a Minute before, and knew his Company. It will be tedious to recite their Activities, how they justled Mens Hands out of their Pockets that were set there purposely as a Guard or Sentinel to secure their Money; how they would pretend to have a Letter read to them, or such like story, while standing behind you, they would Rub the Bung.[371] The many Various neat Tricks they have played upon *Ludgate-Hill*, by making stops of Coaches and Carts; the Money that hath been lost, there being more than sufficient to build up the Houses, and make the way broader without the Aid of an Act of Parliament, which would be highly prejudicial to the Trade. Again, if at any time a Diver was taken in the Fact, and his hand seized; then they had Two or Three in readinesse to Discountenance the Complainer, and to give out that he looks more like a Pick-pocket than their fellow Rogue; and so making a quarrell the Whipster[372] Escapes. There was a device used to catch some of those *Ingeniosi*[373] at the sport, and to that purpose Men have had Fishing Hooks sowed in their Pockets, and some Gudgeons that ventured too deep and plunged into the bottom, have been caught and held fast: and angled up and down for five or six turns in a walk such as the great Hall at *Westminster*,[374] with smart and cutting pains; but the smitten Fish will beware, to prevent that mischief they went afterwards more deliberately to work, and if they suspected any such story would make nothing to cut away the whole side of the Breeches with the Pockets in it; as many have been served in Play-Houses and great Crouds, and concourses of People.

Other times when they had not the opportune and full liberty of their Hands below, they would use them above board in the like presse of the multitude; if they see any Man have a good Beaver,[375] or Silver or Gold Hatband, they would so nimbly and slightly change it, and clap on one of their Musty Felts in the room of it, that the loser could not discerne the Conveyance of it; all these tricks brought Grist to my Mill, but not in the same abundance as formerly; for I did not solely and altogether intend that my former way of dealing, because I was pretty forward in the world, and was a little more serious.

About this time also a great Crony of mine, one *Cheney* a famous Wrastler (for the *North*, though I was for the *West*) which sport I mainly loved: was taken by the Troopers upon the High Way, who had allowance by the State for that very service. He defended himself stoutly, but was over-powred and desperately wounded, and brought to *Newgate*. He would faine have avoided his Tryal by my Counsel of pleading his weaknesse and the sorenesse of his wounds, but that would not passe; They caused him to be brought down in a Chaire,[376] from which they drawed him to a Cart, out of which he was cured of all his Diseases. I offered Fifty Pounds for his pardon because he was a stout fellow, and my old acquaintance; but the Roads were so pestered with frequent Robberies, that I received a rebuke for my pains, and he a worse check for his.

For Colonell *Downes*'s[377] Men, (so they called themselves) were abroad, who suffered no passengers to Travel their wayes; among whom there was one *Horne* a Captain, and a sturdy *Pewterer*, and some other Trades-men whom I very well knew; but with the *Pewterer* I had good Correspondence, some of those Monies came to my hands, which I faithfully kept and delivered at their demand to supply their necessities and occasions of the Prison, where they lay some while before Judgement. They died bravely and gallantly, giving me good cause to speak well of them: for I had some Money of their's in my hand, which by their silence and undisposall thereof, I reckoned my own, this was a good Wind-fall from *Gregories* Plum-tree;[378] and I was so wise as not to speak a word of it to the Sheriffe or any of his Officers.

But my constant intimacy was with Captaine *Hind*,[379] a daring adventurer (whose exploits are many of them publique) yet considering all, there was no such hazard in his pranks, for most of the chief of them I set; both of us concurring to be revenged of Committee Men and Parliament People, by those private assaults, since publique combating of them would not prevaile. The first designe was upon some of their Money that was going to pay their Souldiers at *Oxford* and *Gloucester*; I had employed my Scouts about the Treasury in *Guild-Hall*, who informed me of it, and I gave as speedy notice to *Hind*; withal acquainting him that the Money which was Two Thousand Pounds, was Guarded with a Convoy of Twenty Horse, and therefore to provide accordingly. This was a dangerous Attempt but the love of Money and the pleasure of the spight, excited him to the exployt. He gathers some Twelve of his confident'st associates and withal resolved Men, and way layes the Cash a little of this side *Oxford*; when just at the close of the day, as the Wagon was past *Wheately*, and at the Foot of *Shotover Hill*; he and his fellows rose from Ambuscado in the Twylight, and furiously fell upon the Troopers; who suspecting his number to be far greater than it was, fled away in confusion: while some of them followed the pursuit,[380] and kept them from *rallying* or discovery what they were: while the other fell to ransack the Waggon, and remove the Goods that they might come to the Ferkion[381] where the Money as I advised them was put up.

The Passengers were all in a heavy Fright fearing at the least the losse of all they had; but they rid and freed them of that perplexity and doubt, by telling them they came not to take away any Money, but what did as justly belong to them, as the persons that pretended to it; it being the Commonwealths Money which those great Thieves at *Westminster* had Fleeced out of the Publique to pay the[i]r *Janizaries*, who maintained them in their Tyranny and Usurpation: while the Loyal and the Honest Subject was Ruined and Undone by their Taxes, Plunderies, twentieth part, and Sequestrations of their Estates.

Every one of them took his part of the Money; and having gratified the Waggoner with half a piece, made post hast to

Bedford, and so came by the other end of the Town to *London*; where he acquainted me with the successe of the businesse, and requited my discovery with some of the half Crowns designed for *Red Coats*, who were ready to Mutiny for want of their pay: and I overjoyed with the *booty* and the *vexatios* mischief it did to my *Round headed*[382] *Masters.*

Many such like Feats was done by him, as the robbing the Committee man, &c. But I will not trouble my Reader with what hath been related before as it came in and agreed with his own stories; though I was the Wyer that moved that Engine in all his great prizes, as most of his were such; leaving him in his injurious Grave into which he fell a sacrifice to their revenge and spleen,[383] more than to the Lawes or any-bodies complaint: being betrayed by a Minister sent to prepare him, but indeed to dispatch him.

But out of his *Ashes*, as suddenly after his death arose as great a *Taker* as himself, one that stole as much Money as all the Thievs in *England* for his time; my singular Good Friend *Richard Hannam*,[384] a Fellow that went alwaies habited like, and was reputed, a Merchant. He constantly wore a Watch-Makers and Jewellers Shop in his Pocket, and could at any time command a Thousand Pounds. I put him upon the like employment of seizing Parliament Money on the General Receivers hard at *Reding*; having notice by my Spies that a Thousand Pounds was ready there, expecting an Ammunition Wayn and Convoy to carry it to *London*; but *Hannam* prevented that way of carriage, conveying it up himself on Horseback, having in the night time with his followers brought a Ladder into the Orchard the back way, and set it up just against the Closet Window, in the further-most part of the House, and took away all the Money in bags, leaving some Thirty Pounds or thereabouts in odd and broken Groats[385] and odd Money upon the Table; and leaving the Ladder standing against the Window where they entred, made hast through the Orchard to the Gravell pit where their Horses stood, and mounting them Rode speed for *London*. The notoriety of this Fact was so great, that by strict enquiry it was found that my Friend *Richard* was the principal Verb;[386] whereupon he was way-layd and apprehended, and sent down Prisoner to *Reding*, and from thence at the Assizes carried to *Abington*; whither I procured *Ralph Briscoe* to go down and assist him in what he could; so he packt[387] such a Jury by jugling with the Bailiffs that empanelled it; that though Judge *Jermyn*[388] did what he could to Hang him, there being very good circumstantial proof, as that he was seen in the Town that very night; yet *Richard* so baulked and terrified the simple Jurors, and so affronted the Judge (by bidding him come off the Bench and Swear what he said as Judge, as a Witnesse &c. so he might perhaps Murder him by presumptions of Evidence as he termed it) that the Fellowes brought him in Guiltlesse; though to procure his liberty of the Collector, he confessed he had the Money, but then there was no trying of him again for the same Fact. This was a clever[389] come off, thank honest *Ralph*; the Collector saved himself by discovering the Thieves, and they saved themselves from Imprisonment by discovering their Theft; the honest Collector according to his word procuring their Release.

Many other pranks he did which I was acquainted with, but that Foraigne Robbery of the King of his Plate at *Colen*,[390] which I understood the Villain was in then, so alienated me from him, that I could never after endure the sight of him; but was very glad when not long after for all his promises of giving *Cromwell* some of his *Majesties* Papers which he had taken away at the same time, that discovered the Kings correspondencts here, he was taken and Hanged in *Smithfield* Rounds, having a little before broke out of *Newgate Jayle* by the content of a Convict person, who suffered him to Escape, for which the Foolish Fellow was presently Hanged himself. This *Hannam* was yet fond of me to the last, and I Fingered some Legacy Goods, a Watch and a Ring of his which he sent me from *Newgate*.

But to a more Jocular story: I should have told you that there was one *Rainbeard* a Grocer at *Strand-bridge*[391] and I, who took much pleasure in telling of any silly people we met with, that we were their Godfather and Godmother; and to that purpose if either of us had hit upon a Chouse,[392] whom we had perswaded into that belief, we sent him to one another. He had pickt up a

Costermonger[393] an *Irish-Man*, older than himself, of whom, having ficht out his Parents Name, and the place of his Nativity, he had so deceived him as to make him believe him to be his Godfather; he pretending great kindnesses to his Deceased Friends, and how dearly they Loved one another, insomuch that the Fellow was wrought upon to kneel down and ask him Blessing: and received in Lieu thereof a Brasse half Crown but not discernable, and withal a direction to go to me at my House and do his duty there too, for I was his Godmother; with a Hundred flams what we two would do for him by preferring him to the Court.

The Fellow glad of his good Fortune delayed not coming to me; but when I considered him, and understood his businesse, I could not forbear Laughing; but yet repressing the sudden violence thereof as well as I could, I bid him do his duty: 'twas just at my door, and some of the *Tankard-bearers* perceiving the accost, and knowing my Tricks, fell into such a Hooting at the poor Fellow, jeering him with his Folly and most Grosse ignorance, that the Fellow sensible of it, went with his basket of Pipins into the street against my Windows, and discharged a whole shower of them upon the Glasse, (enough to have made me a Pye) before I could get up: when to give his anger freer passage, I threw off all the Casements which were to every Lyband,[394] and admitted his kindnesse, while the profusenesse of it recalled my Godsons Fury, and set him to vent it another way in Cursing and Swearing.

I had not yet w[r]eakt my spleen upon the Parliament who by undoing my Friends had undone me, being compelled by my good Nature to relieve and lend them Money in their Extremities. What mischiefe I had done them hitherto, was but a Fleabiting, and shewed only the impotence of my hatred; now it was my good Fortune to light upon a Fellow that could make them feel their Losses, and fret at the audaciousness of the Exploit, and yet have no remedy for it neither; with him I communicated my thoughts, and we concurred to Forge and Counterfeite their Commissioners and Treasurers Hands to the respective Receivers and Collectors, to pay the Summs of Money they had in their Hands without further delay, to such as he in his Counterfeits appointed; so that wheresoever we had intelligence of any round Summe in the Countrey, we were sure to forestall the Market. This Cheat lasted for half a Year, till it was found out at *Guildhall*, and such a Politique course taken that no Warrants would passe among themselves to avoid Cozenage.

When the Government was seized and usurped by *Oliver*, we began this Trade afresh, it being very facile to imitate his single signe Manuall,[395] as that ambitious Usurper would have it stiled. My Man therefore, and as fitly too, since they would have it so had his signe Manuall, by which he drawed good Summs of Money out of the Customes and Excise; nay out of the Exchequer it selfe, till *Oliver* was forced to use a private mark to make his Credit Authentique among his own Rascals.

Now appeared that abominable Villany, called *Trapanning*;[396] the blot and blemish of all Bawdery; the leud complices in that Monstrous basenesse, being worse by ten degrees than wittals.[397] It made me commend *Harry Martins*[398] Exposition of the *Rumps* Law against Fornication; that is, provided that people who used that Trade should be sure to keep the doors Locked, and stop all Crannies and Crevises that no body should be able to espy any thing; for it was made to catch fools onely, wise men would be sure to beware. This Roguery raigned a long while before any Remedy could be found; for it was practised upon none but Men of Fashion, Quiet and Fearfull of their Reputation, which those Villains were confident they would preserve at any rate; which they hoisted up sometimes to Five or Six hundred Pounds, upon pretence of Stuprating[399] a fellowes Wife, that is a Common Whore, who was never worth a Farthing. This mischief fell frequently heavy upon Grave Citizens; till at last one that had been served so, and had entred into Four Hundred Pound Bonds, anxiously discovered his Case to his Friend, who prudently advised him to appoint the payment of it in *London*, and when these locusts came, to clap an Action of Two or Three Thousand Pounds upon their back, and lay them in the *Counter*. This was done with success, and the Gallop of this Evil stopt, which made the Trade a little freer than before: no man daring to trust himself in a Womans Company for fear of these Fellowes.

My Trade I am sure was wholy at an end, and my Money gone, get what I would, the Cavaliers my Friends were so needy; so as I was glad to stay at home and play at tick tack[400] for Drink with one of my Companions, and bemoane my decayed Fortunes.

Having run this race, and seeing all things grow every day worse and worse by the desperate evil of the Times; I became weary of them and my self together, so that I wholy relinquished all converse or commerce betaking my self to a sedentary life and to reading; wherein before as I was well versed in *Tale-books* and *Romances*, and the Histories of the Seven *Champions*[401] and the like Fopperies: so now I considered that I had an account of my time to make by spending it in more serious Writings and Contemplations.

He runs long we use to say that never Turnes; it was therefore high time for me of thinking of the way by which I should turn, and that presently offered it self to me; for being grown crazy[402] in my body, and discontented in my mind, I yielded to the next distemper that approached me: which by my bustling and active spirit I had kept off a good while from seizing me; it was a *Dropsie*,[403] a Disease, whose cause you will easily guess from my passed life: but it had such strange and terrible Symptomes, that I thought I was possest, and that the Devil was got within my Doublet.

For what all the Ecclesiasticall quirks, with their Canons and injunctions could not do, this boysterous malady soon effected. I was forced to leave off that upper part of my Garment, and do *penance* again in a Blanket; a Habit[404] distant from the *Irish Rug*, and the *Scotch Plad*, their National Vests for Women of quality, whom my Scoffing Neighbours said I did very much resemble. As for my Belly, from a withered, dryed and wrinckled piece of Skin, it was grown the titest, roundest *Globe* of flesh, that ever any beautuous young Lady strutted with, to the Ostentation of her Fertility, and the Generosity of her Nature. I must tell you I could not but proud my self in it; and thought nature had reserved that kindnesse for me at the last, insomuch that I could have almost been impregnated (as *Spanish Jennets*[405] are said to be begotten by the Wind) with my own Fancy and Imagination, my *conceit* proving the same with *conception*; and to please and maintain me in this delusion a Woman of my Age then living in *London*, was brought a bed of a Son, which was very certainly true; and an old Parson in the *North*, one Mr. *Vivan*, of neer a Hundred years old, was juvenilized again, and his age renewed, as to all his senses he enjoyed before at Fifty. But these were signal Miracles and presages of a *Revolution* in the state (whose hopeful beginnings I lived to see in the Confusions and Distractions of the *Rump revived*,[406] which I could have Eaten without Salt, as stinking as it was;) and this of mine, the certaine forerunners of my *dissolution*: fore there was no blood that was *generative* in my belly, but only that *destructive* of the *grape*, which by my excesses was now turned into water, so that the Tympanied skin thereof sounded like a Conduit door.

I cannot further Anatomize my body, for I dared not to look on my Leggs with the Swan, (though I had nothing in my whole any way aimiable) they did so represent a Bull or Bears stake, and my Head so wrapt up with Cloaths, that I lookt like Mother *Shipton*;[407] so that among all the Looking-glasses my House was furnisht with for Ornaments, I had neer a one big enough to see it altogether and at once. But my self was indeed the best mirrour to my self; for every afflicted part and Member of me did represent and point out the wickednesse, every one of them had been instrumental in, so that I could not but acknowledge the justice of my punishment. My Hands indeed escaped this Vengeance, and I think they were the most innocent; for I never Actually or Instrumentally cut any Mans Purse, though I have often restored it; but oh my *Plotting*,[408] *Match-making* Head in those *Sorceries* of *Lust* I practised! the Leudnesse and Bastardises that ensued, and those frequent Trottings and Runnings up and down to facilitate and bring about those Debaucheries! These I cannot but acknowledge were indigitated[409] to me so plainly, that I was forced to take notice of them; and I hope with a real penitence and true grief to deplore my Condition and former course of Life, I had so profanely and wickedly led.

As an *advantage* thereto, this *disease* lingred with me a long time, which I had solitude enough to improve, all people, but some of my Old and Nearest acquaintance forsaking me. I will not boast of my Conversion, least I encourage other vile people to persist in their sins to the last; but I dare assure the world, I never lived happy minute in it, till I was leaving of it, and so I bid it Adieu this Threescore and Fourteenth year of my Age.

It may be expected I should have made a *Will*, let the Reader therefore understand, that of Fifteen Hundred Pounds which I had of my own in good Gold, which some of my Neighbours can bear witness to have seen, out of my *kind heartedness* to my old Friends, the distressed Cavaliers, to help them in their compositions, and other reliefe they had formerly, I had not a 100*l*. to command, which I thought too small a summe to give to Charitable uses, (as to build an Hospital, &c.) it being no way proportionable to my unjust Gaines, as they were every where esteemed. And I was loath to raise Dust out of my Grave (with the Fly riding upon the Chariot Wheel)[410] by such small Evidences of my Expiating Charity. I very well liked and approved of *Allens*[411] the Players pattern, in building those *Almes Houses*, and endowing of them accordingly, but I could not reach to the imitation. The Money that might have been designed that way, as it came from the Devil, returning to the Devil again, into the *Rumps* Exchequor and Treasury at *Haberdashers* and *Goldsmiths Hall*.

Yet to preserve something of my Memory, and not leave it to the courtesie of an Executor; I anticipated my Funeral Expences, for it being the fashion of the Times to give Rings,[412] to the undoing of the *Confectioners*, who *Live* altogether by the *Dead* and the *New Born*; I distributed some that I had by me (but of far greater value than your pitiful hollow ware of Six or Seven Shillings a piece, that a Jugler would scorn to shew Tricks with) among my chief Companions and Friends.

These Rings (like Princes Jewels) were notable ones, and had their particular Names likewise; as the *Bartholomew*,[413] the *Ludgate*, the *Exchange*, &c. deriving their appellation from the places they were taken in: they needed no admonition of a Deaths Head, for they were the wages and Monument of their Thieving

Masters, who were Enterred at *Tyburn*; and I trust my said Friends will wear them both for my sake and theirs.

In short, for my Breath fails me, I did make no *Will* at all, because I had had it for so long before to no better purpose; and that if I had had my desert, I should have had an *Executioner*, instead of an *Executor*; 'Tis very well I part so fairly, but remember me to *Dun*, and tell him he will not need my *Legacy*; for my divining spirit tells me there's a Glut coming which will make him happy and rich, if he knows how to use it.

I have also already disposed of Thirty Pounds of One Hundred Pounds I have by me, to my Maids, and have charged them to occupy it the best way they can; that and some of my Arts which they have had time to be expert in, will be beyond the advantage of their Spinning and Reeling, and will be able to keep them in repair, and promote them to *Weavers*, *Shoemakers*, and *Taylors*.

The rest of my Estate in Money Moveables and Household *Goods*, my Kinsman *Frith*, a Master of a Ship, dwelling at *Redriffe*,[414] will lay claim to, as next of Kin; whom I advise not to make any adventures therewith, but stay at home and be Drunk, rather than to be Drowned with them.

Let me be lay'n in my Grave on my Belly, with my Breech upwards, as well for a *Lucky* Resurrection at Doomsday, as because I am unworthy to look upwards, and that as I have in my LIFE been preposterous, so I may be in my Death; I expect not, nor will I purchase a Funerall Commendation; but if Mr. *H*———[415] be Squemish and will not Preach, let the *Sexton* mumble Two or Three Dusty Claiy words and put me in, and there's an *END*.

FINIS.

Behold my innocence after such disgrace
Dares show an honest and a noble Face
Hence-forth there needs no mark of me be k
For the right Counterfeit is herein shown—

Ætatis meæ proxcmo 22° Ianuar stilo novo vicesimo primo 1663

Reproduced by permission of the British Library.

THE
CASE
OF
Madam MARY CARLETON,
Lately stiled
The German Princess,
Truely Stated :

With an
HISTORICAL RELATION
OF HER
Birth, Education, and Fortunes ;
IN AN
APPEAL
TO
His Illustrious Highness
PRINCE RUPERT.

By the said MARY CARLETON.

Sic sic juvat ire sub umbra------

London, Printed for *Sam: Speed* at the Rainbow in Fleetstreet, and *Hen: Marsh* at the Princes Arms in Chancery-lane. MDCLXIII.

Great Prince,
To whom should the injured innocence of a Forain & desolate woman address it self but to your Noble and Merciful Protection, who with the *Majestical Glories* of your Relation to this *Crown*, have most *condescending compassions* to the distressed and low *estate* of the *afflicted*.

For when I considered the general report of this your Generosity and Clemencie even in the greatest incitements of passion, amidst the victorious progress of your Arms; I could not but presume Your Highness would open Your ears to the Complaints of an abused Woman, in a Case wherein the Laws are altogether as silent, as in the loudest and clamorous noise of the War.

Besides, the different necessity of my Cause, and the vindication of it, did inevitablie put me upon your Highnesses Patronage. I am traduced and calumniated as an Impostor (and the scandal continues after all the umbrages of it are vanished) and that *I* am not a *German*, nor so well descended there as I have alledged, and do and will maintain: Therefore to your Highness as the sacred and fittest Sanct[u]arie of this truth I have betook my self; whose excellent purity I do so revere and honour, that

I would not soil it with the least tincture of a pretence, or paint of falshood for a world.

Your Highness drew your first Princely Breath, which hath since filled the Trump of Fame, within the limits of that circle of the *Rhine*,[2] where I was born: and within the Confines of your paternal Dominions, my Infant cries were to be heard; and therefore with all alacrity I submit my cause, and my *stronger cries for Justice* to your Highness, who partakes equallie of this and my Countrie.

Notwithstanding I should not have been so bold as to have given your Highness this trouble, but that I have been informed you have been graciouslie pleased to pity my ruines, and to express your resentment of those incivilities I have suffered: And indeed that with the just indignation of other Noble persons, who are pleased to honour my desertion and privacy with their company, is the only support I have against those miseries I indure, the more unsupportable because irremediable by the Laws of this Kingdom made against *Femes Covert*.[3]

I take not upon me to dispute the equity thereof, but in all submiss[ive] obedience do cast myself and my cause at your Highnesses feet, most humbly requesting and beseeching your Grace and Favour in some extraordinary redress to be vouch-safed to

Your Highnesses most
Obedient and most
Devoted Servant,

MARY CARLETON.

Madams,

Be pleased to lay aside that severity of your judgement, by which you examine and castigate the licitness and convenience of every of your actions or passages of moment, and therefore seldom run into the misgovernment of Fortune, and cast a favourable eye upon these Novels[4] of my life, not much unlike those of Boccace[5] *but that they are more serious and tragical.*

The breach that is made in my Credit and reputation, I do feel and understand to be very wide, and past my repayring, what ever materials of defence, excuse, and purgation I can bring to the scrutiny of men; who are not sensible to what sudden changes our natures are subjected, and that from ayry thoughts and motions, things of great influence, sometimes good, somtimes bad, have been exhibited to the world, equal to the most sober and firm resolutions of the valiant and the wise.

It hath been my mishap for one among many others to miscarry in an affayr, to which there are more intrigues and perplexities of kin and alliance, and necessary dependance, than to any other thing in the world, i.e. marriage: (Hymen[6] *is as blind as Fortune and gives her favours by guess) the mistaken advantages whereof, have turned to my real damage: so that when I might have bin happy in my self, I must needs transplant my content into a sterile ungrateful soul, and be miserable by another. Yet have I done nothing dishonourable to your better beloved Sex, there is nothing of leudness, baseness or meanness in the whole carriage of this noised story, nor which I will not, cannot justifie, as the actions of a Gentlewoman; with the account of which, from the beginning of my life, I here present you.*

My Fortune not being competent to my mind, though proportionable to any gentile[7] degree, hath frowardly shrunk into nothing, but I doubt not to buoy both my honor & estate up together, when these envious clouds are dispelled that obscure my brightness; The shadows are at the longest, and my fame shall speedily rise in its due lusture, till then, and ever I am,

Ladies, your devoted Hand-Maid,

MARY CARLETON.

THE
CASE
OF
Madam *Mary Carleton*
The Wife of
Mr. *John Carleton,*
Formerly stiled
A German Princess.

I am so much the more beholden to my Innocence than to my
Fortune, that I dare more confidently appear to the *Vindication* of
the one, than (through the malign deceit and injury of my
Adversaries) to the *v[i]ndication* of the other; And *challenge* my
enemies, and the *Spoils* they have made of me, though I dare not
lay claim to my *Friends*, my *Honour* and my *Estate*, which I shall
keep concealed and inviolable from such rude and mischeivous
hands as my *Person* hath been betrayed to. And yet the suspicious, noxious world doth very hardly conceive of me other
than a Malefactor, and prefer my Wit and Artful Carriage to my
Honesty, and take this untoward passage of my life for some
festivous and merry accident of the times, and look upon me as
a notorious (nay even among the more ingenious, but as a)
notable[8] person.

I can give no other reason for this, but the diligent and
forestalling slanders of my accusers, who by lewd and most false
suggestions have precluded all ways to my justification and
defence; and my own unwearied patience in suffering those
calumnies to pass unrefuted, further than by a legal Trial; not
willing to cast any dirt upon those by way of regesting those

foul-mouthed and libellous scandals by personal reflections; for I concluded that time, and the justice of my Cause and the Laws of the Kingdom would clearly absolve me, and that therefore such exasperations on my part would widen that breach, which the fraudulent covetousness of some Relations had made between my Husband and my self, and render it irreconciliable, when as I had resolved to redintegrate[9] that affection, we were mutually bound to have for each other.

But since I have perceived, and have been fully satisfied and informed of their insatiable and implacable malice against me, not onely in prosecuting me with fresh Indictments after the Jury had acquitted me of the former, (though the grand Jury were so fully sensible of the Injustice and maliciousness thereof, that they would not receive any more) to say nothing also of the Witnesses brought against me, the blind and the lame (as to their tales and stories) procured by most wicked and detestable practices, (whom God forgive) but by advising my Husband after my acquittal to forsake me, and renounce my bed, and so defeating me of my Jewels and other things of value of mine own, and leaving and exposing me destitute to the World, and to the pity or scorn of people, as my condition shall weigh with them: These unsufferable mischeifs have now at last extorted this Narrative from me, which I request the courteous Reader to give Credit to, and equally and seriously consider my Case.

It hath already made a great noyse in the World, sutable to that bluster my Husbands Friends had raised my Fortune and Qualitie to; but those High winds being laid by their weeping showers, I will secretly and clearly tell the World the naked truth of all this story, having premised a short Apology for myself, and given some account of this my (Errant-like) Adventure and Peregrination from the place of my native Country.

I was born at *Collen*[10] in *Germany*, though incredulous people do take that for a pretence, and better concealment from any research that can be made after me; but as I have declared it before that Honourable Judicature in the *Old Bayly*,[11] whose grave and reverend Authority, I hate to prophane and abuse with a lye; so I do again assure the World by the greatest pledges of a Christian, that I am a Native of that place, and did continue in it, or thereabouts, the most part of my life hitherto. They that know it, know it to be one of the Mistresses[12] and compleatest Cities in that Empire, not onely famed for the birth of very Illustrious persons of Ancient Times, and the Honour it hath received from them (as I could largely instance, especially from its Latine adject of *Agrippina*)[13] but for that modern glory it received by the entertainment of the King of Great *Brittain*, who was most Hospitably and Cordially, and with all imaginable respect and Honour treated Here, when by vertue of *Cromwels* League with *France*, he departed that Kingdom.[14]

I mention this at large, because hence I took up those Resolutions, which since, with so much misfortune I have put in Execution. I observed here the courteous civility, and affable good temper of the English Nation, for by those Gentlemen that then attended the King I measured his Kingdom. Those were persons of such winning and obliging carriage, of so easie and familiar address, and yet of that generose and regardful demeanour, that I was hugely taken with such sweet Conditions, and being then young, by their frequent converse in the Town, which was constantly in my eares, came to such an acceptable knowledge of their manners, that I then thought of passing over to that Country, for a fuller satisfaction and delight I had promised my self among such a people.

As to my Parents, who by *Pythagoras* his fancyful Phylosophy,[15] or rather envious Witchcraft, have been transmigrated into I know not what filthy and vile persons, of the most perdite[16] and abhominable[17] sort of men; I do desire pardon of their Ghosts, and shall sprinkle their ashes with my tears, that I have by my unadvised and ungoverned Resolution, raised them from their quiet and Honourable Graves, to be the suspicious and leud discourse of every malevolent and busie tongue. But let such know, that my Fathers name was, *Henry Van Wolway*, A Licentiat[18] and Doctor of the Civil Law, and Lord of *Holmstein*, a man esteemed for his services done to this City of *Colen*, in mediating their Peace and Security and Neutrality, in the *Swedish* and *German War*,[19] and for other effects of his Counsels and Endeavours to our

Ecclesiastical *Prince Elector*, and the House of *Lorrain*,[20] in all those turmoyls of that Country, in the first rupture of the *Spanish* and *French* War.[21]

I instance these remarques, because having been so long dead some nineteen years, I cannot better describe or Characterize him to strangers, though he were known in his own Country by other great and Noble actions, as well as for his long and ancient descent from an honourable Family of that name: which whosoever shall give himself the trouble of curiosity in Enquiring, may yet find preserved from the ruines of a destructive, and but just composed conflagration.

It will seem foolish and sottish flattery in me, to adorn His Monument with any more Elogy, to a strange and perhaps unbeleiving Nation, who have no faith for any thing they see not, or not have heard from plain and undenyable testimony. And if I be taken for uncharitable in this rigid imputation, let the practices of those, who have made their unreasonable incredulity, a pretence to their more barbarous cruelty, be my excuse to the World.

I shall not need therefore to particularize any more of him, for places and circumstances, and the like accidents, will be of no greater demonstration, or convincing verity, than those punctual relations of Sir *John Mandevile*,[22] concerning things that were impossible to be in humanity and nature; and I will not so much as seem to impose upon the reader, with those nearer artifices of a Lye. I am capable of doing my self right, (which I suppose will be too readily interpreted to my disadvantage) by any means, within the compass of a womans understanding, and therefore if I thought I should need more ordinary ways, I would have applyed my self thereunto.

And so I will proceed to a further Narrative of my life, having acquainted the Reader, that it pleased God to take away both my Father and Mother before I was full three years old, but my Father died last suddenly, and left me entirely possest of his estate, without any Guardian or Trustees; the expectation of many people who had long designs both upon it and me.

Being thus an Orphan, and destitute of a Procurator,[23] as we

call it in our Law, the Church as next [of] Kin to such estates
(and claims the right and disposal of the Ward) secured me, and
what I had, in their hands, until such time as I should be of age
and understanding to determine of my self and my Fortunes,
which they hoped by so early a matriculation, and induction of
me into the profession of the Religious,[24] to grasp finally into
their hands.

By them I was put into the Monastery or Nunnery of *Sancta
Clara*,[25] at this Infant age, and educated in all such breeding as
was fit for one devoted to the service of God and his Church,
wherein, if ignorance and innocence might render devotion
acceptable, my young probation-years I may be confident were
not offensive. But growing up to some capable years, and my
active busie soul exerting itself, and biting as it were the bit of
this restraint and confinement; the hours and days of this
solitude and retirement, in which I was as it were buried as soon
as I was born, grew most irksome and tedious to me, though I
was not yet acquainted with the World. I felt some such strong
impulses and natural instincts to be ranging abroad, and in action,
as the first finders of *Terra Incognita*,[26] were urged with, to the
discovery of those Regions, of whose Existence they had no
further assurance than their own hopeful bodings and divinations.

The Discipline also, began now to aggrieve me, and the more
my thoughts wandred and strayed after my roaming and strange
fancy of the worlds bravery (which I began now to take notice
of, from the gallant appearance of persons of quality, who
frequented our Chappel) the more did the orders of the place
streighten and fret me. I began to be weary of my Company, and
the poverty of those *Votaries*, called in derision, as it were the
Bare-footed Clares; and though I suffered none of these hardships,
nor underwent any of those nice penances and mortifications, as
having no inordinacies of youth to quell and subdue, yet the
customary severity of such dealing with that sweetness and
tenderness of our Sex, did much grate me; and I blindly wished
I were (what my inclinations prompted me to) a man, and
exempt from that tedious life, which yet was so much the
worse, because it was altogether passive and sedentary.

Nor could I find when more matured, but that Religion when imposed as a Task, and made an employment, was one of the greatest burdens I could endure; (though I have learned better things by practise and the troubles of the World, and could wish my self safe in such a retreat from the cares of the future, and the doleful thoughts of my past time, and have a zeal for my Religion, the obligations and conduct whereof I have to my sorrow so much in my late unadvised resolutions, abdicated and neglected.) I lookt upon it more as constraint, and not a voluntary act, wherein I had no manner of election; and my Libertine spirit which mistook bold Humanity, and the dictates of a generous nature, for simple and genuine adoration, confirmed me in this opinion, and finally perswaded me and prevailed with my Reason, which grew not up equall with my passion, to abandon this serene and blissful mansion, and venture upon the Worlds alluring, promising vanities.

I was arrived at that age wherein I was capable of being admitted, and professing my self a Nun, and to take upon me the Vows of the Order of perpetual Virginity, and the like requisites of that Monastical life, and therefore the Fathers and Confessors willing to make me a Proselyte, were very urgent that I would take the Habit and devote my self to a religious life, setting before me the many examples of some excellent Ladies and Gentlewomen then in the Cloyster (though it be one of the poorest Convents of all) who had great and noble friends, and great Estates (some of them) and had not withstanding with all readiness of mind separated and estranged themselves from all worldly things, and consecrated themselves to God. But my resolutions of forsaking that melancholy and silent abode, were so far advanced, and so obstinated in me to the prosecution of my masculine conceptions that I obtained my discharge at the same time, as I have partly hinted before, that his Majesty was in *Colen*, whom, with the rest of the desirous world I longed to see: accompanied therefore with my maid who had attended me in the religious house, and a man-servant who was my Steward or Bayliff abroad, and had prepared all things for my secular estate, I went to his Palace, w[h]ere to pass other rencounters, I met with a civil person, one Mrs. *Margaret Hammond*, the Daughter of Sir *Richard Hammond*, living somewhere then in the North of *England*, a very accomplisht woman, who for her Religion had left *England*, intending to have betaken her self to the English Nunnery at *Lovain*;[27] but some difficulties happening therein, she had journied up hither upon the same account, and perceiving me a stranger, did me the civility with her Countrimen, as to procure me the satisfactory view of the King and his Court, which could do no less than oblige me to invite her home, and to desire her while she staid at *Colen* to make use of my house, and what entertainment she found.

She was pleased to accept of this offer, and hereupon my curiosity having attained some part of its wish, we began to be familiar, and I for my part to enquire into her condition, the reason of her travail, and the news of the world, of all which she gave me so delightful an account, insinuating the necessity of her condition, with the perfection of her Endowments; that I told her if she could think it answerable to her content, to stay with me, and be my Governess, she should plentifully partake of my fortunes.

We agreed: but not to weary the Reader with those Instructions and fundamentals of Education she laid, as she was a rare and absolute Mistress of all those Arts, it will be sufficient to declare, that seeing so much vertue in her, my greediness of communicating with it more freely and clearly, put me upon giving her the trouble of teaching me the English tongue, the lockt repository of so many Excellencies.

This by a fond and most pleasing diligence, I pretty well attained in a years time, having my Governess always in my company, whither abroad, as I used to ride some miles by Coach, or else pass in a Pleasure-boat in the Summer, to acquaint my self first with my own Country; the tenderness of my years, offering no man the occasion or thoughts of Love or Marriage, by which means I passed free and unobserved, and then returned again to my Country retirement neer the City.

I now addicted my self to the reading of History, and then to take off the gravity and seriousness of that study, to more facile pastimes of literature; Romances, and other Heroical Adblandiments,[28] which being written for the most and best part in *French*, I made that my next business, though of lesser difficulty, to gain a knowledge in that Tongue, which being counterminous to ours, and spoke promiscuously in the adjacent provinces of the *Walloon* Country,[29] rendred it self at my devotion.

The felicity of these two, put me upon a desire of attaquing the rest of the European Languages, wherein without arrogance, and as many can testifie, I have more than a Smattering, and here was lately an *Italian* (as I have since been told upon discourse and some wonder of my readiness in them) who was one of my Masters; and who might have justified the truth of this and the rest of my story; his name was *Giacomo Della Riva*, well known to many Gentlemen in this Town.

In those and the like Studies, and other befitting Exercises of my sex, I past away the age of nineteen years, when I thought it high time to put all this Speculation and Theory into practice, and being furnished with such a fraught,[30] and store of all Forraign necessaries, to la[u]nch into the World, and see what returnes I could make of this stock, but in the interim of such meditations, an unhappy accident, (at my being at the *Spaw*[31] the last Summer, to drink those medicinal waters) discovered me, and invited two strange Gentlemen, which that place always is furnished with, to enquire further what I was: who having obtained my Country, and some inckling of my quality, made claym to be my servants. I could not in that place, the Mart of good manners, and where there is no nicety of converse, but all persons use their frankest liberty of visit and discourse, refuse their Addresses, but seeing both of them so importunate, and both so disparately and unsociably qualified for my choyce or approbation, I privately withdrew home, but could not so be rid of my odd payre of Gallants, who quickly haunted me and my House.

I was thus of a suden encompassed with two evils, of so indifferent a choyce, that I could not tell which was worse: one was an old Gentleman that had fair demeasnes about *Leige* or

Luyck[32] not many miles distant from *Colen*, a man of serious gravity and venerable aspect for his gray hayrs, but disfigured with some scars his youthful luxury had given him, which were repayred and supplemented by Art, but so that he plainly spoke his infirmity through the ruined Arches[33] of his voyce. He accosted me the rude military way, for he had been a *Soldado*, and had caught as he said, that rotten hoarse cold, and snuffling in the Trenches of *Breda*, in the Brigade of Count *Henry* o[f] *Nassaw* in *Spinolas* Army,[34] and had afterwards served Mounsieur *Tilly* against the King of *Sweden*, whom he had seen fall at *Lutzen*,[35] and therefore by no means must be said no, or denyed his suit, since he had never known what a repulse meant in his life.

The other was a young and pale Student in the Mathematicks, Chymistry, and Magick, like a fellow here that pretends to be Secretary to God and Nature, and had exhausted a plentiful estate, and was like to be a second Dr. *Faustus*, and like my Lord, threatned either a contract with me, or with the Devil:[36] for having lost his Projection of the Philosophers Stone,[37] and decanted all his money and estate, his magical Glass shewed him me, who should by my fortune make him up again. In short, the one said he would storm and force me, and the other would make me yeild or else he would set *Archimedes* his unexperimented Engine[38] at work, to remove me with him into some unknown World, to which he added the efficacy of his Spels and Conjurations.

I had by my Servants and some distant friends account of such a design as carrying me away, and forcing my consent by the Gouty Cavalier, who had some Castellanes and Governours in *Alsatia*[39] his friends, and there was no less danger from my Magical Sweet-heart, but the open violence of the one, and the secret mines of the other were in prudence to be prevented by my absence, which I now concluded on by my self.

I shall not be obliged to give you any further account of my parentage or cond[it]ion, for by such means my disaster here, may reach the ears of some Friends and Acquaintance, from whose knowledge my purpose is yet to estrange my self, (and to

general enquiries *Collen* is too spacious and populous to afford
any discovery)[.] It will suffice, that I was liberally and honourably educated, and such principles laid, that I wonder at the
super-structure[40] of my fortune. I knew not what belonged to
vulgar and Plebeian customes or conditions, and they that idlely
tax my discourses and behaviour with mimick pendantry, know
not the generous emanations of a right born soul. And so, that
which probably makes me obnoxious to the censures of the
multitude, as it hath to the hatred of my new Relations, is the
low spiritedness, and pityful ignorance of such Mechanick[41] and
base people.

I would not be thought to boast of any accomplishments,
which some persons (who favour my distrest estate, and they
are of honour also) do please to acknowledge in me, all the use
I can make of them, shall serve onely for an Argument against
that vile and impertinent falshood, that I am of a most sordid
and base extraction in this Kingdom, no better than the Daughter of a Fidler at *Canterbury*.[42]

The Blasphemous lye was first broached in an Anonymous
Libel, Entituled the *Lawyers Clark trappanned by the crafty Whore of
Canterbury*,[43] but at whose instigation I could never tell, nor
did I make enquiry, but at last spontaneously the Roguery
discovered it self at my being in custody neer *Newgate*,[44] where
I understood the Devil and necessity with the Writer, and
undertaker, were as instrumental as the Devil and Covetousness, in the Occasioner of that report; but that fellow is of so
leud and miserable an infamy, for such defamatory Pamphlets,
that his name will poyson the eyes of the Reader, and fester
even my charity in forgiving him, to proceed.

The time of my deliberated departure being come, and other
intervening accidents having confirmed me to the pursuance of
that journey, [(]some p[i]ece-meal rumours whereof have been
scattered up and down, not far distant from the truth, namely
Constraint and awe of an unliked and unsutable match, which
the freedom of my soul most highly abhominated and resented)
I privately by night withdrew from my Governess, and by the
way of *Utrecht*, where I stayed a while incognito, thence passed

to *Amsterdam*, and so to *Rotterdam*, I came to the *Brill*,[45] and there took Shipping for *England*, the *Elyzium*[46] of my wishes and expectations being in hope to find it a Land of Angels,[47] but I perceive it now to be, as to me, a place of Torments.

I am not single,[48] or the first woman, that hath put her self upon such hazards, or pilgrimages, the stories of all times abound with such Examples, enough to make up a volume. I might as well have given lustre to a Romance as any[49] of those supposed *Heroina's*: and since it is the method of those peices, and the Art of that way of writing to perplex and intricate the commencement and progress of such adventures, with unexpected and various difficulties and troubles, and at last bring them to the long desired fruition of their dear bought content, I am not altogether out of heart, but that Providence may have some tender and more courteous consideration of me; for I protest I know not what crime, offence or demerit of mine hath rendred her so averse and intractable as she hath proved to my designs.

Nor do the Modern and very late Times want Examples of the like adventures. I could mention a Princess,[50] and great Personage out of the North, who not long since came into my Country, and hath passed two or three times between *Italy and France*, and keeps her design yet undiscovered, and is the onely Lady Errant in the World. I could mention another of a far worse consequence in this Country, a She-General, who followed the Camp to the other World in *America*,[51] &c. and was the occasion of the loss of the designe. Mine compared with those are meer puny stories, and inconsiderable, I neither concerned my travail in negotiating peace, or carrying war, but was meerly my own free *Agent*.

Nor can I be blamed for this course, for besides the necessity and enforcements of forsaking my Country, without running into a more unsupportable condition of Marriage than this I am now in, (for my patience and suffering, and Continence I have, I trust in my own power, and shall endeavour to keep them undisturbed and uncorrupted, what ever temptations or occasions, by reason of this unjust separation, now are, or shall be put upon me hereafter; but my life is not in my disposal or preservation, which I had certainly endangered at home, if I had been bedded to him whom my heart abhorred:) and besides other reasons, which I cannot in prudence yet render to the World, the very civility and purity of my design, without any lustful or vicious appurtenant, would fairly excuse me.

What harme have I done in pretending to great Titles? Ambition and Affection of Greatness to good and just purposes was always esteemed and accounted laudable and praiseworthy, and the sign and character of a vertuous mind, nor do I think it an unjust purpose in me to contrive my own advancement by such illustrious pretences as they say I made use of, to grant the Question, that I am not so honourably descended as I insinuated to the Catchdolt[52] my Father in Law, (which yet by their favour they shall first better and more evidently disprove than as yet they have done, before I relinquish my just claym to my Honour) I think I do rather deserve commendation than reproach; if the best *things are to be imitated*; I had a good precept and warrant for my assumption of such a personage as they were willing to beleive me to be; If indeed by any misbecoming act unhandsome and unbefitting such a person, I had prophaned that quality, and bewrayed and discovered any inconsistent meanness therewith (as it was very difficult to personate greatness for so long a time without slips or mistakes) I had deserved to be severely punished and abhominated by all Gentlemen; whereas after all these loads of imputations which my enemies have heaped upon me, I do [(]with my acknowledgements to them for it) enjoy, and am happy in many of their loves and good estimation.

And I will yet continue the same respects, and make the World to know that there is no possibility of such perfections, without a more intent care and elegancy of learning, to which I have by great labour and industry attained.

I need not therefore engage further in this preliminary part of my defence, onely as an irrefragable confutation of the poorness of my birth, and in this Kingdom, I would have my Adversaries know, as some of them do, though they don't well understand, that the severall languages I have ready and at my command, as the *Greek*, *Latine*, *French*, *Italian*, *Spanish*, *English*, and something of the Oriental Tongues, all which I pronounce with a Dutch Dialect and Idiome, are not common and ordinary endowments of an English Spinster, no not of the best rank of the City. And since I must praise my self, in short, I came not here to learn any thing for use or ornament of a woman, but onely the ways to a better fortune.

I come now to the matter of fact, the first place I touched at was *Gravesend*, where I arrived towards the end of *March*, and without any stay took a Tide-boat[53] came to *London* in company with a Parson or Minister, who officiously, but I suppose out of design, gave me the trouble of his service and attendance to the *Exchange-Tavern* right against the *Stocke*, betwixt the *Poultry* and *Cornhil*,[54] the house of one Mr. *King*, not having any knowledge, of the Master or his acquaintance, and free, God knows from any design, for I would have entred any other house if I had found the doors open, or could have raised the folks nearer to my landing, for I was distempered with the nights passage; but it was so early in the morning, five a clock, that there was no body stirring elsewhere, onely here by mishap Mr. *King* himself was up and standing at the Bar, telling of brass farthings, whom the Parson desired to fill a pint of wine, which he readily performed, and brought to a room behinde the Bar. While the wine was a drinking, (which was Rhenish wine, the complement being put upon me by the Parson as the fruit of my own happy Country) Sir *John* very rudely began to accost me, and to offer some incivilities to me, which I found no other way to avoid, than by pretending want of rest to the Master of the house, and acquainting him with my charge of Jewels, and that I was as I do justifie my self to be a person of Quality. Hereupon a room was provided for me to repose myself in, and the Clergyman took his leave with a troublesome promise of waiting upon me another day to give me a visit, which I was forced to admit & to tell him, I would leave word where-ever I went; but he considering as I suppose of the unfeasibleness of his desires, and the publiqueness of the place, neglected his promise and troubled me no more.

He being gone, *Mr. King* began to question me, what Country woman I was, and of what Religion, I frankly told him; and acquainted him with all what charge I had about me, which to secure from the danger of the Town, that was full of cozenage and villany, he advised me to stay with him till I could better provide for my self.

I rested my self here till eleven a clock at noon: when I arose, and was very civilly treated by *Mr. King*, who well knowing I was a stranger and well furnished with money, omitted no manner of respect to me, nor did I spend parcimoniously, and at an ordinary rate, but answerable to the quality and account, at their fetching and itching questions, I gave of my self.

This invited him earnestly, with all submiss[ive] address to request my staying with them till I had dispatched, and had provided all things for my publique appearance, for the better furnishing and equiping whereof, I acquainted Him I would send by Post to my Steward, for the return of some moneys to defray the expences thereof, which Letters he viewed, and conceived such imaginations in his Head thereupon, that it never left working till it had wrought the effect of his finely begun and hopefully continued Enterprise.

These Letters he himself delivered at my desire, to have them carefully put into the Male, to the Post-House;[55] and thereafter observed me with most manifest respects. In the *Interim* of the return of these moneys, I was slightly, and as it were by the by, upon discourse of my Country (wherein they took occasion to be liberally copious) engaged into some discovery of my self, my estate and quality, and the nature of both, the causes of my coming hither, &c. but I did it so unconcernedly, and negligently, as a matter of no moment or disturbance to me, though I had hinted at the discontent of my match, that this did assure them that all was real, and therefore it was time to secure my estate to them by a speedy and secret marriage.

Let the World now judge, whither being prompted by such plain and publique signes of a design upon me, to counterplot them, I have done any more than what the Rule, and a received principle of Justice directs: *to deceive the deceiver, is no deceit.*

I knew not nevertheless, which way their Artifices tended, till Master *King*, brought into my acquaintance old Mr. *Carleton* his Father in Law, and soon after Mr. *John Carleton* his Son: it seems it had been consulted, to have preferred *George* the Elder Brother: He troubled with a simple modesty, and a mind no way competent to so much greatness, was laid aside, and the younger flusht and encouraged to set upon me. By this time they had obtained my Name from me, *viz. Maria de Wolway*, which passage also hath suffered by another leuder Imposture, and allusory sound of *De Vulva*: in the language of which I am better versed, than to pick out no civiller and eleganter impress.

To the Addresses of Mr. *John Carleton*, I carried my self with so much indifference, not superciliously refusing his visits, or readily admitting his suit, not disheartening him with a severe retiredness, or challenges of his imparity, nor encouraging him with a freedom or openness of Heart, or arrogance of my own condition, that he and his friends were upon the spur to consummate the match, which yet I delayed and dissembled with convenient pretences, but herein I will be more particular in the ensuing Pages.

In the mean while, to prevent all notice of me, and the disturbance of their proceedings, that might be occasioned thereby, they kept me close in the nature of a Prisoner, which though I perceived, yet I made no semblance thereof at all, but colluded with them in their own arts, and pretended some aversness to all company, but onely my enamourate, Mr. *Carleton*: nor was any body else suffered to come near me, or to speak with me; Insomuch, as I have bin informed, that they promised 209*l.* to one *Sackvil*, whom for his advice, they had too forwardly, as they thought imparted the business, the sum of 200*l.* to be silent, lest that it should be heard at Court, and so the Estate and Honour which they had already swallowed, would be lost from their Son, and seized by some Courtier, who should next come to hear of this great Lady.

After many visits passed betwixt Mr. *Carleton* and my self, Old Mr. *Carleton* and Mr. *King* came to me, and very earnestly pressed the dispatch of the Marriage, and that I would be pleased to give my Assent, setting forth with all the qualities and great sufficiencies of that Noble person, as they pleased to stile him. I knew what made them so urgent, for they had now seen the answers I had received by the Post, by which I was certified of the receipt of mine, and that accordingly some thousands of Crowns should be remitted instantly to *London*, and Coach and Horses sent by the next Shipping, with other things I had sent for, and to reinforce this their *commendamus*[56] the more effectually, they acquainted me, that if I did not presently grant the suit, and their request, Mr. *Carleton* was so far in love with me, that he would make away with himself, or presently travail beyond Sea, and see *England* no more.

I cannot deny, but that I could hardly forbear smiling, to see how serious these *Elders* and *Brokers* were in this *Love-killing* story, but keeping to my business, after some demurs and demands, I seemed not to consent, and then they began passionately, urging me with other stories, some of which long repetition I will now insert:

Wednesday the first of *April*, Mrs. *King* made a great Feast, where the divers persons of quality, as she said, amongst the rest, her Brother Mr. *John Carleton*. At which entertainment Mrs. *King* did advise me to call her Cozen, the which I did. *Thursday* the second of *April*, Mr. *John Carleton* came in his Coach, with two Footmen attending on him, calling him my *Lord*, and Mrs. *King* did also call him my *Lord*. With that I asked Mrs. *King*, if it was not the same person that dined with us yesterday; she said, True, it was so, but he was in a Disguise then, and withal, that in a humour he would often do so: *But*, saith she, *I do assure you he is a Lord*. Upon that I replied, *Then his father must be an Earl, if living*. She affirmed, that he was a person of great honour. The same time my Lord presented me with a rich box of Sweetmeats: I could do no less than thankfully accept thereof.

My Lord came every day to *Mr. Kings*, and by this importunity would carry me abroad in a Coach to *Holloway* and *Islington*.[57] *Mrs King* would often ask me, what my Lord did say to me; I told her, *nothing that I observed, but his Lordship abounded in civility, mixt with complements. How*; said she, *Madam, He loves you. Loves me, for what Mistris King?* I replied. She said, *For your great parts and Endowments.* I asked her, *How my Lord could tell that I had either.* I[58] said, *My Lord must have very good eyes if he could see within me, or else I must be very transparent.*

After which, I did order the matter so, that his access to me was not so easie: Mistris *King* importuneth me to admit my Lord to visit me; I told her plainly, *That I did not understand his Lordships meaning.* He provided me a great Banquet, at which his Lordships mother was very fine drest, who questioned what I was. I told my Lord, *That I had received civilities from him, and he had the like from me, and that I had no necessity to give any account to any person what I was, for any thing that I intended; and that if any design or affair of his required any such thing out of convenience, or otherwise he might forbear it.* His Lordship excused his mothers inquisition, by saying, *She was his Mother, and that Parents did think themselves concerned, in looking after the good of their children.* But (said he) *Madam, Wave all this, however I will marry you to morrow.* What (said I) *my Lord, without my consent:* my Lord, *I desire your Lordship not to come near me any more, I will not lye under such questioning and scrutiny: Your Lordship will be safe in following my advice, in not coming at me any more.* Upon this his Lordship wept bitterly: I withdrew my self from his presence: He writ a Letter of high Complements to me (the which Letter was lost in that violent surprize of me and my things, by the force of *Mr George Carleton,* my Husbands Father.) At the same time I had a Gown making upon my own account, by *Mrs. Kings* Taylor in the *Strand,* I took a Coach and went thither; all this while the young Lord not knowing where I was, remained impatient until my return, where I found him standing at the Bar (in a very pensive and melancholy manner, as if he had been arraigned for not paying his reckoning)[59] at the *Exchange-Tavern,* and suddenly claspt about my middle, and violently carried me to my Chamber. I asked his meaning: He answered, *That I had forbid him my presence; that it had almost made him mad; that he desired nothing more of me, than but to let him look upon me.* Upon that he did, with a very strange gesture, fix his eyes upon me: In compassion to him, I askt him what his Lordship meant, and intended; he replied in a kind of discomposed manner, *I would have you to be my Wife*. I answered him, *My Lord, I rather think you have courted me for a Mistress, than for a Wife: I assure you, that I will never be a Mistris to the greatest of Princes, I will rather chuse to be a Wife to the meanest of men*.

Upon which, he uttered divers asseverations in confirmation of the real[i]ty of his intentions, and earnest desire of the Honour in making me his Wife, without any respect to what I had.

After my Lord had insinuated his affections so far, that I began to understand him, and did mix and scatter some such like acceptable words, which put him into some confidence of obtaining me; he began like other Lovers to set forth the amplitude of his Fortunes, and those brave things he would do if I would finish his suit; among many other finenesses and Grandures he would bestow on me, I well remember, he told me that he had given order for a great Glass Coach of the new fashion to be presently made, against our wedding was over, where eleven or twelve might conveniently sit, and that he would sute it with a set of Lacquies and Pages, the neatest and handsomest of the Town for their Liveries and persons. That I might see I had married a person that not onely dearly loved me, but would also highly honour me, with the most splendid accom[m]odations that *England* yeilded.

At the very same time, he had changed as he told me (and part of it I saw) two hundred pound of silver, into two hundred peices of Gold, for the better portableness thereof, that his Princess might see nothing of meanness belonging to him, and that as soon as the Coach was made and all things fitted to it, he would presently go to Court, and carry me with him, and introduce me to the King and Queen: his further intention being, which as yet he concealed to me, to get a *Knight-hood*, and have something of honour to oppose the envy of men, that so great an Estate was conferred on a private person.

And now my Lord spoke nothing but Rodomantadoes[60] of the greatness of his Family, of the delights and stateliness of his Lands and houses, the game of his Parks, the largeness of his stables, and convenience of Fish and Foul, for furnishing his liberal and open Housekeeping, that I should see *England afforded more pleasure than any place in the World*, but they were (without the Host)[61] reckoned and charged beforehand to my account, and to be purchased with my estate, which was his, by a figure of anticipation, when we two should be all one, and therefore he lyed not, but onely equivocated a little.

But he did not in the lest mention any such thing to me, nor made any offer of enquiry what I was, no not the least semblance or shadow of it; he seemed to take no notice of my fortunes, it was my person he onely courted, which having so happily and accidently seen, he could not live, if I cherisht not his affections. Nor did I think it then convenient or civil to question the credit of his words, and the report given me of him. His demeanour I confess was light, but I imputed that to his youth, and the vanity of a Gallant, as necessary a quality, and as much admired as wit in a Woman.

The last day of my virgin state, *Easter* Eve, the Taylor brought me my Gown to my Lodging, I being drest and adorned with my Jewels, he again renewed his suit to me; with all importunity imaginable: His courteous Mother was also now most forward, pressing me to consent, by telling me, that *she should lose her Son, and* [he] *his wits,* he being already impatient with denyals and delays, adding withal, that he was a person hopeful, and might deserve my condiscention: I withstood all their sollicitation, although they continued it until twelve of the Clock that night: The young Lord at his taking his leave of me, told me he would attend me betimes the next morning, and carry me to St. *Pauls* Church,[62] to hear the Organs, saying, that there would be very excellent Anthems performed by rare voices, the morrow being Sunday, the 19. of *April* last: in the morning betimes, the young Lord cometh to my Chamber-door, desiring admittance, which I refused, in regard I was not ready; yet so soon as my head was dressed, I let him have access: he hastned me, and told me his Coach was ready at the door, in which he carried me to his Mothers in the *Grey-fryers, London,*[63] where I was assaulted by the young Lords tears, and others to give my consent to marry him, telling me that they had a Parson and a License ready, which was a meer falshood, and temporary falacy to secure the match.

So on *Easter* morning, with three Coaches, in which with the Bride and Bridegroom were all the kindred that were privy to the business, and pretended a Licence,[64] they carried me to *Clothfair* by *Smithfield*,[65] and in the Church of Great St. *Bartholomews*,[66] Married me by one Mr. *Smith*, who was well paid for his paynes: and now they thought themselves possessed of their hopes, but because they would prevent the noise and fame, of their good fortune from publique discourse, that no sinister accident might intervene, before Mr. *Carleton* had bedded me, offence being likely to be taken at Court, (as they whispered to themselves) that a Private Subject had Married a Forraign Princess, they had before determined to go to *Barnet*[67] and thither immediately after the celebration of the Marriage we were Driven in the Coaches, where we had a handsome treatment, and there we staid Sunday and Munday, both which nights Mr. *Carleton* lay with me, and on Tuesday morning we were Married again, a License being then obtained to make the match more fast and sure, at their instance with me to consent to it.

This being done, and their fears over, they resolved to put me in a garb befitting the Estate and dignity they fancied I had; and they were so far possessed with a beleif of it, that they gave out, I was worth no less than 80000*l. per annum*, and my Husband, as I must now stile him, published so much in a Coffee-house; adding withal, to the extolling of his good hap, that there was a further Estate but that it was my modesty or design to conceal it: And that he could not attribute his great fortune to any thing but the Fates, for he had not any thing to ballance with the least of my Estate and Merits: So do conceited[68] heighths of sudden prosperity and greatness dazzle the eyes and judgement of the most, nor could this young man be much blamed for his vainglorious mistake.

My Cloaths being made at the charge of my Father in Law, and other fineries of the mode & fashion sent me by some of his

Kindred and friends (who prided themselves in this happy affinity, and who had an eye upon some advantages also, and therefore gave me this early bribe, as testimonies of their early respect[)], & as for Jewels I had of mine own of all sorts, for Necklaces, Pendants and Bracelets, of admirable splendor and brightness. I was in a Prince-like attire, and a splendid equipage and retinue, accoutred for publique view among all the great Ladies of the Court and the Town on *May* day ensuing. At which time in my Lady *Bludworths*[69] Coach, which the same friends procured for my greater accommodation, and accompanied with the same Lady with Footmen and Pages, I rode to Hide-Park,[70] in open view of that celebrious[71] Cavalcade and Assembly, much gazed upon by them all, the eximiousness[72] of my fortune drawing their eyes upon me, particularly [that] noble Lady gave me precedence, and the right hand, and a neat Treatment after our divertisement of turning up and down the park.

I was altogether ignorant of what estate my Husband was, and therefore made no nicety to take those places his friends gave me, and if I be taxed for incivility herein, it was his fault that he instructed me no better in my quality, for I conceited still that he was some landed, honorable and wealthy man.

Things yet went fairly on, the same observances and distances continued, and lodgings befitting a person of Quality taken for me in *Durham Yard*,[73] at one mr. *Greens*, where my husband and I enjoyed one another with mutual complacency, till the return of the moneys out of *Germany* failing the day and their rich hopes, old Mr. *Carleton* began to suspect he was deceived in his expectation, and that all was not gold that glistered: but to remove such a prejudice from himself, as if he were the Authour of those scandals that were now prepared against my innocence, a Letter is produced, and sent from some then unknown hand, which reflected much upon my Honour and Reputation; and thereupon on the fifth or sixth of *May* ensuing, *I* was by a Warrant dragged forth of my new Lodgings, with all the disgrace and contumely that could be cast upon the vilest offender in the World, at the instigation of old Mr. *Carleton*, who was the

Prosecutor, and by him and his Agents devested and stript of all
my cloaths, and plundred of all my jewels, and my money, my
very bodyes, and a payr of silk Stockings, being also pulled from
me, and in a strange array carried before a Justice.

But because this story hath not yet been fully discovered,[74] I
will more manifestly here declare it; That Letter above said,
came from one Mr. *John Clay*, the younger Son of Mr. *Clay* a
Drugster[75] at the Bear and Mortar in *Lumber-street*,[76] a Servant[77]
and Admirer of Mrs. *King* my fine Sister in Law, who because
her Husband hath a weak head, (though he sat like a Parliament man once in *Richard Cromwel* time for three days,[78] as
since I have been informed) must have an assistant to carry on
the business. The contents of this Letter were neer to this
purpose,

SIR,

I *Am unknown to you, but hearing that your Son Mr.* John Carleton
*hath married a Woman of a pretended great Fortune and high birth, I
thought fit to give you timely notice of what I know, and have heard
concerning her, that she is an absolute Cheat, hath Married several men
in our County of* Kent, *and then run away from them, with what they
had; If it be the same woman I mean, she speaks several languages
fluently, and hath very high Breasts,* &c.

I was at the Exchange Tavern, as it was designed, when this
Letter was brought, and thereupon their countenances were set
to a most melancholly look, and pale hue, which shewed a
mixture of fear and anger: presently I was brought before the
inquisition of the Family, and examined concerning the said
Letter, which I constantly, innocently, and disdainfully denyed,
so that they seemed something satisfied to the contrary, and so
my Husband and I went home in a Coach, but that very same
night, all the gang, with one Mrs. *Clark* a Neighbour to *King*,
came to my lodging where after most vile language, as Cheating
Whore, and the like, they pulled me up and down, and kept me
stript upon a bed, not suffering my Husband to come neer me,
though I cryed out for him to take my part, and do like a man

to save me from that violence, who at a distance excused it, by putting all this barbarity upon his Father; In fine they left me not a rag, rincing every wet cloath out of the water,[79] and carrying them away[.] The whole, was a most unwomanly and rude Action at the best of it, if I had been such as they pretended me to be, and not to be parralleld, but by a story I have lately heard of the six woman shavers in *Drury Lane*.[80]

See the fickleness and vanity of humane things, to day *embellished*, and adorned with all the female Arts of bravery and gallantry, and courted and attended on by the best rank of my sex, who are jealous observers what honour and respect they give among themselves, to a very punctilio;[81] and now disrobed and disfigured in mishapen Garments, and almost left naked, and haled[82] and pulled by Beadles,[83] and such like rude and boysterous fellows, before a Tribunal, like a leud Criminal.

The Justices Name was Mr. *Godfrey*,[84] by whose Mittimus,[85] upon an accusation managed by Old Mr. *Carleton*, that I had married two Husbands, both of them in being, I was committed to the *Gate-house*.[86] Being interrogated by the Justice, whither or no I had not two Husbands as was alledged, I Answered, if I had, He was one of them, which I beleive incensed Him something the more against me, but I did not know the Authority and dignity of his place, so much am I a stranger to this Kingdom.

There were other things and crimes of a high nature objected against me besides, That I cheated a Vintner of sixty pounds, and was for that committed to Newgate,[87] but that lye quickly vanished, for it was made appear, That I was never a Prisoner there, nor was my name ever recorded in their books; And that I pickt a Kentish Lords pocket, and cheated a French Merchant of Rings, Jewels and other Commodities, That I made an escape, when sold and shipt for the *Barbadoes*, but these were urged onely as surmises; and old *Carleton* bound over to prosecute onely for Bigamy, for my having two husbands.

Thus the world may see how industrious mischeif is to ruine a poor helpless and destitute Woman, who had neither money, friends nor acquaintance left me; yet I cannot deny that my Husband lovingly came to me at the Gatehouse the same day I

was committed, and did very passionately complain of his
Fathers usage of me, meerly upon the disappointment, as he
said, of their expectations, and that he could be contented to
love me as well as ever, to live with me and own me as a wife,
and used several other expressions of tenderness to me.

Nor have I less affection and kind sentiments for him, whom
I own and will own till death dissolve the union, and did
acquaint him with so much there, and protested my innocence
to him, nor do I doubt could he have prevailed with his Father,
but that these things had never happened.[88] If now after my
vindication he prove faithless and renege me, his fault will be
doubly greater, in that he neither assisted my innocence when
endangered, or cherished it when vindicated by the Law.

In this prison of the Gatehouse I continued six weeks, in a far
better condition than I promised myself, but the greater civilities I ow to the Keeper: as I am infinitely beholding to several
persons of quality, who came at first I suppose out of curiosity
to see me, and did thereafter nobly compassionate my calami-
tous, and injurious restraint.[89]

All that troubled me was an abusive pamphlet which went
under my Husbands name,[90] wherein, most pitifully he pleaded
his frailty and mi[s]fortune, and intituled it to no lesser prece-
dent than *Adam*, which I suppose was had out of the new *Ballad*,
of *your Humble Servant*,[91] a hint whereof, please the Reader to
take in this Abridgement.

Reader,

*I shall not give my self the trouble, to recollect and declare the
several motives and inducements that deceitful, but wise enough, Woman
used to deceive me with, &c. Her Wit did more and more ingage and
charm me: Her Qualities deprived me of my own; Her Courteous
Behaviour, her Majestick Humility to all persons, her Emphatical
speeches, her kind and loving expressions; and amongst other things, her
high detestation of all manner of Vice, as Lying, &c. Her great Pretence
to zeal in her Religion; her modest Confidence and Grace in all
Companies, Fearing the knowledge of none; her demeanour was such, that
she left no room for Suspition, not onely in my opinion, but also in others*

both Grave and Wise. And all this is real and not feigned, and more convincingly and apparently true, by this foil of his own setting[;] As for his undertaking to tell the Story of the management of the business betwixt us; he is so far from doing me justice herein, that he wrongeth me and his own soul by lying.

For Confutation of which, I refer the Reader to the ensuing Tryal; Onely there is one passage that I am unwilling to let slip, that is, he saith there, that my Father was in Town upon my Commitment, and did acknowledge me to be his Daughter, and that I had played many such tricks. It's strange this Father of mine could not be produced at the Tryal, if that had been true.

And yet a little before this, upon his visiting me in the *Gate-house*, where I was destitute of money and subsistence, at my first coming in he seemed very tender of me, and charged the Keeper I should want nothing, for as far as 40*sh*. went, he would see him payd, which I beleive he must ere long, and after that sent me a Letter, which is the onely paper I have by me of his, the other amorous and loving scriblings being lost and taken from me, the same time that they plundered me of my Jewels, I do not know what I may do for them, but I hope I shall never cry for those Epistles. This done in these words, so that my Love and my Dear, could be hot and cold almost in an instant.

My Dearest Heart,

Although the manner of your Usage may very well call the sincerity of my Affection and Expressions to you in question; Yet when I consider, That thou art not ignorant of the Compulsion of my Father, and the Animosity of my whole relations, both against You and my self for Your sake, I am very confident your goodness will pardon and pass by those things which at present I am no way able to help; And be you confident, That notwithstanding my Friends aversion, there shall be nothing within the reach of my power shall be wanting, that may conduce both to your liberty, maintenance, and Vindication. I shall very speedily be in a condition to furnish you with Money, to supply you according to your desire. I hope Mr. Bayly will be very civil to you; and let him be assured,

*he shall in a most exact measure be satisfied, and have a Requital for his
Obligation. My dearest, always praying for our happy meeting,*

I rest, Your most affectionate Husband.

May the 11th.
    1663.

John Carleton.

Other of my Husband's Friends came to Visit me in the *Gate-
house*, (of the many hundreds of other I shall say nothing) one of
them said, Madam, I am one of your Husbands Friends and
Acquaintance, I had a desire to see you, because *I* have heard of
your breeding. Alas, said I, *I* have left that in the City amongst
my Kindred, because they want it.

Another in his discourse delivered as an Aphorism, *That
marriage and hanging went by Destiny. I told him, I had received from
the Destinies Marriage, and he in probability might Hanging.* To waive
many others of the like nature.

My innocence furnished me with several of those answers,
and repartees to the mixt sort of visitants, who either for
novelty or designe came to trouble me. I was advised indeed to
seclude my self from such company, but because there might be
no disadvantage pretended by reason I kept close, and evidence
might be puzled, not having seen me in so long a time, as
afterwards at my Tryal might have been suggested, I gave all
persons the freedom of my Chamber. But for the Nobler sort, I
may in some measure thank my stars, that out of this misfortune
extracted so much bliss, as the honour of their acquaintance,
which otherwise at large I had been in no capacity to attain.

The time of the Sessions of the Peace for *London* and *Middlesex*
being arrived, I was conveyed from the Gate-house to Newgate;
where by the civility of the Master of the prison I had lodgings
assigned me in his own house, which adjoyns to the Sessions-
house-yard; and there I was publickly seen by all comers: that

my enemies might want no advantage of informing their witnesses of my Person, Age and condition, and so square their Evidence: but my innocence and my good Angels preserved me from the worst of their malice.

From thence, on Wednesday, *June* the third, in the evening, the first day of the Courts sitting in the *Old-Bayly*,[92] I was brought down to the Bar: and there an Indictment upon my Arraignment[93] was read against me; to which I pleaded Not guilty: and, as instructed by my friends, and a good conscience, (being altogether ignorant of the Laws and Customs of this Kingdome) put my self for my Triall upon God and the Country, without making any exception, or ever so much as examining what my Jury were.

And because they approved themselves men of honesty, judgment and integrity, and did me so much justice, I can do no less than take occasion here to return them my humble thanks, that they would regard the oppressed condition of a helpless prisoner; and not give credit to the wicked asseverations of a wretch, who onely swore to the purpose against me: and to let the world know my particular gratitude, I will transcribe into this my *Case*, as one of the happiest and fairest remarks therein, the names of those upright Jurors, *viz.*

William Rutland,
Arthur Vigers,
Arthur Capel,
Tho. Smith,
Fran. Chaplin,
Robert Harvey,
Simon Driver,
Robert Kerkham,
Hugh Masson,
Tho. Westley,
Richard Clutterbuck, and
Randolph Tooke.

The Indictment was *in hæc verba.*[94]
That she the said Mary Moders, late of London *Spinster, otherwise*

Mary Stedman, *the wife of* Tho. Stedman *late of the City of* Canterbury *in the County of* Kent *Shooemaker,* 12 May, *in the Reign of his now Majesty the sixth,*[95] *at the Parish of St.* Mildreds *in the City of* Cant[erbury] *in the County aforesaid, did take to husband the aforesaid* Tho. Stedman, *and him the said* Thomas Stedman *then and there had to husband. And that she the said* Mary Moders, *alias* Stedman, 21 April, *in the* 15 *year of his said Majesties Reign, at* London, *in the Parish of* Great S[t.] Bartholomews, *in the Ward of* Farringdon *without, feloniously did take to husband one* John Carleton, *and to him was married, the said* Tho. Stedman *her former husband then being alive, and in full life: against the form of the Statute in that case provided, and against the Peace of our said Soveraign Lord the King, his Crown and Dignity,* &c.

After which being set to the Bar, in order to my Trial, I prayed time till the morrow, my witnesses not being ready; which was granted: and all persons concerned were ordered to attend at nine of the Clock in the Fore-noon.

Being returned to my lodging, where some Gentlemen gave me a visit to counsell and advise me; my Husband Mr. *Carleton* came thither to take his leave of me, as I understood afterwards by his complement: but my Keeper knowing of him, thought him not fit company for me, who was one of the causers of my injurious usage: but notice at last being given me of it, I gave order for his admittance, and treated him with that respect which became my Relation to him; though he, to add trouble to me, fell into more impertinent discourses concerning the shortness of my dayes, and speedy preparation of Repentance for another world; and that he would pray for me, and the like: to the which I replied, Pray my lord let none of those things trouble you; I thank God I am as well as ever in my life, and do of all things least fear hanging: and as for your prayers, are you righteous or no? if not, they will so little availe me, that they will not profit your self. Hereupon a Gentleman to break off this discourse drank to him in a glass of Canary;[96] which my Lord unhandsomely declining to accept, I could not forbear to tell him, I was sorry to see his Lordship's slender breeding could not suffer him to be civill.

Thus the world may see how these mine Adversaries had already swallowed my life and my credit, and devoted them to the Gibbet without redemption: the onely security of all their past injustices towards me. – *Per scelera sceleribus estiter*:[97] they must end as they have begun. Thus the Devill and his imps were here frustrated.

For, on Thursday *June* the fourth, I proceeded to Trial, according to appointment; but my fathers bandogs[98] being not ready, my husband came into the Court very spruce and trim in, one of his wedding-suits, and prayed the Court, that in respect his father and his witnesses were not yet come together, or rather had not concinnated[99] their lies to be found in one tale, that the Trial might be deferred for halfe an hour. I could not but smile to see my deare husband labour so to make sure of my death, and with so little regard to pass by his dear Princess without so much as vouchsafing a look to her; as if he were angry at his eyes for having beheld so much already. But to abrupt these thoughts, and to continue the discourse: the Court growing impatient of these uncivil delayes, and telling my father-in-law that they were not bound to wait on him or his witnesses; they were now produced before them, and sworn; and with old *Carleton* himself were six in number: namely, *James Knot*, one that will almost cleave a hair; *William Clark*, and *George Carleton* [his] brother-in-law; Mr. *Smith* the Parson, and one *Sarah Williams*; which for fuller information of the world, I will give, with a review of the whole Triall, according to the exactest copy of it, which was taken in short-hand at my desire.

James Knot. My Lord, and Gentlemen of the Jury, I gave this woman in Marriage to one *Thomas Stedman*, which is now alive in *Dover*, and I saw him last week.

Court. Where was she married?

Knot. In *Canterbury*.

Court. Where there?

Knot. In St. *Mildreds*, by one Parson *Man*, who is now dead.

Court. How long since were they married?

Knot. About nine years ago.

Court. Did they live together afterwards?

Knot. Yes, about four years, and had two children.

Court. You gave her in marriage but did the Minister give her to her husband then?

Knot. Yes, and they lived together.

Jury. Friend, did you give this very Woman?

Knot. Yes.

Court. What company was there?

Knot. There was the married Couple, her sister, my self, the Parson and the Sexton.

Court. Where is that Sexton?

Knot. I know not, my Lord.

Court. You are sure they were married in the Church, and this is the woman?

Knot. Yes, I am sure of it.

Court. How long ago?

Knot. About nine years ago.

Court. Did you know this woman before the Marriage? and how long?

Knot. Yes, I knew her a long time; I was an Apprentice seven years near her Mothers house in *Canterbury*.

Court. Then she's no forreign Princess? Of what Parentage was she?

Knot. I did not know her own father (and in that he might be believed) but her father-in-law was a Musician there.

Court. You see her married: what words were used at her marriage, and in what manner?

Knot. They were married according to the order of the Land, a little before the Act came forth touching Marriages by Justices of the Peace.[100]

Court. Was it by the Form of Common-Prayer, any thing read of that Form?

Knot. I did not take notice of that: I was but a young man, and was desired to go along with them.

William Clark being sworn, said, My Lord, I was last week in *Dover*, in company with this *James Knot*, and *Thomas Stedman*, and he the said *Stedman* did own that he did marry one *Mary Moders*, a daughter of one in *Canterbury*, and that *Knot* gave her, and that he had two children by her, and declared his willingness to come up to give evidence against her, but wanted money for his journey: And I have understood that a person here in Court was of a Jury at *Canterbury*, at a Triall between *Day* and *Mary Stedman* at the Bar for having two husbands.

Court. Was she cleared?

Clark. I cannot tell.

Young *Carletons* father sworn.

My Lord, I was at *Dover* the last week on Wednesday; I saw the husband of this woman, and the man acknowledged himself to be so; and did say that *James Knot* was the man that gave her in marriage to him.

Court. Where is this man her husband? Hearsays must condemn no man: what do you know of your own knowledge?

Carleton the Elder. I know the man is alive.

Court. Do you know he was married to her?

Carleton. Not I, my Lord.

Sarah Williams. My Lord, This Woman was bound for *Barbadoes*, to go along with my husband, and she desired to lodge at our house for some time, and did so; and when the ship was ready to go, she went into *Kent* to receive her means, and said she would meet the ship in the *Downs*;[101] and missing the ship, took boat and went to the ship. After severall dayes remaining there, there came her husband with an Order and fetched her ashore, and carried her to *Dover*-Castle.

Court. What was his name that had an Order to bring her on shore again?

Sarah Williams. His name was *Thomas Stedman.*

Court. Have you any more to prove the first marriage?

Carlton the Elder. No, none but *Knot*; there was none but three, the Minister dead, the Sexton not to be found, and this *Knot* who hath given Evidence.

Court. What became of the two children, *Knot?*

Knot. They both died.

Carlton the Elder. *Stedman* said in my hearing, that he had lived four years with her, had two children by her, and both dead; five years ago last *Easter* since she left him.

Court. Mr. *Carlton*, What have you heard this Woman say?

Carlton. My Lord, she will confess nothing, that pleases him.

Court. Mr *Carlton*, did you look in the Church-Register for the first marriage?

Carleton. I did look in the Book, and he that is now Clerk, was then Sexton (just now not to be found;) he told me, that Marriages being then very numerous, preceding the Act before mentioned, the then Clerk had neglected the Registry of this Marriage. If she intended this Trade, she likewise knew how to make the Clerk mistake Registring the Marriage.

Young *Carlton*'s brother sworn, who said,

My Lord and Gentlemen of the Jury, I was present at the Marriage of my Brother with this Gentlewoman, which was on or about 21 *April*, 1663. They were married at Great St. *Bartholomews*, by one Mr. *Smith* a Minister here in Court, by Licence.

Mr. *Smith* the Parson sworn.

My Lord, all that I can say, is this, that Mr. *Carlton* the younger told me of such a business, and desired me to marry them; they came to Church, and I did marry them by the Book of Common Prayer.

Court. Mr. *Smith*, are you sure that is the Woman?

Parson. Yes, my Lord, it is; I believe she will not deny it.

Prisoner. Yes, my Lord, I confess I am the Woman.

Court. Have you any more witnesses?

Carlton. We can get no more but *Knot* to prove the first Marriage; the last is clear.

Judge *Howel.* Where is *Knot?* Remember your self well what you said before. You say, you know that Woman at the Bar; that you had known her a great while; that she was born near you in *Canterbury*; that you were present at her Marriage; that Parson *Man* married them; that none were present but your self, the married couple, Parson, Sexton, and her sister.

Knot. Some others came into the Church, but none that I knew; I am sure none went with her, but those I named.

Court. Who gave her in marriage?

Knot. I did.

Court. How came you to do it?

Knot. I was *Stedmans* shop-mate, and he desired me to go along with him.

Court. Were her Parents then living, or no?

Knot. Her Mother was.

Jury. How old are you?

Knot. Two or three and thirty years.

Jury. How long ago was this marriage?

Knot. About nine years since.

Court. Then he was twenty three, and might do it. What is your Trade of life?

Knot. I am a Cordweyner,[102] otherwise, a Shoomaker; *Stedman* was so too: we wrought both together.

Jury. We desire to know whether she had a Father and Mother then living.

Knot. She had a Father-in-law.

Court. Did you know her Mother?

Knot. Yes.

Court. How long before that Marriage did her own Father die?

Knot. I did not know him. [I] said so before indeed.

Court. What age was she when married?

Knot. I suppose nineteen or twenty.

Prisoner. May it please your Honours, and Gentlemen of the Jury, you have heard the several witnesses, and I think this whole Country cannot but plainly see the malice of my Husbands Father against me; how he causelessly hunts after my life: when his Son, my Husband, came and addressed himself to me, pretending himself a person of honour, and upon first sight pressed me to marriage; I told him, Sir, said I, I am a stranger, have no acqaintance here, and desire you to desist your suit: I could not speak my minde, but he (having borrowed some thred-bare Complements) replied, *Madam*, your seeming virtues, your amiable person, and noble deportment, renders you so excellent, that were I in the least interested in you, I cannot doubt of happiness: and so with many words to the like purpose, courted me. I told him, and indeed could not but much wonder, that at so small a glance he could be so presumptuous with a stranger, to hint this to me; but all I could say, would not beat him off: And presently afterwards he having intercepted my Letter, by which he understood how my affairs stood, and how considerable my means were, he still urged me to marry him; and immediately by the contrivance of his friends, gaping at my fortune, I was hurried to Church to be married; which the Parson at first did without Licence, to secure me to my Husband, and sometime after had a Licence.[103]

And my Husbands Father afterwards considering I had a considerable fortune, pressed me, that in respect I had no relations here, and because, sayes he, we are mortall, you would do well to make over your Estate to my Son your Husband; it will be much for your honour, satisfaction of the world, and for which you will be chronicled for a rare woman: and perceiving he had not baited his hook sufficient (with some fair pretences) to catch me then, he and his Son, who were both willing to make up some of their former losses in circumventing me of what I had, they robb'd me of my Jewels, and Clothes of great value, and afterwards pretended they were counterfeit Jewells; and declared, that I had formerly been married to one at *Canterbury*, which place I know not; and this grounded on a Letter (of their own framing) sent from *Dover*, with a description of me; that I was a young fat woman, full brested; that I spoke severall languages; and therefore they imagined me the person; and so violently carried me from my lodging before a Justice of Peace, only to affright me, that I might make my Estate over to them. The Justice having heard their severall allegations, could not commit me, unless they would be bound to prosecute me; which my husband being unwilling to, the Justice demanded of his Father whether he would prosecute me, saying, they must not make a fool of him; and so after some whisperings, the Father and his Son were both bound to prosecute; and there-upon I was committed to prison: And since that, these people have been up and down the Country, and finding none there that could justifie any thing of this matter, they get here an unknown fellow, unless in a prison, and from thence borrowed, you cannot but all judge, to swear against me. My Lord, were there any such Marriage as this fellow pretends, methinks there might be a Certificate from the Minister, or place; certainly if married, it must be registred: but there is no Registry of it, and so can be no Certificate, no Minister nor Clerk to be found: and if I should own a marriage, then you see that great witness cannot tell you, whether I was lawfully married, or how? but it is enough for him (if such a paultry fellow may be believed) to say, I was married. I was never yet married to any but *John Carlton*, the late pretended Lord: But these persons have sought alwayes to take away my life, bring persons to swear against me, one hired with five pounds, and another old fellow perswaded to own me for his Wife; who came to the prison, and seeing another woman, owned her, and afterwards my self, and indeed any body. If such an old inconsiderable fellow had heretofore wooed me, it must have been for want of discretion, as *Carleton* did for want of money; but I know of no such thing. Several scandals have been laid upon me, but no mortall flesh can truly touch the least hair of my head for any such like offence: they have framed this of themselves. My Lord, I am a stranger, and a forreigner; and being informed there is matter of Law in this Trial for my life, my innocence shall be my Counsellor, and your Lordships my Judges, to whom I wholly refer my Cause. Since I have been in prison, several from *Canterbury* have been to see me; pretending themselves (if I were the person as was related) to be my school-mates; and when they came to me, the Keeper can justifie, they all declared that they did not know me.

Court: *Knot*, You said she lived near you at *Canterbury*; What woman or man there have you to prove she lived there? have you none in that whole City, neither for love of Justice nor Right, will come to say she lived there?

Knot. I believe I could fetch one.

Court. Well said, are they to fetch still?

Prisoner. My Lord, I desire some Witnesses may be heard in my behalf.

Elizabeth Collier examined. My Lord, my Husband being a Prisoner in the *Gatehouse*, I came there to see my Husband, and did work there a dayes; and there came in an old man, his name was *Billing*, he said he had a wife there; says Mr. *Baley*, Go in and finde her out; and he said I was his wife, turned my hood, and put on his spectacles, looks upon me, and said I was the same woman his wife; and afterwards said I was not, and so to others: I can say no more.

 Jane Finch examined.

My Lord, there came a man and woman one night, and knockt at my door; I came down, they asked to speak with one *Jane Finch*. I am the person, said I. We understand, said they, you know Mistress *Carleton* now in prison. Not I, said I, I onely went to see her there. Said they, Be not scrupulous: if you will go and justifie any thing against her, we will give you 5*l*.

 Court. Who are those two?

 Finch. I do not know them, my Lord.

 Mr. *Baley* examined.

My Lord, there has been at least 500. people have viewed her; severall from *Canterbury*, fourty at least that said they lived there; and when they went up to her, she hid not her face at all, but not one of them knew her.

 Court. What Country-woman are you?

 Prisoner. I was born in *Colen* in *Germany*.

 Court. Mr. *Carleton*, How came you to understand she was married formerly?

 Carlton the elder. I received a Letter from the Recorder of *Canterbury* to that purpose.

 Prisoner. They that can offer five pound to swear against me, can also frame a Letter against me: they say I was nineteen years of age about nine years ago, and I am now but one and twenty.

 Court. Mr. *Carlton*, you heard what *Knot* said; he said she lived near him four years a wife: why did not you get some body else from thence to testifie this?

 Carleton. Here was one *Davis* that was at her Fathers house, and spoke with him ——

 Court. Where is he?

 Carlton. I know not; he was here.

 Court. You were telling the Court of a former indictment against her, what was that for?

Carlton. She was indicted for having two husbands, *Stedman* of *Canterbury* her first Husband, and *Day* of *Dover* Chirurgion, her second Husband. The indictment was Traversed the year before His Majesty came to *England*, she was found not guilty.

Court. Who was at that Trial?

Carlton. One here in Court was of the Jury; but that party said there was such a trial, but knows not that this is the Woman.

Judge *Howel.* Gentlemen of the Jury, you see this indictment is against *Mary Moders*, otherwise *Stedman*, and it is for having two husbands, both at one time alive; the first *Stedman*, afterwards married to *Carlton*, her former husband being alive. You have heard the proof of the first marriage, and the proof doth depend upon one witness, that is *Knot*; and he indeed doth say, he was at the marriage, gave her, and he names one *Man*, the Parson that married her, that he is dead; none present there but the married couple that must needs be there, the Parson, this witness, her sister, and the Sexton; that he knows not what is become of the Sexton. All the Evidence given on that side to prove her guilty of this Indictment, depends upon his single testimony. It is true, he says she was married at *Canterbury*, but the particulars, or the manner of the marriage he doth not well remember; whether by the Book of Common-Prayer, or otherwayes: but they lived together for four years, had two Children. If she were born there, married there, had two children there, and lived there so long, it was easie to have brought some body to prove this; that is all that is material for the first marriage.

For the second, there is little proof necessary: she confesses her self married to *Carlton*, and owns him; the question is, Whether she was married to *Stedman*, or not?

You have heard what defence she hath made for her self, some Witnesses on her behalf; if you believe that *Knot*, the single witness, speaks the truth so far forth to satisfie your conscience, that that was a marriage, she is guilty. You see what the circumstances are, it is penal; if guilty, she must die; a Woman hath no Clergy,[104] she is to die by the Law, if guilty. You heard she was indicted at *Dover* for having two husbands,

Stedman the first, and *Day* the second. There it seems by that which they have said, she was acquitted; none can say this was the woman: that there was a Trial, may be believed; but whether this be the woman tried or acquitted, doth not appear. One here that was of that Jury, says, there was a Trial, but knows not that this is the Woman. So that upon the whole, it is left to you to give your Verdict.

The Jury went forth, and after some short Consultation, returned to their places.

Clerk, Mary Moders, alias *Stedman*, hold up thy hand; look upon her Gentleman, what say you? Is she guilty of the Felony whereof she stands indicted, or not guilty?

Foreman. Not guilty. And thereupon a great number of people being in and about the Court, hissed and clapped their hands.

Clerk. Did she flie for it?

Foreman. Not that we know.

Afterwards I desired, that my Jewells and Cloaths, taken from me, might be restored to me: The Court acquainted me, that they were my husbands, and that if any detained them from me, he might have his remedy at Law. I then charging old Mr. *Carleton* with them, he declared they were already in the custody of his Son her husband. So that if they had been counterfeit, as they all along pretended, I doubt not but that they would have had so much confidence and justice for themselves, as to have acquainted the Court with so much, to the bettering the envy and scandal of their gross abuses: but concerning the real worth of those Jewels, I shall have further occasion to speak presently.

Being thus fairly acquitted, *I* was carried back to my former Lodgings; where, among other visits, *I* had one from my Husbands near Friend, who but two hours before had swore and threatned my death: yet to feel my temper in this disappointment of their bloody designe against me, he was sent with an impertinent story into my company, where he began to glaver,[105] and offer me a glass of Wine; (above which their generosity yet never reached:) but my passions were so high at the very sight of him, that *I* bid him get him out of the room, and not trouble me with his company: which he did, by slinking from me, as the Dog in the Proverb that had lost his Tayl.

They thought being thus freed *I* would have ranted and vapoured, and gave them some further unwary hint of my condition, as being now out of danger: but *I* (that knew my self not to be in any) was transported with no such exultation, but kept the same equanimity and constant tenour; no less affected with the triumphs of Justice, than those of my Honour and Reputation.

Hitherto they have not found any thing unbecoming the person I am, or what they made me to be, except in my necessities, and that frequency of company to which they have subjected me by false imprisonment, and other scandals; which I could not better remove, than by my bare-fac'd appearance to all comers: so that that which other women hide and mask for modesty, I must shew and set to publick view for my justification.

On the sixth of *June*, being Saturday, I was discharged of my confinement, (having been all along most civilly used by the Masters and Keepers of both the Prisons where I was in durance; but indeed rather in the suburbs of a Prison, than a Prison it self; for which I am their Debtor) and did expect that my husband, by whom I was committed, that is, by his Relations, would have brought me out; and I stayed there to that purpose two days after my acquittal and purgation: but no such matter; they had got my Estate, I might do what I would with my person; the groundless slaunders they had cast upon that, should yet serve turn to infame my bed; and the Counterfeit, though after conviction of the falshood thereof, must be separated and divorced: but the counterfeit Jewels they'll *Hug* and *Embrace*, and *part* withal at no rate.

And therefore in stead of my lawful and true Husband, they endeavoured to put a counterfeit upon me: but too much are they stupified, in stead of being sublimed in this mysterious way of cheat, which as in melancholy people, works still in their fancy that they sent me the most ridiculous Dotard for Husband-

Gentleman-Usher,[106] that ever woman laid eye on: a Fellow that could be no younger than brother to Mother *Shipton*,[107] and had his Prophetical Spectacles[108] to fit him for a Legacy.

It was one of my pretended husbands, by whom a Bill was preferred (but not found, as I said before) by *Billing* the Brick-layer. Upon *Whitsun-Monday*, the 8th of *June* instant, the said *Billing* came to *Newgate*, demanded of the Keepers to deliver his Wife to him. The Turn-key, and other subordinate Officers of the Gaol,[109] told him, They had none of his Wife. He insisted upon it, and with-stood all denial, mentioned my name, and the particulars of my Trial. The Keepers remembring there was a former mistake of the same person, given in Evidence on my behalf at the Trial, called one *Grizel Hudson* a Convict, a pretty Woman, and in good habit: the Turn-Key asked *Billing*, Whether this was his Wife? *Billing* replied, *Yes*; and askt her, Why she did not come to him upon his first sending for her? She told him, That the Keepers would not permit her to stir out of the Prison, in regard her Fees were not paid. *Billing* said, He would pay the Fees; and whispered her in the Ear, saying, That they had a minde to hang her (meaning the *Carletons*) but he would not persecute her. True it was, he had put in an Indict-ment against her, but he could not help that. Well *Moll*, said he to her, *Have ye all your things?* She said, *Yes*. But, said he, *Moll, Why do you stay here amongst such wicked company, Rogues and Whores? I see their Irons about their Legs*. Why, said she, *I have left some Linnen ingaged in the Cellar*. To the Cellar the Keeper carried them both; and there *Billing* left a note under his hand, to pay five shillings to the Tapster:[110] Which Note he hath to produce, to satisfie any that shall make further Enquiry in this particular.

He further said, That she had cheated him of fourty pounds, and that he would pawn the Lease of his house, rather than she should want Money, although she was a wicked Rogue, if she would but live with him: she promised she would. He told her he would give her a Sky-colour'd Silk Petticoat and Wastcoat, and a Podesway Gown, new *Holland* for Smocks, and all other things necessary. *Billing* turning himself to the Company there present, said merrily, *That she had cost him much before when he*

married her, but he never lay with her, but he had kist her, *and felt her*
a hundred times. Billing askt her again, if she would leave these
wicked Rogues, and go along with him. She said, she had
another Debt to pay: He askt what it was; She said, twenty
pounds to such a one, a stranger then present, unto which
person he gave a note to pay 20*l.* in one moneth after the Date
thereof: (it's more than probable he will be made so to do.)

He further said to her, *That now it will trouble me to pay all this*
Money, and then you to run away from me in a short time. Withall,
said he, *Moll, You need not, for I have a better estate than the young*
man that tried you for your Life. So gave the particulars of his
Estate, what in Money, Houses, Leases and Land. He added
moreover, that he did love her out of measure, notwithstanding
she had done him other mischiefs, than what he had before
mentioned. She askt him, what they were? He said, She had
stollen from his Daughter a Knife and a wrought Sheath, a
Handkercher, and a Seal'd Ring. With that, the standers by told
him, that he was mistaken, that this *Grizell Hudson* was not the
person. He swore it was, and that he knew her well enough;
that he saw her in the *Gate-house*, and that she knew what passed
between us there: *But*, said he, *Moll, Thou art a cunning Rogue; I*
desire nothing of thee but to be honest, and live with me; the which she
promised, and he parted with great content thereupon.

This affront and indeed disgrace *I* put to the other; but am
very sorry the poor old Fellow should be abused so by my
Relations; the second part or worse of the cheat of a cunning
Gypsie, who having inveagled his affections, and set him on edge
by some lascivious gesture, entangled him in a marriage; and for
the better port and celebration of the Nuptials, procured him
twenty pound from a friend of hers, for which he gave Bond
(the Duplicate of this story) and when bed-time came, and the
rusty Bridegroom had prepared himself, [s]he ran away in the
dark with most of the money, and some odd things, as Linen,
and the like, and never after appeared, till those skilful Conjurers of *Grey Fryars*[111] (*in quo peccamus, in eo plectimur*;[112] where
my fault was in deserting my first station among the Religious,
from the like demolished place am *I* punished) raised up my

white name, and made me personate the baseness of that Imposture.

To proceed: I might now very well be said to be set at liberty, having no where to go, or where to betake my self: for the Verdict did not reach to give me possession of my Husband, whose Wife *I* was declared to be, (the Jury telling my young Lord, upon his asking of them the Verdict, as they were coming through the Garden of their Sessions-House into the Court, *That he must make much of his Princess, and keep her to himself:*) Nor was it easie to avoid the trouble of twenty several Courtiships for Lodgings, which *I* well considered might give further occasion of reproach, and abuse of my Credit.

But Mr. *Carleton* not appearing, which gave me suspition of some further designe, I took Lodgings in *Fullers Rents*,[113] where in privacy I resolved to wait the reduction of him to better and honester thoughts; and that when they his friends had all prejudice laid aside, and considered the duty and obligation that lay upon him, they would have restored and returned him to me. But this neither had its designed end, though the danger that I threatned his father with, brought him to me.

This was on Sunday in the Evening, *June* the sixth, when he came to me, accompanied with Mr. *George Hewyt* his Master, a Barrister of *Grays Inne* in *Coney*-Court; where after some discourses, and perseverance of my resolved manner of proceeding against his Father in the same method, and at the same Bar where he had arraigned me; he did most submissively supplicate me, and adjure me by all respects to him, falling upon his knees to move me the sooner, that I would promise him not to prosecute his father for my Jewels, or any other account: adding moreover, That if I did it, he should presently murther himself; with such-like cowardly Bravado's as he had used to the overruling of my affections, when he pretended he would do an hundred more mischiefs to himself, If *I* would not consent to marry him.

And now he resumed his first kindnesses, in hope *I* would do what he intreated; kissed me, and offered his embraces: though I could not so easily admit such danger into my bosome, having so lately felt the viperous sting: but this loving humour, like a time-serving passion, soon abated by the interposition of Mr. *Hewyt*.

I do suppose, that if he had been alone, and out of the custody and tuition of that person, he would have stayed with me all night, and perhaps for the future; but that person who hath surfeited may be, and hath had too much of a woman, had now so little repects for our sex, as to curse it in generall: but let him beware, as froward and as great a woman-hater as he is, lest he expiate those Maledictions, by some notable feminine revenge a steeping and preparing for him.

Next day I sent a Letter to my husband, and left it for him at Master *Hewits* Chamber: but through his means, as I can conceive no otherwise, I received no word of any answer; so that I resolved once for all to go and make a demand of my said goods and Jewels of old Mr. *Carlton*; which I did on *Fryday* night, the 19th of *June*, at his house at *Gray-Friars*; and knocking at Door, he himself asked who was there: I answered, Your Daughter when a Princess, but now your sons wife: he demanded my business; I told him I came to demand my Jewells, and other things he had taken from me, and also my husbands Person. He replied in short, the old Gentlewoman pulling him back from further discourse, That for the Jewels, my husband had them; and for himself, he was gone.

There being no more to be said or done, I bid them look to their hits, and departed: having on all occasions, after so many injuries sustained, proffered a reconciliation, being willing to cohabit with him, and have left no means unattempted to bring us together, that the world might see I am not such a loose irregular leud woman as I am slandered to be, by my carriage and demeanour in that relation of a wife, which title I am more ambitious of than any other yet put upon me: but since it must be otherwise, I doubt not so prudently and innocently to behave my self, as I shall not want a husband, much less the trouble of so impertinent and fickle a person as my husband, whom I would willingly exchange for my Jewels, and give him liberty to look after another Princess where he can finde her.

And now for that *Hocus Pocus*, the delaying of those counterfeit Jewels, as they talked, I shall make it no difficulty to prove that those Gems they had of me were none of their Bristol-stones,[114] or such-like trumpery: for not long after my tryal, they were offered in *Cheap-side* to the view of a Goldsmith, and he demanded what they might be worth; who having steadily and considerately lookt them all over, said, they were worth 1500*l*. At which the Trustee, or Fiduciary, in whose hands they were, askt the Gold-smith if he was mad, or knew what he said. Yes, that I do, replied he, and will presently lay you down so much money for them, if you have power to sell them: whereupon my Gentleman put up his counterfeit ware with a more counterfeit face, saying, he came only to try his skill, and departed.

And now let all the world judge of the Cheat I have put upon this worshipfull family of the *Carletons*. I have of theirs not a thred, nor piece of any thing, to be a token or remembrance of my beloved Lord, which I might preserve and lay up as a sacred relique of a person dear to me (I think indeed the dearest that ever woman had.)

But it may be they intend to furnish my Lord with this portable and honourable furniture to the second part of this *Gusman*[115]-story, against he shall knight-errant it abroad; and having found the way, marry some other great forreign Lady, and in stead of Boys whooping and hallowing at him here, be revered and adored by subjects, as his great spirit always divined and suggested to him he should be some-body, though to little purpose: but I hope to prevent that designe, and to have speedy redress against all this fraud and violence that hath been acted against me.

And now I have concluded the Narrative, and I hope to the satisfaction of the world: and if there be any thing not so elegantly and clearly expressed as my cause requires, let it be known it is my fathers, not my fault, which hath in some places disturbed and muddled my fancy, and in others reserved a hiding place and obscurity for my pursued honour.

I hope the ingenuous will pardon and admit of this defence,

considering the nature of it. No man is bound by any law to set forth more than what he is directly interrogated and questioned to; and there I have for my innocence sake exceeded. And for the ignorant and malicious, let them wonder and slander on; and when they shall give me worthy occasion, which is not in the capacity of their shallow brains, or in their dishonest intentions, to a further vindication; that is, when my relations shall have returned me what they took from me, and leave me in *statu quo*, by any handsome expedient, I shall not faile of making this discourse most evident demonstration, and descend to such undeniable proofe of every particular here, that shall make their impudence and rash folly one of the leudest stories of the Age.

The world usually and frequently judges as it likes and affects, and is altogether swayed by interest and humour; and even by that, amidst all those industrious calumnies, I dare stand or fall. Let my quality and condition alone, and he is not weighed in the common scales; yet the fair conduct and the harmless example deserves no censure. Let both alone, my sex is to be pittied and respected, and my person not to be hated. But I will not prostitute my fame to them: to his Highness I have appealed, and to him I shall go. Not doubting but what the strictness and nicety of the Law doth at present withhold him, we shall by his gracious protection of innocence be freed from such incumbrances; and some easier solution found for those intricacies, than my Lawyers at present expedite.

I am advised howsoever to prosecute my adversaries in the same manner, and at the same Bar where they arraigned me for a suspition, of a real suit of Felony, for that riot against the publick peace committed upon my person: which I am resolved to do, in case I receive not better satisfaction from them before the Sessions: nor shall my husbands dilating intreaties and perswasions befool me any longer.

> *Either love me, or leave me,*
> *And do not deceive me.*

The fashions and customs here are much different from those

of our Country, where the wife shares an equal portion with her husband in all things of weal and woe, and can *liber intentare*,[116] begin and commence, and finish a suit in her own name; they buy and sell, and keep accounts, manage the affairs of houshold, and the Trade, and do all things relating to their severall stations and degrees. I have heard and did believe the Proverb, *That* England *was a Heaven for women:*[117] but I never saw that Heaven described in its proper termes: for as to as much as I see of it, 'tis a very long prospect, and almost disappears to view; It is to be enjoyed but at second hand, and all by the husbands title; quite contrary to the custome of the *Russians*, where it is a piece of their Divinity, that because it's said that the Bishop must be the husband of one wife, they put out of orders, and from all Ecclesiastical function such Clergy men, who by the Canon being bound to be married, are by death deprived of their wives; so that their tenure to their Livings and Preferments clearly depends upon the welfare and long life of their yoake-fellows, in whose choice, as of such moment to their well-being, they are very curious, as they are afterwards in their care and preservation of them.

I could instance in many other customes of nearer Nations, in respect to female right and propriety in their own Dowers, as well as in their husbands estates: but, *cum fueris Romæ, Romano vivite more.*[118] I will not quarrel [with] the English Laws, which *I* question not are calculated and well accommodated to the genius and temper of the people.

While *I* mention these customes, *I* cannot forbear to complain of a very great rudeness and incivility to which the mass and generality of the English vulgar are most pronely inclined, that is, to hoot and hallow, and pursue strangers with their multitudes through the streets, pressing upon them even to the danger of their lives; and when once a cry, or some scandalous humour is bruited among them, they become Brutes indeed. A Barbarity *I* thought could not possibly be in this Nation, whom *I* heard famed for so much civility and urbanity. This I experimented the other day in *Fanchurch*-street,[119] as *I* was passing through it upon some occasion, which being noised and scattered among the Prentices, *I* was forced to bethink of some shift and stratagem to avoid them, which was by putting my Maid into a Coach, that by a good hap was at hand, and stepping into an adjoyning Tavern; which the Herd mistaking my Maid for me, and following the Coach as supposing me there for the convenience thereof, gave me the opportunity of escaping from them. A Regulation of this kind of uproar by some severe penalties, would much conduce not onely to the honour of the Government of the City, but the whole Nation in general;[120] having heard the French very much complain of the like injuries and affronts: but those to me *I* may justly place to my husbands account, who hath exposed me to the undeserved wonder, and to be a May-game[121] to the Town.

And to his debility and meanness of spirit, I am likewise beholding for some other scandalous Libels and Pasquils[122] divulged upon this occasion of our marriage; chiefly for the Ribaldry of some pitiful Poetry, entituled, *A Westminster-wedding.*[123] which equally reflects as much upon himself as me. This tameness of his doth hugely incense me; and I swear, were it not for the modesty of my sex, the bonds of which I will not be provoked to transgress, I would get satisfaction my self of those pitiful Fellows, who by this impudent and saucie scribling, do almost every day bespatter my honour. At least, I wonder my husband doth not vindicate himself, and assert his own individual Reputation, having threatned so much in print against a civil person that formerly & first of all endeavoured to clear and justifie mine.[124]

But when I consider how apt his kindred are to return to their vomit of slandering me, and reckoning the nine days wonder of their great cheat discovered is over, are like those that have eat shame and drank after it; I did the less wonder at his stupidity and senselessness of those indignities done him: and commonly those that have no regard to anothers honour, have as little respect for their own; as he is Master of another mans life, that is a Contemner of his own.

I shall therefore omit all the subsequent sneaking Lyes, raised by the same kindred, when they saw their more mighty and potent Accusations helped forward with such predjudices, noise and ostentation, were at once disappointed and blown to nothing: such as those Chimæra's of their framing and fancying, that *I* was seen in mans apparel, with a Sword and Feather, in designe to do mischief to some body; and that I have used to do so: and so punctual are they in this Lye, as to name both the time and place: that I resolved to set up a Coffee-house, and at last to turn Player or Actor: with an hundred other flams[125] to sully my Name, and of a mulititude of the like, to make one or other of those Calumnies and Reproaches to stick upon me.

Whereas on the contrary I do resolve, as soon as my cause is heard, and justice done me by the supreme power, if I cannot otherwise attain it, to retire and return back, though not immediately to my own home, yet to make such approaches at necessary distance for the present, that I might be in readiness and view of all transactions there, as soon as this bluster shall be so laid here, that I shall not fear the tayl of this Hurricane pursuing me: yet shall I always have my heart and my Arms open to Mr. *Carleton*, as a person whom for his Person and Naturals I do and shall ever affect, as his wife and my husband, maugre all those practices (as for my part) of rendring us mutually hateful and suspect to each other.

And while *I* thus open the way to a composure of this unhappy business, and am willing to put up so many private injuries, and publick contumelies and disparagements, in tendencie to, and in consideration of the relative state of marriage, which my conscience commands me to prefer before any advantage, respect or honour of mine own individual particular; and have not refused, but rather by all fair means, and too mean condescensions have courted an Accommodation and Agreement; what Injustice is it upon Injustice, Oppression upon Cruelty, refined Malice like Salt upon Salt, to pierce and exasperate that bosome which is full of so much indulgence to, and dallyance with their worst of injuries, in expectation that time would give them to see their mischievous errour?

But neither Time nor Truth it self will reclaim them, without Angels appear to confirm them in it. And *I* do in some part not blame them for it: for the excess and lofty structure of their hopes hath so dazled their looks downwards, that they can see nothing aright, nor in any true proportion or colour. Their dejection and fall from the pinacle of their ambition, hath quite stunned them, that they will hardly recover the dizzie mistake that lies between a *Princess* and a *Prentice*.

They are angry their golden Mountains have travelled and been in labour with a Mouse,[126] and that they cannot finger any of my Estate; and very importunate they are for me to declare it; and this they say is the onely argument to prove me no Cheat, and *I* say and believe it is the onely argument to prove me a fool; and with that, of all other their slanders and durtiness, they shall never abuse me.

But may not *I* with a great deal more reason enquire for, and demand my Joynture and Dowry? and those Mannors, Leases, Parks, Houses, and the like Rhapsodies and Fictions of an Estate, meer castles in the Air; and as one merrily since told me, he believed they were Birds Nests? It is sure a greater imputation and shame to them to be found such Cheats and Lyars, than it can be the least blur to me, who never avowed any such thing, nor boasted of my Quality and Fortune.

As to the Letters they intercepted of mine from my Steward, I wonder they do not produce them: but they are ashamed of their most ridiculous simplicity therein. I knew very well the uncertainty of my condition here; and therefore the Letters were meerly Cyphers, and under those terms of Moneys, &c. an account was given me of another affair at home: the distaste whereof made me comply with, and so soon yeild to those importunate and love-sick sollicitations of my Lord.

But what will they be the better for a Rent-roll, or particulars of an estate in *Germany*, the Tenure and Customes of whose propriety and nature of claime if they did know, yet could they not tell how to make their Title to it? I could easily name places, and discover my own Hereditaments perhaps without danger, and they never the wiser: nor will the impartial Reader be better satisfied. But if my sister *King*, or any of my kinsfolk long for some *Baccharach* grapes,[127] I'll send to my Steward for them, and he will convey them from mine own vineyard as soon as they are ripe; and I can furnish her husband with *Westphalia* Hams;[128] which run in my woods gratis. All those fine things I have store of: and when Mr. *Carlton* pleases to make it a surer match, and be married the third time, all things shall be done in ample manner: I will make a resignation of my whole estate, and have nothing setled in lieu of it, but a necessitous despised condition of life, and be taught to sing *Fortune my foe* to the pleasant new tune, or eccho of a *Cheat*.

But I trust Providence will better govern me, and put me upon no necessity of abandoning good and just resolutions I have made to myself, whether in case of separation or re-union, which I shall not over-fondly press, or urge from them who love not me but mine, and require signes and wonders, and love to be no less than Principalities.

FINIS.

NOTES

THE LIFE AND DEATH OF MAL CUTPURSE

[1] 'Tyburnian Sibyl' on the analogy of, e.g., 'Cumaean Sibyl'. Sibyls – a number of women who in antiquity were believed to have access to divine mysteries. Tyburn, then still a village, was the site of the gallows where felons were hanged (near modern Marble Arch).

[2] Picking pockets.

[3] When Tarquin II refused to pay the high price asked for nine prophetic books by the Cumaean Sibyl, she burnt six of them.

[4] Offal (for the bear to eat). 'Not fit to carry guts to a bear' was a proverbial phrase.

[5] Wanton or prostitute, with an allusion to the Roman goddess called *Bona Dea*, whose rites were practised at night.

[6] The sybils of antiquity.

[7] With the characteristics of both sexes.

[8] Sudden changes.

[9] 'Characterized, influenced, or prompted by excessive and mistaken enthusiasm, *esp.* in religious matters' (*OED*). Frith's eccentric attitudes are here paralleled with religious extremism that she did not share.

[10] Flavius Josephus, *Works*, trans. Thomas Lodge (London, 1655) recounts that for seven years before the fall of Jerusalem (70 AD), a poor countryman went about the city prophesying woe.

[11] Messages.

[12] Daughter of King Priam of Troy, Apollo's love brought her the gift of prophecy; when rejected, the angry god ensured that her predictions were never believed.

[13] Matched.

[14] The two chief nonconformist groupings. Anthony à Wood (1632–95) characterises the Presbyterians as severe in life, manners, conversation and apparel, and preaching damnation; the Independents as more free, frolicsome and gaily dressed and advocating liberty. They united, he says, only against 'the common enimy' (the royalists and a Laudian Church of England).

[15] The original text reads 'that in that'.

[16] In 1649 the House of Commons was 'purged' of those who wanted to

negotiate with the king. The remainder or 'Rump' of about fifty members then set up a court to try the king and established a Commonwealth. Removed by Cromwell in 1653, the Rump Parliament was recalled after his death six years later, then dissolved at the Restoration. With a pun on her own rump, which breeches would have revealed.

[17] Those born under the sign of Mercury, thieves.

[18] Heroic woman, female warrior.

[19] Oliver Cromwell (1599–1658), ruler of England under the Commonwealth; also with an allusion to the Oliver who, with Roland, was one of the heroes of legends about Charlemagne's knights.

[20] Thomas Deloney tells the story of the Princes Crispine and Crispiane, who become apprentice shoemakers to escape death at the hands of the Roman Emperor. Crispine eventually marries the Emperor's daughter, Ursula; it is his brother who becomes a knight (*The Gentle Craft*, Part I, 1597; Part II, 1598). Various forms of romance recounting knightly adventures were popular throughout the sixteenth and seventeenth century (see Introduction pp. viii–ix).

[21] Thieves.

[22] Robbers.

[23] Rumpadders or highwaymen.

[24] While avoiding the danger of being corrupted in the search for fuller information.

[25] Female director.

[26] Coming to an agreement (rather than standing out for 100%); a form of plea-bargaining was practised.

[27] Hanging.

[28] Deal in prostitutes.

[29] Modesty.

[30] Ingenuous.

[31] Various unrelated elements.

[32] Latin: Farewell.

[33] Notorious as the chief criminal prison in London, it occupied one of the city's main gatehouses.

[34] Ambidexter or double-dealer.

[35] Roman god, one of whose roles was patron of thieves. Those born under his planet were quick-witted, lively and ingenious.

[36] Resourceful.

[37] Mary Frith died in 1659, and according to her *Diary*, said farewell to the world at the age of 74.

[38] Aldersgate Street runs north past the Barbican (an area retaining the name of an outer fortification of ancient London); in the seventeenth century this street was considered particularly handsome and included a number of noble mansions.

[39] Claim to be of noble origin.

[40] Agency for second-hand goods.

[41] In classical mythology, rapacious female monsters.

[42] Politician, crafty intriguer.

[43] It was believed that a woman called Joanna concealed her sex and became Pope in the ninth century.

[44] One acquainted with esoteric doctrine, a secret intriguer.

[45] Slit in front of a garment beneath which a separate pocket could be worn: often used with sexual innuendo.

[46] Tomboy.

[47] Probably connected with 'romp', a boisterous girl, a hoyden.

[48] Romping.

[49] Kerchief; probably worn around the neck.

[50] Hooks for suspending cooking-pots over the fire would be blackened and greasy; driven snow is proverbially white and pure.

[51] Kinsmen.

[52] With an unfortunate disposition.

[53] Tax of a tithe or tenth part of a parishioner's annual profit had to be paid to the Church.

[54] Astrologers divide the heavens into twelve parts or 'houses'. Venus is the goddess and planet of love.

[55] William Lilly (1602–81), a well-known astrologer who published many almanacs and pamphlets.

[56] Cheating.

[57] The inauguration of a new Lord Mayor of London has for many centuries been marked by an elaborate procession through the streets of the city.

[58] Nativities (an astrological term).

[59] Just outside the wall, to the east of the Fleet Ditch, numerous contemporary references suggest that Turnmill Street was a centre of organized thieving.

[60] Swindlers, especially those who decoy their victims.

[61] The thugs and rowdies common in the streets of contemporary London.

[62] A wide street running east from St Paul's Cathedral, Cheapside was the chief centre for commerce, and site of processions and public punishments.

[63] This street, which passed the site of the Royal Exchange, is still in the commercial centre of the city of London. In the seventeenth century it was also a place of recreation, with May Day festivities and, later, coffee houses.

[64] The area now distinguished by the British Museum was then known as a place for picking up 'poor whores'.

[65] A better class of prostitute was to be found here, offering clients 'fine habit and manners'.

[66] The original reads 'ure'.

[67] 'One who follows his own inclinations or goes his own way; one who is not restricted or confined' (*OED*).

[68] A quarterstaff, long and iron-tipped, was the poor man's weapon; fighting with it was a favourite sport.

[69] Staff and sword.

[70] Share expenses with.

[71] As long as.

[72] An impartial explanation of the way she conducted herself can hardly be found in her natural tendencies.

[73] Kickshaws, fancy dishes.

[74] To expiate a murder, this hero of classical legend had to serve Queen Omphale (sometimes Iole) as her slave; she set him to perform women's work. The episode, a favourite image of monstrous reversal of the natural order, is usually depicted with Hercules spinning while Omphale wears his lion-skin and carries his club.

[75] Roman emperor (AD 54–68); Suetonius (*Lives of the Caesars* VI) suggests the bridegroom was his freedman Doryphus.

[76] The last king of Assyria (seventh century BC); he was believed to have wallowed in luxury and effeminacy until an attempt to dethrone him (eventually successful) spurred him into military action.

[77] Mocked.

[78] Garments.

[79] Chaste.

[80] Proverbial name for a fool.

[81] A chlorotic disease believed to affect unmarried girls who had reached sexual maturity; a symptom was a craving for substances such as lime and coal.

[82] Agent.

[83] Swindles (see also pp. 28 and 67).

[84] Deliberation.

[85] Taste, smattering.

[86] Casting horoscopes.

[87] Wondered at.

[88] Curtsy.

[89] Taste.

[90] This huge statue of Apollo was supposed to have stood with one foot on each side of the harbour at Rhodes.

[91] Mateo Alemán's *Guzmán de Alfarache* (published in English translation in 1622) had, with other picaresque narratives purporting to be autobiography, such as its predecessor *Lazarillo de Tormes*, created an association between Spain and rogue literature.

[92] Court.

[93] A ninth-century Arab astronomer transmuted into magician and cheat in a comedy by Tomkis (1615, revived 1668 with a prologue by Dryden).

[94] Traditionally depicted as a female figure who carried the illustrious away on her wings.

[95] Human cunning.

[96] Probably the voyage to Jamestown in 1609. See Introduction, pp. x–xi.

[97] *OED* gives a seventeenth-century meaning of the verb 'spirit': 'to kidnap, in order to transport to the plantations in America'. Carrying off both children and adults to be sold as servants and labourers could be expedient as well as profitable.

[98] Fights or contests.

[99] A port on the right bank of the Thames, opposite Tilbury. It was both a favourite place for excursions from London and the point at which outward-bound ships paused to take on supplies and wait for tide and wind to be favourable.

[100] Enticed.

[101] Ship.

[102] The original text reads 'halling'.

[103] Knowledge.

[104] Officer of the law.

[105] Money Frith had meant to use for betting at the 'matches' she had been falsely promised.

[106] The coxswain, a petty officer in charge of a ship's boat and its crew, would be responsible for rowing anyone needing transport between a ship lying at anchor and the shore.

[107] Rash.

[108] Pickpockets.

[109] Ships.

[110] Markets.

[111] Measuring, probably with some other slang sense.

[112] See note 86.

[113] A branch of mathematics; used here with a pun on other associations of the word.

[114] Set free; they are looking to see whether Frith has been branded after a conviction. (See also p. 46 and note 281.)

[115] Handicraft.

[116] Muscles.

[117] Cutting.

[118] Quacks.

[119] This earlier form of the word 'surgery' makes clear its basic sense of healing by manual operation (Gk. *cheir* – hand), and gives the narrator yet another opportunity for a play on words.

[120] Drop the money.

[121] Use to signify.

[122] Until recently 'work' when used in connection with women meant needlework, and rejection of the needle a rejection of femininity.

[123] Imagined.

[124] Originally a palace, this building between St Bride's Church and the Thames became a house of correction for malefactors. A whipping post was installed in 1633, providing a popular weekly spectacle.

[125] Exposure.

[126] The original text reads 'an'.

[127] Coin worth five shillings (one fourth of a pound sterling).

[128] Noblemen.

[129] Highwaymen.

[130] Acceptance as a tenant, usually involving some payment.

[131] Etna, a notoriously active volcano in Italy, near Naples.

[132] Explosive artefacts are suggested, but the words were also applied to such ingenious tricks as Frith uses elsewhere for revenge or amusement.

[133] Trading station.

[134] Financial settlement (see Introduction, pp. xvii–xviii).

[135] A percentage of the whole for acting as agent.

[136] Ownership.

[137] Impartial.

[138] Ill-gotten gains.

[139] Hold.

[140] Partners.

[141] Judgement.

[142] Notorious as base and trading post for the Barbary pirates who preyed on towns and shipping around the Mediterranean.

[143] Distribution of profits.

[144] Craft.

[145] Vermin.

[146] During the Interregnum parliamentary reforms included abolition of the monarchy, the House of Lords, bishops, censorship, and almost all forms of public entertainment.

[147] Prisoner in Newgate.

[148] When coins were of precious metal, it was profitable but illegal to trim small quantities from the edge.

[149] The monarchy was abolished in March 1649 and England proclaimed a commonwealth in May. There was resentment against the direct taxation of the Interregnum – higher than at any period before the twentieth century.

[150] The Royal Exchange (between Cornhill and Threadneedle Street) was one

of the most important buildings in London, serving as bourse, shopping precinct and social centre.

[151] Water was available to Londoners at a number of conduits, some of them impressive structures. This one (opposite the end of Milk Street) consisted of a square pillar with statues around the sides and the figure of Fame on top.

[152] One that may very properly be asked for.

[153] A large and fashionable tavern on the north side of the street, to the west of Shoe Lane.

[154] Running west from Ludgate to Temple Bar, Fleet Street was one of the most important thoroughfares of seventeenth-century London. On the royal route from Westminster to St Paul's and adjacent to the Inns of Court, it was home to some eminent people. Associated with printing and publishing from their beginning, there were also numerous taverns.

[155] Mentioned by Pepys as a landmark, the water flowed from a stone tower in the centre of the street, which had a chime of bells, and was decorated with images of saints and angels.

[156] Cautious.

[157] Indulged.

[158] One of the main city gates; Frith would have needed to pass through it to approach Fleet Street from the east. It had a statue of King Lud, legendary founder of London.

[159] A 'translator', or cobbler who mended old shoes, would have less prestige than a shoemaker.

[160] Citizen appointed to keep the peace in his parish.

[161] The counters or compters were city corporation prisons for those who committed civil offences.

[162] 'B.E. *Dict. Cant. Crew*, a Drunken Man or Woman taken up by the Watch...and carried to the Counter' (*OED*).

[163] Group of watchmen who patrolled the streets at night before the introduction of a police force.

[164] Dungeon; 'the name of one of the worst apartments in the Counter prison in Wood Street, London' (*OED*). Frith chooses this 'cheap experience' out of curiosity; she would have been able to pay for better prison accommodation.

[165] Excuse me.

[166] Jailer.

[167] Place where arrested persons were locked up.

[168] Money extracted from new prisoners as jailer's fee or to buy drinks.

[169] Entreat.

[170] Pawn.

[171] Petty constable.

[172] Boasted.

[173] Fool.

[174] Messenger-god of classical mythology (see also note 35 above).

[175] London's central criminal court was in the street of this name, opposite Fleet Lane, in Frith's day. The present Old Bailey is nearby, on the site of what was Newgate prison.

[176] (Also chiaus and chouse) a Turkish official messenger, a swindler (see also pp. 15 and 67).

[177] Perplexity.

[178] Abductor.

[179] Stopped trying to hide his feelings.

[180] Spanish wine of the sherry type.

[181] To the south of Smithfield, Pie (i.e. Magpie) Corner was well-known for its cookshops. It was the corner between Cock Lane and Giltspur streets and must have adjoined a labyrinth of narrow alleys in which crime flourished.

[182] An apt mocking nickname for this cobbler; the word could mean a great, a rich and mean, or a lumpish man.

[183] Literally, 'good-place'; this spelling appears to have been used interchangeably with the 'Utopia' ('no-place') of Sir Thomas More's ideal country.

[184] Cinquanter, 'A man of fifty, an old stager' (*OED*).

[185] Generic name for a rough, lower-class woman.

[186] Cover great distances each day.

[187] Sancho Pança or Panza, Don Quixote's peasant-squire (see p. 37 and note 232).

[188] Physician as well as fortune-telling astrologer, John Lambe's most eminent patient was well known to be George Villiers, the unpopular first Duke of Buckingham. The latter was closely associated with Charles I in his attempts to gain more absolute power. During the tense summer of 1628 Lambe was attacked as he left the theatre and so severely beaten and stoned that he died the following day; two months later his patron was assassinated.

[189] Those entrusted with secret business.

[190] Random.

[191] See note 55; the loyal Frith would also have disliked Lilly as a supporter of Parliament against the king.

[192] Horoscope.

[193] Frith's Fleet-Street house must have been very near the corner with Shoe Lane, which runs north from near St Bride's Church. The cockpit there attracted a wide variety of people.

[194] A large open space north west of the City, its many uses included as a market for livestock and horses, and as the site of the famous Bartholomew Fair.

[195] See also p. 21, where the narration makes the meaning clear.

[196] Being cleaned or mended.

[197] Pocket.

[198] Crime.

[199] Warrant directing a gaoler to receive and keep a prisoner until further notice.

[200] Come to an amicable arrangement.

[201] The officials felt able to demand a large sum as the price of Frith's freedom as the crime of which she was accused carried the death penalty.

[202] Legal question.

[203] If not quite a Fagin, it is clear from this, and references to her 'imps', that Frith controls and profits from the services of a number of delinquent children.

[204] Books containing business records.

[205] Coins.

[206] What it was worth to them.

[207] Promoting, i.e. setting a case in motion.

[208] Court officer.

[209] Of whose identity I could never be certain.

[210] Ecclesiastical court, where offences against religion and morality were tried.

[211] Procurator or attorney.

[212] An open-air pulpit in St Paul's Churchyard. A letter of 12th February, 1612 (*The Letters of John Chamberlain*, ed. McClure, vol. I, p. 334) describes Moll-Cutpurse, the 'notorious bagage (that used to go in mans apparell...) ', as penitent and weeping there the previous Sunday, and the sermon as so bad that most of the congregation departed.

[213] Members of city guilds wore distinctive garments on special occasions. This inappropriately dressed citizen would have been impressing his country cousins: it has been customary to travel 'down' into the country and 'up' to London.

[214] The wearing of a distinctively priestly garment was a matter of controversy in the highly-charged religious atmosphere of the time.

[215] A wooden structure set up in public view in which the neck and wrists of malefactors were locked. No market or fair could legally be held without a pillory.

[216] Rumour.

[217] Trick.

[218] Arrest.

[219] For the illegible portions of this paragraph Nakayama conjectures 'was [one] offended' and 'others [of my s]ex'. The syntax of the whole paragraph is particularly loose and confusing, making elucidation as problematic for the modern editor as it may have been for the original compositor. Close examination of the original print (not seen by Nakayama) suggests an attempted correction superimposed on an earlier reading. Interpretation of the result is entirely speculative. It is possible that some words from the

original manuscript had been accidentally omitted and the printer tried unsuccessfully to remedy this.

[220] Minutely inquisitive.

[221] Joking.

[222] Four pence.

[223] A little bit at a time.

[224] Sweated in acid to remove some of the precious metal.

[225] Bizarre.

[226] Recorded as a London innkeeper in the 1630s, Banks had showed Morocco, his performing horse, in England and abroad. Shakespeare refers to the famous animal (*Love's Labours Lost*, I: ii. 53).

[227] Charing Cross (with a monument to Edward I's queen until it was destroyed in 1647) was one of the most important public places in London. At the junction of Whitehall, Haymarket and the Strand, and on the route from Westminster to the city, it was a conspicuous departure point for Frith's ride. Shoreditch was a parish to the north-east of the city with an unsavoury reputation. The ride would have taken Frith right across London, through all the busiest streets.

[228] From head to foot.

[229] This could be the 'Mr *Atturney Noy*' mentioned later, (see p. 48 below and note 291); he had a dry wit.

[230] This gate was the exit point for traffic going north towards Cambridge. A spacious street with good shops led up to the gate; on the other side lay a sort of shanty town with a very mixed population.

[231] In the chivalric romances popular in the sixteenth and seventeenth centuries, female messengers are frequently sent galloping off alone on such errands, while both male and female knights may be attended by female squires.

[232] Miguel de Cervantes's satire of chivalric romance, recounting the adventures of Don Quixote and his comically plebeian squire Sancho Panza; Part I was published in 1605 (English translation 1612).

[233] Whims and devices.

[234] (d. 1527?) wife of a goldsmith and powerful mistress of Edward IV. Like Frith in that she was imprisoned, and she was thought to be a sorceress, the reference here is to the fact that she too was made to do public penance at Paul's Cross (see p. 34).

[235] Then a village outside London; its location away from legal jurisdiction made it an attractive base for highwaymen.

[236] Dogs with long shaggy fur, popular as ladies' pets.

[237] Beraying, i.e. befouling.

[238] The devil.

[239] Idiot.

[240] Spout.

[241] Several of the 'cotemporaries' who figure in this text also appear in others, and continue to do so over the years. Their lives and doings often seem to have been mythologised in their own lifetimes (see p. 65 below and note 379). There also appear to be a number of free-floating 'rogue' stories; a later version of the theft of Lady Fairfax's watch (see p. 62 below) attributes the crime not to Walker, but to a character called Cottington and nicknamed 'Mull-Sack'.

[242] Amusing.

[243] An expression of indignation.

[244] '*to tread the shoe awry*: to fall from virtue, break the law of chastity' (*OED*).

[245] Stick.

[246] 'A stick with a basket-hilt used instead of a sword in fencing, a single-stick' (*OED*).

[247] Mirthful.

[248] Causing trouble or mischief.

[249] Large Fleet Street hostelry near Temple Bar and St Dunstan's church, once frequented by Ben Jonson and his circle.

[250] 'As much as one can "carry" of drink' (*OED*).

[251] Usually 'routing': (of pigs) turning over with the snout in search of food.

[252] Gutter.

[253] Stray livestock were (and still can be) legitimately 'impounded', i.e. temporarily enclosed in the finder's field or stable or in a public 'pound'.

[254] Heavily pregnant ('pig' denoted only very young swine or hogs).

[255] 'A drink or dose of medicine given to an animal' (*OED*).

[256] The Guinea or river hog (Potamocharus pictus) had been introduced to Europe from the West Coast of Africa.

[257] Female and male cronies.

[258] Then a village on the Great North Road with pastures and dairies, a favourite place for outings from London.

[259] Made an appalling noise.

[260] Obsolete variant of 'own'.

[261] An account of this episode appears in a pamphlet of 1638 (*Stripping, Whipping, and Pumping. / Or, the five mad Shavers of / Drury-Lane...*). A Drury Lane barber called Evans is said to have been seen drinking with the young woman who had nursed his wife in child-bed. The nurse (Joan Ilsley) is then invited to a roast-pig supper, but instead, the jealous Mrs Evans and four other women strip her, gag her, and whip her with birch-rods till her flesh is raw; shaving tackle is sent for, and as she struggles, Ilsley is cut with a razor. Dragged downstairs and held under first one pump, then another, the victim is held under the water and 'shamefully used'. When the pamphlet was being written, the perpetrators were apparently on bail pending trial, having been pelted with dirt by other women on their way home from the

initial hearing. Despite such goings-on, Drury Lane was still a fashionable street in the seventeenth century. (See also Mary Carleton p. 103.).

[262] Fully indulged myself in.

[263] Making merry with.

[264] Adulteration.

[265] Sedge.

[266] In the nick of time.

[267] Inconsiderable.

[268] Charles I had actually failed in his attempt to impose episcopacy and the English prayer book on Scotland by force of arms.

[269] Extensive stone piers or breakwaters.

[270] A famous Greek courtesan, who was herself said to have served as a model for statues of Venus to both Praxiteles and Apelles.

[271] Charles I must have been familiar with the independently-minded heroine of Shakespeare's *Much Ado About Nothing* as he amended the title to 'Beatrice and Benedick' in his personal copy of the Second Folio.

[272] Almost always.

[273] Associates and household.

[274] Reluctant.

[275] Taste.

[276] The original text reads 'apathany'.

[277] Numbness.

[278] One of the four legal societies with the right to admit to the English bar; Briscoe could have been servant to a lawyer there as a child.

[279] Chum.

[280] A King and Queen of Misrule were chosen to preside over the festive disorder of Christmas revels.

[281] Felons could sometimes be released after having their left palm branded as a record of the conviction.

[282] Though the courtiers, failing to honour the itemized accounts sent them by the city merchants, have been lucky enough to cheat them of their wares and goods. 'Imprimis' (first) would introduce the initial entry in a bill and 'item' (also) the subsequent articles.

[283] In the seventeenth century, 'Cavalier' was used in a number of French, Spanish, Italian and (as here) Portuguese forms.

[284] Noblemen.

[285] Dashing gentleman.

[286] Sign a binding contract.

[287] Financial extravagance.

[288] Old man.

[289] Retired.

[290] Official discharge.

[291] William Noy or Noye (1577–1634), Attorney General to Charles I; he seems to have been witty, grim and cynical.

[292] *DNB* recounts that on being offered the post of Attorney General by the king, Noy first asked what his wages would be.

[293] The middle figure might be either '0' or '2'; Nakayama reads 'one hundred twenty pounds'. 100 is more probable both because '100 *l.*' is more likely to be preceded by 'a' than '120 *l.*' (which appears twice below with no article) and because the point of the story is the dishonesty of the dealer's oath. He has lost £100, and promises £20 to the finder; the countryman who finds it is then given only £1 reward, the dealer pretending that the amount lost was £120 and the finder must have pocketed the difference. Each swears an oath to his own version, and Frith interprets the contradiction as indicating that the £100 found had no connection with the £120 that the dealer claimed to have lost, and that the finder should therefore keep it all.

[294] Written statements, confirmed by oath, to be used in judicial proof.

[295] The English Civil War (1642–9) between Parliament and supporters of Charles I.

[296] Conjuring or trickery.

[297] Republic.

[298] John Pym (1584–1683); political radical and anti-catholic, though not opposed to the institution of monarchy, Pym was a central figure in the House of Commons at the outbreak of the Civil Wars. His friends controlled the financial centre of London and put their wealth at the disposal of Parliament.

[299] Dupes.

[300] Puritanical.

[301] (Originally 'anothergates') another kind of.

[302] Name for the devil.

[303] Sleight of hand or deception.

[304] Thomas Wentworth, first Earl of Strafford (1593–1641). Chief advisor to Charles I, he opposed Parliament's desire to seize executive power, and was planning to impeach popular leaders when he was himself impeached by Pym. Despite the king's promise and wish to save him, fear of the yelling mob led Charles to agree to Strafford's execution in May 1641.

[305] Oliver St John (?1597–1675), lawyer and politician; he was a leading parliamentarian, but refused to sit on the tribunal which tried the king.

[306] Religious maniacs; used by royalists as a derogatory term for those refusing to conform to the Church of England.

[307] The former was an amphitheatre on the Bankside, used for bull- and bear-baiting and fencing matches; the latter was the medieval great hall of the palace of Westminster, and the setting for important trials, such as those of Strafford and Charles I.

[308] Officer of the Houses of Parliament responsible for enforcing commands and arresting offenders.

[309] (See also pp. 55, 62.) Dorset House was in Salisbury Court, off Fleet Street, almost opposite where Frith lived. Her protector and client was probably Edward Sackville, fourth Earl of Dorset (1591–1652; 'one of the handsomest men of his time' [*DNB*]). As a regent during the king's absence in the north, he would have had 'Power and Authority'; in 1642 Dorset joined the king at York, then took the queen to Holland ('occasion to leave *London*' – p. 55). He was said never to have left his London house after the king's execution.

[310] Amusing.

[311] Involved in prostitution.

[312] Mistress of a brothel.

[313] A famous brothel run by Elizabeth Holland in an old manor house on the Bankside. It may have gained the name 'leaguer' (a besieged military camp) when under siege by the authorities, but it is also a joke on its mistress's name, as the term was a Dutch one. The Bankside was an area of theatres and brothels south of the river and outside city jurisdiction.

[314] She became the 'madame' of a seamen's brothel, and according to Pepys 'the most Famous Bawd in the Towne'. Certain naval commanders apparently relied on her to keep them supplied with men, to the horror of Pepys and Evelyn.

[315] Interloping, trading illicitly.

[316] Market.

[317] Tailors specializing in women's clothes.

[318] When returning home from the east, down Ludgate Hill, Frith would have had to cross this bridge over the Fleet river (now covered by Farringdon Street).

[319] Affectedly refined.

[320] 'Caressing treatment' (*OED*).

[321] (1617–1670). A Welsh nonconformist divine, he preached in and around London during the Interregnum. The royalist Frith would also have disliked his republicanism.

[322] Corrupt.

[323] See note 352.

[324] Sinful, requiring expiation.

[325] The god of fertility, Priapus's symbol was the phallus. Mary Frith's house was frequented by both men and women in search of sexual partners.

[326] By chance.

[327] A personification of money.

[328] See note 309.

[329] Well-born.

[330] Blunt.

[331] Large groups of city apprentices assembled on Shrove Tuesday for

organized assaults on brothels, which they sacked and sometimes even demolished.

[332] The beadle was the official responsible for whipping miscreants, naked to the waist, until they were bloody. They might be tied either to a whipping post (of which there were a great many in London) or to the back of a cart which was paraded through the streets. The hog may be a variant of the horse or wooden barrel on which victims were sometimes tied as an alternative to the cart. The throwing of repulsive missiles by spectators was an important feature of such public punishments.

[333] Type of Spanish wine, sweetened, spiced and heated.

[334] Spirits.

[335] With a pun on 'torrid'.

[336] One of the rivers of Hades; drinking its waters brought oblivion.

[337] At the junction of the Brent and Thames rivers, Brentford is only ten miles from St Paul's; news of Prince Rupert's troops sacking it in November 1642, soon after relative success at Edgehill, terrified Londoners and the militia was mobilized. As trained bands and Edgehill veterans stood defending the approach to London, the Lord Mayor requested that congregations should be asked to contribute part of their Sunday dinner to feed them.

[338] Half-boiled.

[339] Food, especially army provisions.

[340] Cloth.

[341] The original text reads 'rawing'.

[342] Peters or Peter (1598–1660), a puritan who became an active pastor and citizen in Massachusetts; he returned to England to help the parliamentary cause and was executed at the Restoration.

[343] Charlatans' assistants, mountebanks' buffoons.

[344] See note 59; the worthy burgesses are the thieves, now outdone by the supporters of the parliamentary cause.

[345] Civic Hall of the Corporation of London, used as a treasury by the parliamentarians.

[346] Picaro or rogue.

[347] The royalist James Howell commented mockingly on contributions to the parliamentary cause including the sempstress's silver thimble, the chambermaid's bodkin and the cook's silver spoon.

[348] Church treasury, originally that of the Temple at Jerusalem.

[349] (Turkish) personal troops or bodyguard.

[350] Proverbial phrase, from the faithlessness attributed by the Romans to their Carthaginian enemies.

[351] Citizen army, as opposed to professional troops.

[352] Robert Devereux, third Earl of Essex, (1591–1646), was appointed to command the parliamentary forces in the summer of 1642. His house was at the end of the Strand on the south side, just before the road became Fleet

Street at Temple Bar. Sensational and bitter legal proceedings in 1613 had finally declared his marriage to Frances Howard null because unconsummated. He had married again, but lived apart from his wife. Mrs Anne Turner (see p. 53 above) allegedly supplied the Countess of Essex with potions to decrease her husband's love and increase that of her lover (Sir Robert Carr, later Earl of Somerset). Turner was hanged in 1615 for her part in the poisoning of Sir Thomas Overbury, who was antagonistic to the Countess and knew too much of her affairs.

[353] Tools for loosening hard ground.

[354] One responsible for military machines and earthworks; an inventor of plots and traps.

[355] See note 352.

[356] Authority to raise a military force, revived by Charles I.

[357] Social intercourse.

[358] Mandragora, a poisonous plant whose forked roots can make it look human, was formerly believed to shriek when pulled from the ground.

[359] Fine gallant.

[360] Joker.

[361] Cavaliers or royalists.

[362] See note 309.

[363] Financial agreements; see note 364.

[364] The Committee for the Advanced Monies, which sat in Haberdashers' Hall, was established in 1643, and was responsible for raising funds for the army by taxing any suitable person, royalist or neutral, who had failed to contribute to the parliamentary cause. The Goldsmiths' Hall Committee was established the following year to negotiate with royalists who wished to regain their sequestered estates. As the fine payable for their return varied from one tenth to two thirds of the value of the property, the process of 'compounding' was obviously of vital importance.

[365] Anne Vere, a woman of strong presbyterian sympathies, had married Thomas, third Baron Fairfax (eventually commander-in-chief of the parliamentary forces) in 1637.

[366] William Dugdale believed that such lectures or sermons, given by 'turbulent spirits' appointed by the parliamentary leaders, incited rebellion.

[367] Thomas Jacombe (1622–1687), a presbyterian minister who received the living of St Martin's, Ludgate Hill in 1647 when the incumbent was ejected, then lost it himself at the Restoration. Narcissus Luttrell considered him a 'fanatick parson' (February 1684/5).

[368] Puritans, punctilious nonconformists.

[369] Crime.

[370] Gregory Brandon, the public hangman.

[371] Extract the purse.

[372] B.E. *Dict. Cant. Crew*, 'a sharp or subtil Fellow'.

[373] Experts.

[374] When not being used for official purposes, this was one of the most important public spaces in London. There were seamstresses, booksellers and other traders and men of affairs went there for news and gossip. Crowded and noisy, it was also a notorious haunt of pickpockets.

[375] Hat made of beaver's fur.

[376] A sedan or enclosed chair, carried on poles.

[377] John Downes (?1635–66); one of the regicides, he was a colonel of militia in the parliamentary army.

[378] The gibbet (see note 370).

[379] James Hind or Hinde, a royalist highwayman whose exploits were printed in many forms, was executed in 1652. (See Lincoln B. Faller, *Turned to Account* [Cambridge, 1987] for an examination of narratives of Hind's life and deeds.).

[380] The original text reads 'parsuit'.

[381] Firkin or barrel.

[382] Parliamentarians were so called from the puritan custom of cutting men's hair short, in contrast to the long curls of many royalists.

[383] Hind was executed not for highway robbery, but for treason to the republican regime.

[384] Hannam was hanged in 1656; there are a number of contemporary accounts of the life and death of this 'Witty Rogue' and 'Incomparable Thief', including details of robberies committed on various royal personages and all over Europe.

[385] See note 222.

[386] Chief or most important thing' (*OED*).

[387] Arranged (for a partial jury).

[388] Philip Jermyn (called to the bar 1612) remained a judge on the King's Bench during the Interregnum.

[389] The original text reads 'cleaver'.

[390] Cologne (Koln). Charles II left Paris for Cologne in the summer of 1654 and remained there for about sixteen months.

[391] A lane near Somerset House and the landing stage at its foot were still called 'Strand Bridge', though no bridge remained.

[392] Someone easily deceived (cf. notes 83, 176).

[393] A street seller of apples (costards).

[394] A 'leyband' was a fastening-string.

[395] 'An autograph signature (*esp.* that of the sovereign) serving to authenticate a document' (*OED*).

[396] A trapan or trepan was a person used as a decoy when ensnaring a victim for criminal purposes.

[397] Complaisant cuckolds.

[398] Henry Marten (1602–1680), parliamentary radical, republican and regicide; contemporary comment on Marten's private life does not suggest that

fornication was an institution he would have wished to abolish. The Rump Parliament introduced the death penalty for female adulterers in 1650, and the law proved quite unenforceable.

[399] Violating.

[400] 'An old variety of backgammon' (*OED*).

[401] *The Famous Historie of the Seven Champions of Christendom* (a widely-read romance by Richard Johnson, printed about 1597) relates how Saint George of England releases six other national 'champions' from enchantment.

[402] Sickly.

[403] 'A morbid disease characterized by the accumulation of watery fluid...in the body' (*OED*).

[404] Garment.

[405] Small Spanish horses.

[406] The Rump Parliament (see note 16) was recalled in May 1659 after Richard Cromwell's failure as Protector.

[407] A supposed prophetess and witch, she was pictured as a hideous old woman.

[408] The original text reads '*Plodding*'.

[409] Pointed out.

[410] 'It was prettily devised of Aesop, "The fly sat upon the axletree of the chariot-wheel and said, what a dust do I raise".' (Francis Bacon, Essays, 58: *Of Vicissitude of Things*.)

[411] Edward Alleyn (1566–1626), a famous actor who used the wealth he acquired from the theatre and from property (including brothels), to establish a charitable foundation including a school (now Dulwich College) and almshouses. The source of Alleyn's money, like Frith's, was considered evil.

[412] Mourning rings (often gold with a black enamelled skull) were distributed at funerals; provision for them is frequently made in seventeenth-century wills. The rings distributed by Frith are named after crowded places notorious for robberies.

[413] This enormous fair, with all sorts of entertainment as well as buying and selling, was held annually at Smithfield.

[414] Ratcliff; a hamlet with an unsavoury reputation to the east of the city of London, on the riverside between St Katherine's and Wapping. It seems to have been inhabited mainly by those concerned with various forms of water transport.

[415] John Herring had been incumbent of St Bride's, Fleet Street, for eight years when, unable to accept the Act of Uniformity, he resigned in 1662. There was much in Frith's life to make such a nonconformist 'intruder' feel 'squemish' if asked to preach at her death.

THE CASE OF MARY CARLETON

Facsimile frontispiece. Mary Carleton gives the date in the new style. Since England was still mainly using the old style, the usage would underline her claim to foreign birth.

Facsimile title page. Latin: 'So, so I am pleased to go beneath the shades'. The words are Dido's just before her suicide following Aeneas's abandonment. See *The Aeneid*, bk IV, l. 660.

[1] Prince Rupert (1619–82) was the son of the Elector Palatine of Bohemia and Elizabeth, daughter of James II. He came to England to assist his uncle Charles I in 1642, becoming the dominant figure in the first Civil War ending in 1646. He then for a time lost the confidence of Charles although he later became commander of the fleet. At the Restoration he settled in England and received an annuity from his cousin, Charles II.

[2] One of Prince Rupert's titles was Count Palatine of the Rhine.

[3] This phrase indicated a married woman's assumption into her husband for legal purposes. The *Lawes Resolution of Womens Rights* (1632) declares that 'A woman as soone as she is married is called covert, in Latine *nupta*, that is, vailed, as it were, clouded and over-shadowed'.

[4] The word at this time could mean both fiction and reports.

[5] Giovanni Boccaccio (?1313–75) was an Italian writer of fiction and poetry, whose most famous work was the *Decameron*, a collection of a hundred tales narrated by different characters.

[6] The god of marriage.

[7] Genteel or appropriate to a gentlewoman.

[8] Attracting notice, conspicuous.

[9] Restore.

[10] Cologne or Köln on the banks of the Rhine was ruled by an archbishop-elector and formed one of the provinces of the Holy Roman Empire. It is spelt Colen or Collen throughout the text.

[11] The main criminal court in London, close to Newgate prison.

[12] Probably mistressest i.e. the best.

[13] Agrippina, the wife of the Emperor Claudius, was born in Cologne. After her it was named Colonia Agrippina or Agrippinensis.

[14] Despite his nominal Protestantism Charles II was in exile in the Catholic city of Cologne for a year and a half beginning in September 1654. In October 1655 Cromwell, the Protector of England during part of the Interregnum, made a treaty of friendship with Cardinal Mazarin of France. One of its clauses was that France should not receive Charles II and his brothers.

[15] Pythagoras, a philosopher of the sixth century BC, believed in the metempsychosis or transmigration of souls.

[16] Damnable.

[17] The seventeenth-century spelling of 'abominable' as if the word came from *ab homine*.

[18] Someone who holds a licence to exercise a profession.

[19] Sweden was at war with Germany during the Thirty Years' War which ended in 1648 with the Treaty of Westphalia and again when a war with Poland expanded into general European war during the reign of Charles X; this ended in the Peace of Oliva in 1660.

[20] Cologne was ruled by an archbishop-elector who was also archduke of Lorraine.

[21] Spain was at war with France on several occasions between 1621 and 1665. Eager to create a landroute between their country and the territory of Flanders, the Spanish were often in alliance with the rulers of the German states who gave them free passage.

[22] Sir John Mandeville was the name taken by a French compiler of exotic travels in the fourteenth century. The book which has some factual elements and many fantastic ones was translated into several languages and became extremely popular.

[23] Mary Carleton's use of legal terms gives support to John's claim in *Ultimum Vale* that she became a pupil of a Greys Inn lawyer.

[24] A nun. If Mary became a nun her fortune would go to the Church.

[25] St Clara (1194–1253) was the founder of the Franciscan nuns; they espoused the primitive rule of poverty.

[26] An unknown or unexplored region.

[27] English Catholics had established convents in this Flemish town; during the Interregnum the daughters of the Catholic Viscount Stafford were edcuated at one of them.

[28] The word is not in the OED. The neologism might again be intended to suggest Mary Carleton's learning.

[29] South eastern provinces of Flanders where people spoke a dialect of French.

[30] A variant of freight.

[31] A fashionable watering and meeting place in the province of Liège in Flanders, famous for its mineral springs.

[32] He had property near Liège, capital of the province of Liège on the banks of the Meuse in Walloon country. In German the town was called Luik.

[33] Among other effects, syphilis attacked the roof of the mouth. The disease was treated with mercury which, given in excess, made the jawbones disintegrate and produced a quantity of saliva.

[34] Ambrose Spinola, Marquis de Los Balbases (1569–1630), was a general serving Spain in the Thirty Years' War. He gained the most renowned victory of his career in 1621 during war with Holland when he captured the Dutch town of Breda in Brabant from Frederick Henry, prince of Orange and Nassau.

[35] The Count of Tilly was the general of the Catholic League during the Thirty Years' War. One of his opponents was Gustavus Adolphus of Sweden

who defeated him at the battle of Breitenfeld in 1631. Gustavus Adolphus was killed during the battle of Lützen in the following year.

[36] Faustus or Faust was a sixteenth-century magician. In legend and literature he was famous for making a compact with the devil to sell his soul in return for superhuman knowledge.

[37] A reputed substance supposed by alchemists to be able to change other metals into gold or silver.

[38] The Greek mathematician and inventor Archimedes was credited in tradition with several magical engines.

[39] Alsace, on the border of France and Germany.

[40] Built on something else as foundations.

[41] Vulgar and low.

[42] See Introduction, pp. xxvii, xxxii.

[43] The Lawyer's Clarke Trappan'd by the Crafty Whore of Canterbury. In rogues' slang trepan meant to trap or trick.

[44] Newgate prison on the east side of the Old Bailey was used to house debtors and felons.

[45] Brielle, a Dutch port.

[46] The longed-for goal of ideal happiness.

[47] An allusion to the famous story of Gregory I who, on seeing fairheaded Angles from England, is supposed to have said 'Non Angli sed Angeli'. He sent Augustine on a mission to convert England to Christianity in the late sixth century.

[48] Singular or unique.

[49] The text reads 'any any any'.

[50] Christina (1626–89), daughter of Gustavus Adolphus, became queen of Sweden when still a child. After some years of misrule she abdicated in 1654 and entered a 'vagabond' life, wandering through Europe often scandalously in male attire. Her story was current in A Relation of the Life of Christina Queen of Sweden (1656). In the work she is described as a Lady Errant, the term Carleton uses for herself.

[51] In The Female Hector the author asserted that Mary Carleton would make a 'stout General att the head of an Army of Amazonian Ladies'.

[52] Swindler.

[53] A boat that travelled with the tide up the Thames.

[54] The Royal Exchange was one of the principal buildings of the City; it had covered walks and shops selling luxury wares and it served as a place of business for merchants and traders. Cornhill ran east from Poultry past the Royal Exchange. It was celebrated for its coffee houses and taverns and it also housed the stocks and pillory.

[55] Charles II had tried to regulate the mail service and to make it impossible for anyone without permission from the secretaries of state to intercept or tamper with letters. The original text reads 'put into the Male'.

[56] A recommendation or what is given in trust as a deposit.

[57] At this time Holloway and Islington were villages outside London, places for outings and rendezvous.

[58] The original reads 'she', probably from a slip in transcribing from *An Historical Narrative* which has 'She said, my Lord, could see within me. I answered that my lord must have very good eyes if he could see within me...'.

[59] Bill.

[60] The word comes from the name of the boastful Saracen leader in Ariosto's *Orlando Furioso*. It indicated extravagant bragging.

[61] 'Reckon without the host': to calculate a bill without consulting the landlord; and so to come to conclusions without taking into consideration some important cirumstance of the case.

[62] Before the Fire of London in 1666 St Paul's had been a huge gothic cathedral. There were plans for its restoration when it was burnt down.

[63] Greyfriars was an area consisting of old ecclesiastical buildings which, in the seventeenth century, housed many families.

[64] They pretended that they had a licence or they had a fake licence which they pretended was authentic.

[65] A public space north west of the City outside the walls; the site of fairs and markets.

[66] St Bartholomew the Great in West Smithfield.

[67] A village to the north of London.

[68] Imagined.

[69] Possibly a name used to suggest high rank and birth.

[70] Hyde Park, extending from Piccadilly to Kensington Gardens, was a place of fashionable rendezvous. Maying was a favourite custom there. On 1 May 1661 Evelyn 'went to Hyde Park to take the air; where was his Majesty and an innumerable appearance of gallants and rich coaches, being now the time of universal festivity and joy'.

[71] Fine and crowded.

[72] Excellence. Mary Carleton's use of unusual words added to the impression of her learning.

[73] Durham Yard, formerly the town residence of the bishops of Durham, extended from the Strand to the Thames. It was a well-to-do and fashionable part of the town.

[74] Disclosed.

[75] A seller of drugs.

[76] In *The Life and Character of Mrs. Mary Moders, alias Mary Stedman, alias Mary Carleton, alias——* this is corrected to Lombard Street. There were many famous taverns there such as *The Cardinal's Hat*, and just off it *The Pope's Head Tavern*.

[77] A lover or suitor.

[78] Richard Cromwell, the son of Oliver, succeeded his father in 1658. Between then and his fall in 1659 there was much antagonism between the army and parliament, with the result that the parliaments called did not long survive. In the parliament that sat between January and April 1659 a Thomas Kinge sat for Harwich.

[79] They took the clothes that had been soaking in the wash.

[80] See note 261 to page 42. In this text the shavers have been increased to six.

[81] A minute detail.

[82] Harried or molested.

[83] An inferior parish officer.

[84] This is the famous Edmund Bury Godfrey whose murder in 1678 after taking a statement from the informer Titus Oates did much to precipitate the furore of the Popish Plot. He was a justice of the peace for Westminster.

[85] Latin: we send, i.e. a warrant ordering the keeper of a prison to receive someone into custody.

[86] The Gate-House of Westminster was used to hold prisoners, on the east side, clerks-convicts, and, on the west, state and parliamentary offenders, as well as felons and debtors.

[87] See note 33 to p. 7.

[88] If these things had not happened.

[89] Most notably Samuel Pepys on 29 May 1663.

[90] John Carleton's *The Replication, or Certain Vindictory Depositions*.

[91] Probably a reference to *The Westminster Wedding; or Carlton's Epithalamium*; or possibly to *Vercingetorixa*.

[92] See note 11 to p. 82.

[93] Accusation.

[94] Latin: these words.

[95] Although on the throne only from 1660 Charles II dated his reign from the death of his father in 1649.

[96] A light sweet wine from the Canary Islands.

[97] Latin: The journey is through wickedness.

[98] Ferocious dogs on leads: hired villains.

[99] Put together properly.

[100] Cromwell's Marriage Act of 1653 introduced a new civil ceremony as part of its assault on the Roman Catholic sense of marriage. Marriages would henceforth be celebrated by a Justice of the Peace and all litigation concerning it was removed from the jurisdiction of the ecclesiastical courts. The civil marriage differed from that contained in the Book of Common Prayer, no longer in use, since it omitted the phrase 'till death us do part', so suggesting to some that divorce might just be possible. At the Restoration this act became void although the powers of the ecclesiastical courts continued to wither and Parliament retroactively declared marriages contracted under the Act legal.

[101] Part of the sea near the Goodwin Sands off the East coast of Kent, used as a rendezvous for ships.

[102] A worker in cordwain or Spanish leather, so a shoemaker.

[103] The first wedding must have occurred without banns or licence and might therefore have been questioned. But in fact before 1753 a simple public exchange of vows could constitute a valid marriage.

[104] Benefit of clergy was the privilege allowed to clergymen of exemption from trial by a secular court, later extended to everyone who could read. It was usually confined to men but there are examples of women using it.

[105] Talk deceitfully and flatter.

[106] Suggesting a person of low degree.

[107] Mother Shipton was a supposed prophet and witch known for her great age. She lived at the end of the fifteenth century and was said to have foretold the Fire of London and other national events.

[108] A reference to Mother Shipton and her prophecies.

[109] The original text reads 'Goal'.

[110] The keeper of a tavern or one who draws the beer.

[111] The Carltons lived in Greyfriars.

[112] Latin: It is where we sin that we are punished.

[113] Fulwood's Rents, commonly known as Fuller's Rents, was a court in Holborn nearly opposite Chancery Lane close to Greys Inn. It had several taverns and coffee houses, as well as private lodgings and houses.

[114] Transparent rock-crystal found in the Clifton limestone near Bristol, so not precious.

[115] Gusman is the hero of a Spanish picaresque romance by Alemán. It was translated into English as *The Rogue* in 1622.

[116] *liber intendare*. Latin: free to bring an action against someone.

[117] This was a frequently quoted idea. See Fynes Moryson, *Itinerary* of 1617: 'England in generall is said to be the Hell of Horses, the Purgatory of Servants and the Paradice of Weomen.'.

[118] Latin: 'When in Rome do as the Romans do', St Ambrose's advice to St Augustine.

[119] Fenchurch Street was a wide street between Aldgate Street and Gracechurch Street.

[120] The behaviour of the London mob was a constant source of civil commotion in the seventeenth century.

[121] This was merry-making associated with May 1st; she feared she would be made into sport for others.

[122] Lampoons.

[123] *The Westminster Wedding; or Carlton's Epithalamium*.

[124] Presumably the author of *A Vindication of a Distressed Lady* answering *The Lawyer's Clarke*.

[125] Tricks and fabrications.

[126] An allusion to Horace's famous line in *Ars Poetica* 139: 'Parturient montes, nascetur ridiculus mus' (the mountains will be in labour and a ridiculous mouse will be born).

[127] Famous grapes from the town of Bacharach used to make Rhenish wine.

[128] Westphalia is a province of western Germany between Hanover and Prussia, famous for its production of hams.

APPENDIX 1

Table of Dates for Mal Cutpurse

(There may be minor inconsistencies in the dating given below, caused by the failure of some accounts to make it clear whether the Gregorian or the Julian calendar is being used. Under the Gregorian calendar, used in England and America until 1752, the year began on 25 March; the Julian reform also involved advancing the date by ten days.)

1586   Mary Frith born (according to age given in 'Diary' [p. 72]; 1589 according to the writer of the Preface [p. 8]).

1603   Death of Elizabeth I and accession of James I.

1609   Nine vessels set sail for Jamestown, Virginia. One of these may well have been the ship from which Frith escaped [pp. 18–20].

1610   August. Entry in Stationers' Register, 'A Booke called the Madde Prancks of Merry Mall of the Bankside, with her Walks in Mans Apparel and to what Purpose. Written by John Day'. There is no surviving copy; it may never have been printed.

1611   Publication of Middleton and Dekker, The Roaring Girl (first performance likely to have been earlier).

1612   27 January. Frith confesses to a number of misdemeanours before the London Consistory Court.
9 February. Frith does penance at Paul's Cross [pp. 33–4].
12 February. Letter of John Chamberlain to Sir Dudley Carleton: '. . . and this last Sonday Mall Cut-purse a

notorious bagage (that used to go in mans apparell and challenged the feild of divers gallants) was brought to the same place, where she wept bitterly and seemed very penitent . . .'.

18 February. First entry of *The Roaring Girl* in *Stationers' Register* (referred to as 'a booke concerning Mall Cutpurse'); elsewhere there is a record for the same day of a fine for having printed the book without entering it. Publicity provoked by Frith's punishment had probably drawn attention to printer's omission.

1618   First publication of Nathan Field, *Amends for Ladies.*

1621   Suit of complaint of wrongful arrest and imprisonment brought against several people, including 'Mary Markham alias Frith, alias Thrift, alias "Malcutpurse"'.

1625   Charles I succeeds his father as king.

1628   Dr Lambe stoned and beaten on leaving theatre (Friday, 13 June); he dies the following day. (Buckingham, king's unpopular favourite, assassinated 23 August) [p. 30].

1629   King dissolves Parliament after a bitter struggle; governs without a parliament for next eleven years.

1633–7   Banks keeps a tavern in Cheapside [p. 36].

1638   August. Episode of the Women Shavers of Drury Lane [p. 42].

1639   Publication of Nathan Field, *Amends for Ladies. With the merry prankes of Moll Cut-Purse: Or, the humour of roaring* . . .

1641   Execution of Strafford, who was working against Parliament for an absolute monarchy (12 May) [p. 50]. Soon afterwards Frith seeks protection of 'a Nobleman my Neighbour' when threatened with arrest after organising a royalist bear-baiting. The fifth Earl of Dorset would have been in London; he was made regent during the king's absence in north in 1640; on 23 November 1641, he ordered the Middlesex trained banks to fire on a mob intimidating Parliament. In 1642 he was in York with the king ('occasion to leave London' [p. 124]), then in Holland with the queen before rejoining the king and finally returning to London [pp. 51, 55, 62].

1641 25 November. Charles I's triumphal entry into London on his return from Scotland. He was acclaimed in Fleet Street and the conduit ran with wine; several pamphlets given an account of this ambivalent event. The 'Diary' gives the year 1638, however; as the king, determined to enforce episcopacy and the English prayer book, had made previous attempts to control Scotland, there may have been earlier rejoicing on his return, or Frith may be confusing different occasions [pp. 43–4].

1642–5 First Civil War.

1642 Robert Devereux, third Earl of Essex, appointed to command parliamentary army in summer of this year [p. 59].

1642 August–1643, June. Women work on the construction of fortifications around London [p. 59].

1642 12 November. Prince Rupert takes Brentford by storm [p. 57] – a point at which it has been argued that Charles I might have taken London and won the war (the battle of Edgehill on 10 October had been indecisive). Houses of those on both sides plundered; Milton's Sonnet VIII, 'When the assault was intended to the City', asking for his house (then in Aldersgate Street) to be spared, dates from this same moment, when an advance on London seemed imminent.

   13 November. Parliamentarian forces drawn up on Turnham Green across royalist line of advance on London. The Lord Mayor requests ministers to ask from the pulpit that every household should contribute part of their ready-cooked Sunday dinner to feed the troops. Carts ordered to stand ready in every parish and a great deal of food and drink contributed [p. 57].

1643 Committee for the Advanced Monies established in Haberdashers' Hall to raise supplies and taxes for Parliament [pp. 62, 72].

   8 and 9 August. Violent scenes when women (wearing white silk ribbons in their hats) petition Parliament for peace [p. 60].

1644   Goldsmiths' Hall Committee established (to deal with sequestrations) [pp. 62, 72].

1647–8   Second Civil War; Parliament held London throughout.

1649   Execution of Charles I (30 January).
        Proclamation of a republican Commonwealth.

1650   Parliament introduces death penalty for female adulterers [p. 69].

1652   James Hind the royalist highwayman executed for treason to the republican regime [p. 66].

1653   Oliver Cromwell made Lord Protector, though he had been effectually in control for several years: 'Government seized & usurped by *Oliver*' (or Frith may have had the execution of Charles in mind as the moment of usurpation) [p. 69].

1658   Death of Oliver Cromwell; succeeded as protector by his son Richard.

1659   Rump Parliament recalled (7 May) after Richard Cromwell's failure as Protector [p. 71].

1659   Death of Mary Frith, at 73 according to her own account ('Threescore and Fourteenth year of my Age' [p. 72]).

1660   Restoration of the monarchy and coronation of Charles II.

1662   *The Life and Death of Mrs. Mary Frith* published.

APPENDIX 2

The Mary Carleton Pamphlets

The Man in the Moon, no 2, May 1663.

The Lawyer's Clarke Trappan'd by the Crafty Whore of Canterbury, or, a True Relation of the whole life of Mary Mauders, the daughter of Thomas Mauders, a fidler in Canterbury. With her strange and unparallel'd pranks, witty exploits, and unheard of stratagems, touching her being a wife for a week, and a lady of pleasure. London; Printed for J. Johnson, 1663.

A Vindication of a Distressed Lady. In Answer to a pernitious, scandalous, libellous Pamphlet; Intituled, The Lawyers Clarke Trappan'd by the Crafty Whore of Canterbury. London, Printed 1663.

The Replication, Or Certain Vindicatory Depositions, Occasioned by Way of Answer, to the Various Aspersions, and False Reports of Ignorant and Malicious Tongues, and the Printed Sheets and Pamphlets of Base Detractors, concerning the Late Acted Cheat. Written by *John Carleton* of the Middle Temple London, Gent. Printed by the Authors Appointment in the Year, 1663.

The Articles and Charge of Impeachment against the German Lady, Prisoner in the Gate House, to be Exhibited According to the Records of the City of Canterbury, in Order to her Trial at the Session-House in the Old Bailey. With the Confession of the Witnesses, and Her Father in Law, Touching Her Strange Pranks and Unheard of Designs, As Also a True Narrative of Her Proceedings since the 25th Day of March Last, to the

161

Time of the Contract of Marriage, betwixt This Rare Inchantress and That Worthy Gentleman Mr. Carlton. London, Printed for G. Winnam, 1663.

The Arraignment, Tryal and Examination of Mary Moders, Otherwise Stedman, now Carleton, (Stiled, The German Princess) At the Sessions-house in the Old Bayly, being brought Prisoner from the GatehousE Westminster, for having two Husbands; viz., Tho. Stedman of Canterbury Shooemaker, and John Carleton of London, Gent. Who upon a full Hearing was acquitted by the Jury on Thursday, June 4. 1663. Lond: Printed for N. *Brook*, at the Angel ub *Cornhil*, near the Royal Exchange. 1663. (another edition includes the words 'Taken more largely by special Appointment' and adds a woodcut.

The Great Trial and Arraignment of the late Distressed Lady otherwise called the late German Princess. Being brought to her trial in the Old Bailey on Thursday last the 4th instant of this month of June before the Rt. Hon, the Lord Mayor, the Lord Chief Justice of Common Pleas, the Rt Worshipful, the Court of Alderman, and all the rest belonging to that most Honourable bench. The tenure of her indictment, of having two husbands and her answer to the same. Also the several witnesses which came in against her, with her absolute confutation upon each of their evidences by her acvute wit and impregnable reasons, whereby she was acquitted by public proclamation. London, 1663. For W. Gilbertson.

A True Account of the Tryal of Mrs Mary Carlton, at the Sessions in the Old Bayly, Thursday the 4th of June, 1663. She being Indicted by the Name of Mary Mauders alias Stedman. Sometime supposed by Mr. Carlton and others, to be a Princess of Germany. Published for her Vindication, at Her own Request. London, Printed for Charls Moulton.

The Tryall of Mis Mary Carleton, (formerly the German Lady, Henereta Maria de Woolva) at the Old Baily, Thursday Morning June the 4: between Eight and Eleven of the Clock: Wherein You have the Substance of All That Was Said... London, Printed in the Year, 1663. (see Hazlitt's third biographical series).

An Historical Narrative of the German Princess, containing all material passages, from her first arrivall at Graves-End, the 30th of March last past, untill she was dischanrged form her imprisonment, June the 6th instant wherein also is mentioned, sundry private matters between Mr. John Carlton, and others, and the said Princess; not yet published. Together with a brief and notable story of Billing the brick-layer, one of her pretended husbands coming to New-Gate, and demanding of the keeper hjer dleiverance, on Monday the eight instant. Written by her self, for the satfisfaction of the World, at the request of divers persons of honour. London, Printed for Charles Moulton, 1663.

The Westminster Wedding; or Carlton's Epithalamium. To the Tune of, The Spanish Lady. London: printed for S.B. 1663.

Vercingetorixa: or, the Germane Princess Reduc'd to an English Habit. By F.B. Gent. '*Why* Vercingetorix *we give/ Unto this Book for Name,/ Know,* German Princess doth derive/ As By-Blow *from the same.* London: Printed in the Year MDCLXIII.

The Case of Madam Mary Carleton, Lately Stiled The German Princess, Truely Stated: With an Historical Relation Of Her Birth, Education , and Fortunes; In An Appeal to His Illustrious Highness Prince Rupert. By the Said Mary Carleton. London, Printed for Sam: Speed at the Rainbow in Fleetstreet, and Hen: Marsh at the Princes Arms in Chancery-lane. MDCLXIII.

Ultimum Vale of John Carleton, of The Middle Temple London, Gent. Being A true Description of the Passages of that Grand Impostor, Late a Pretended Germane-Lady. Published by the Order and appoint- ment of the aforesaid right worthy and ingenious Author Mr. John Carleton. London, Printed for J. Jones, 1663.

A Witty Combat: Or, The Female Victor. A Trage-Comedy. As it was Acted by Persons of Quality in Whitson-Week with great applause. Written by T.P. Gent. London, Printed for Tho. Roberts, and are to be sold at the Royal-Exchange, Fleet-Street, and Westminster-Hall, 1663.

The Female Hector, or, the Germane Lady turn'd Mounsieur. With the manner of her coming to the White Hart Tavern in Smithfield like a young lord in Man's Apparel..How she deceived the gentry at Amsterdam..How she deceived an inn keeper at Sandwitch in Kent..How she made her escape from the Kings-bench. London, N. Dorrington, 1663.

News from Jamaica in a Letter form Port Royal Written by the German Princess to Her Fellow Collegiates and Friends in New-Gate. London, Printed by Peter Lillicrap, for Philip Brigs, Living in Mer-maid Court near Amen Corner in Pater Noster Row, 1671.

Some Luck, Some Wit, Being a Sonnet upon the Merry Life and Untimely Death of Mistriss Mary Carlton, Commonly Called the German Princess. To a New Tune, Called The German Princess Adieu. London, Printed for Philip Brooksby near the Hospital-Gate in West-Smith-field.

An Exact and True Relation of the Examination, Tryal and Condemnation of the German Princess, Otherwise Cal'd Mary Carlton, at Justice-Hall in the Old Bailey, January 17: 1672. Also, an Account of the Pretended Treachery Which She Was to Discover to the Bench; and the Reason of Her Return from Jemeca. London, Printed for R.O. 1672.

An Elegie on the Famous and Renowned Lady for Eloquence and Wit, Madam Mary Carlton otherwise styled the German Princess. London Printed for Samuel Speed. 1673.

The Deportment and Carriage of the German Princess, Immediately before her Execution: And Her last Speech at Tyburn: Being on Wednesday the 22th of January, 1672. London. Printed for Nath. Brooke at the Angel in Cornhill, near the Royal-Exchange 1672.

The Memoires of Mary Carleton, Commonly Stiled, the German Princess. Being a Narrative of Her Life and Death Interwoven with Many Strange and Pleasant Passages, from the Time of Her Birth to her Execution at Tyburn. Being the 22th of January 1672. With her Behaviour in Prison. Her Last Speech, Burial & Epitaph. London, Printed for Nath.

Brooks, at the Angel in Cornhill near the Royal Exchange, and Dorman Newman at the Kings Arms in the Poultry, 1673. *(another version gives the author as G., J. or John Goodwin).*

Memories of the Life of the Famous Madam Charlton; Commonly Stiled the German Princess. Setting forth the whole Series of her Actions, with all their Intrigues, and subtile Contrivances form her Cradle to the fatal period of her Raign at Tiburn. Being an account of her Penitent behaviour, in her absteining from food and rest, in the Prison of Newgate, from the time of her Condemnation to her Execution, January 23. 1672 Taken from her own Relation, whilst she was Prisoner in the Marshalsea, and other certain information. With her Nativity Astrologically handled, and an Epitaph on her Tomb. London, Printed for Phillip Brooksby, next door to the Ball inn West-Smith-field, near the Hospital-Gate, 1673.

The Life and Character of Mrs. Mary Moders, alias Mary Stedman, alias Mary Carlton, alias Mary—— The Famous German Princess: Being an Historical Relation of Her Birth, and Fortunes, with the Havock and Spoil she committed upon the Publick in the Reign of King Charles the Second. Together With her Tragical Fall at Tyburn, on the 22nd of January 1678; added by way of Appendix. (second edition) London: Printed for J. Cooke in High Holborn, and Sold by the Booksellers, and Pamphlet-Sellers in the Cities of London and Westminster.

The Counterfeit Lady Unveiled. Being a full Account of the Birth, Life, most remarkable Actions, and untimely Death of Mary Carleton, Known by the Name of The German Princess. London, Printed for *Peter Parker*, at the *Leg*, and *Star*, over against the *Royal Exchange* in Cornhill, 1673.